The Man Called
CASH

The Man Called CASH

The Life, Love and Faith of an American Legend

STEVE TURNER

BLOOMSBURY

First published in Great Britain 2005

Copyright © 2004 The John R. Cash Revocable Trust

The moral right of the author has been asserted

Bloomsbury Publishing Plc, 38 Soho Square, London W1D 3HB

All Scripture quotations, unless otherwise indicated, are taken from The Holy Bible,
New International Version. Copyright © 1973, 1978, 1984. International Bible Society.
Used by permission of Zondervan Bible Publishers.

All lyrics by Johnny Cash are used by permission of the John R. Cash Estate.
For a list of songs and albums by Johnny Cash, see the Discography in the back of this book.
All lyrics by other Cash family members are used by permission.

Reviewed for accuracy by John Carter Cash, Lou Robin, Karen Robin, and Mark Stielper

Special thanks to Laura Cash, The House of Cash, and Rhonda Hogan of Creative Solutions,
Arlington, Texas, for compiling photographs for this book

A CIP catalogue record for this book is available from the British Library

ISBN 0 7475 7953 9
ISBN-13 9780747579533

10 9 8 7 6 5 4 3 2

Printed in Great Britain by Clays Ltd, St Ives plc

All papers used by Bloomsbury Publishing are natural, recyclable products
made from wood grown in well-managed forests. The manufacturing processes conform
to the environmental regulations of the country of origin.

Q: Did you ever have an imaginary friend?

A: Yes. Sometimes I am two people. Johnny is the nice one. Cash causes all the trouble. They fight.

—Entry in Tara Cash's personal book
Dad, Share Your Life with Me

Contents

Foreword by Kris Kristofferson   ix

Acknowledgments   xiii

1. First to Cross   1

2. The Promised Land   13

3. Leaving Home   31

4. Walking the Line   45

5. Amphetamine Blues   65

6. Going Down, Down, Down   81

7. Busted   101

Contents

8. The Voice of America   121

9. Personal Jesus   141

10. The Beast in Me   159

11. Riding the Highway   171

12. American Recordings   187

13. The Man Comes Around   201

14. Touched by Grace   219

    Interview with Johnny Cash   231

    Chronology   243

    Discography   259

    Personal Interviews by the Author   267

    Endnotes   269

    Bibliography   273

    Index   281

Foreword

KRIS KRISTOFFERSON

JOHNNY CASH IS A TRUE AMERICAN HERO, who rose from a beginning as humble as Abraham Lincoln's to become a friend and an inspiration to prisoners and presidents—respected and beloved the world over for his courage, his integrity, and his genuine love for his fellow man. Like Muhammad Ali, he was bigger than the profession that brought him to the world's attention, and his spirit transcended the boundaries of ordinary artistic stardom. But he was wonderfully, charmingly human.

I am told that when Bob Dylan met John—I think it was at the Newport Folk Festival—he circled John, bent slightly forward and smiling up at him with pure admiration. It's a reaction with which anyone who ever met him can identify. I first saw him in person in June 1965, backstage at the Ryman Auditorium. I was still in uniform, but when Marijohn Wilkin introduced us, his electric handshake was the final nail in the coffin of my army career. John was and always would be larger than life, as powerful and unpredictable as lightning, the deep thunder of his voice a perfect match for his craggy, Lincolnesque features. June, his partner for life, was the beautiful, effervescent youngest daughter of the legendary Carter Family, as bright and shining as he was dark and dangerous, and the two of them were head over heels in love and unquestionably the answer to each other's dreams. The Wildwood Flower may not have tamed the Holy Terror, but she definitely smoothed the rough edges of the wildest force of nature running loose in the magical world of music at the time, and together they would become a rock-solid sanctuary and source of inspiration, not only for each other and their beloved children, but for the extended family of lost souls and songwriters they took under their wing.

The first words John said to me when we were introduced at Columbia Recording Studios where I was working as a janitor were, "It's always nice to get a letter from home, isn't it, Kris?" Cowboy Jack Clement had told him of a letter I'd received from my mother disowning me for pursuing a career in a music "nobody over the age of fourteen ever listens to and, if they did, they wouldn't be anyone we'd want to know." It might have been why he always encouraged me in my songwriting (he carried the lyrics of one of my songs in his wallet).

Although it would be years before he ever recorded one of my songs, I continued to pitch him every song I wrote, giving them to June or Luther Perkins so I wouldn't get fired for bothering him. Once he went to bat for me when his producer's assistant tried to get me fired for letting two songwriters into his session (they had cornered him in a hallway and were trying to get him to listen to a whole album of religious songs they wanted him to cut). My boss told me he wasn't going to fire me because he knew I wasn't responsible for letting them in, but he advised me to stay away from the studio where John was recording. So I was hiding in the basement busying myself with erasing tapes for reuse in demo sessions when John suddenly appeared and asked how I was doing (as if he always came down to the basement to see how the janitor was doing). I said I was okay, and he asked if I was coming up to the session. I said I was pretty busy and he said, "Well, I heard you had some trouble, and I just wanted you to know that I'm not going to start the session until you get there." So I went back upstairs with him, watched the session, and tried to ignore the glare coming from the producer's assistant in the control room.

Years later when I was a performer (thanks to John putting me onstage with him at the Newport Folk Festival—against their wishes), I was taking a lot of heat in a country music magazine for work I was doing to protest the U.S. terrorizing of Nicaragua. John wrote a letter defending my patriotism and pointed out that I'd served my country in the army. He did the same thing for Bob Dylan when Bob was criticized in *Sing Out!* for the direction his music was taking ("leave him alone; he knows what he's doing"). John was never afraid to jeopardize his own career by defending what he thought was right.

Some years later I was opening for him in Philadelphia and dedicated a song to Mumia Abu Jamal (who was on death row). Some officials went ballistic, and after I'd left the stage they sent word that I needed to go back out and apologize. I felt awful because it was John's show I was hurting. John said, "You don't need to apologize for anything you say on my show. I want you to come onstage with me at the end of my set when we're doing the gospel songs and sing "Why Me."

Speaking of "Why Me," John once told the guys in his band that Jesus wrote a song called "Why Me, Kris."

John never lost his sense of humor. When June slipped away from us without warning, he was devastated. At the funeral home where people were paying their last respects to her, I was sitting next to John near her casket as people filed by to offer their condolences. One of the mourners spoke with John, then noticed me and proceeded to tell me what a great singer he thought I was. When he left, John leaned over to me and said, "Well, that's *one.*"

I will always be grateful to John and June for the kindness they showed to me and my wife and children. He wrote some very funny letters to his namesake, Johnny, and he was always writing them poems and giving them pictures he'd drawn and toys and books. A lot of books. He had a gift for making everyone he was talking to feel like they were the most important person in the world.

His last words to me were, "I love you, Kris." I will always love you, John.

Acknowledgments

I AM FIRST OF ALL GRATEFUL TO MY EDITOR, Kate Etue, and publisher, David Moberg, for taking me on. I was originally going to cowrite this book with Johnny Cash, and we were due to begin working together in late October 2003. He died on September 12. Fortunately, for me, his estate still wanted the project to proceed, and that's how *The Man Called Cash* evolved.

Thanks are due to Johnny's manager, Lou Robin, and his wife, Karen, for clearing the way for some of my interviewees and for giving constructive feedback on the manuscript. Thanks to Johnny's attorney, Bob Sullivan, for liaising between the various parties involved, and to Kelly Hancock and Karen Adams at the House of Cash for supplying me with phone numbers, books, cuttings, DVDs and insights.

In Nashville, the *Tennessean* newspaper allowed me free access to its archives, and this proved to be an invaluable resource. Particular thanks to editorial assistant Beverley Burnett and text archivist Christine Irizarry for making this possible. The Johnny Cash files in the archives of the Country Music Hall of Fame and Museum were also extremely useful.

I wouldn't have had such an insight into life in Dyess, Arkansas, if Everett Henson and his brother A. J. hadn't driven me from Memphis to their old hometown and then shared a wealth of material with me, including copies of the *Colony Herald* from the 1930s and yearbooks from Dyess High School. Everett is the closest Dyess has to an official historian, and he keeps former residents and other interested parties in touch through his Web site.

Likewise, I wouldn't have been able to track down so many former USAF colleagues who served in Germany if it weren't for Gayle Stelter, keeper of the Master List for the 12th/6912th Radio Squadron Mobile (RSM). Gayle was always obliging and quick, and I hope I've helped swell the size of the reunions by passing on the contact details of previously untraced men.

Mark Stielper's encyclopedic knowledge of Johnny's and June's lives was invaluable to me, as was his willingness to give me comprehensive answers to all my questions simply because of his love of the people involved and his concern for historical accuracy. Every legend deserves a Mark Stielper, as does every biographer.

Thanks to Annie McCaig for interview transcriptions, Stephen Aucutt for helping sort out the contract, and Steve Taylor for introducing me to my publisher. Thanks to Lou Freeman for letting me use the letters Cash wrote to her late husband, Ted. My interviewees are listed separately in the back of the book, and I thank all of them for sharing their memories.

—

ABOVE ALL I have to thank the Cash children—John Carter, Rosanne, Kathy, Tara, and Cindy—who gave me so much of their time, never flinched from any question, and have always been helpful and cheerful. There were aspects of their father's life that were painful for them to read, but they never tried to conceal his weaknesses or to mythologize his strengths.

—

I WAS NATURALLY DISAPPOINTED not to have worked on this project with the man himself. My only consolation is that not having him around has made me dig deeper for the truth. If he had spoon-fed me the information, I might have been tempted to pass it on without subjecting it to the normal rigorous tests.

I hope that, in the spirit of honesty and self-examination that he promoted in his work, he would approve of *The Man Called Cash*. When I met him in 1988 I gave him a copy of my book *Hungry for Heaven*, which was a study of the various religious influences on rock-'n'-roll throughout its history. On the tour bus back from Brighton to London I spent the journey talking to June, while Johnny sat across the aisle engrossed in reading the book. Two or three days later he phoned me to tell me how much he'd enjoyed it. The one sentence I can remember from all he said was, "In that book you told me things I didn't know about people I've known all my life." I'd like to think that he'd say something similar if he read *The Man Called Cash.*

The Man Called Cash

He's a poet, he's a picker—
He's a prophet, he's a preacher—
He's a pilgrim and a preacher and a problem when he's stoned—
He's a walkin' contradiction
Partly truth and partly fiction
Takin' ev'ry wrong direction on his lonely way back home.[1]

—"THE PILGRIM; CHAPTER 33"
Kris Kristofferson

1

First to Cross

WHEN JOHNNY CASH LOST HIS WIFE, June Carter Cash, in May 2003, the public took a sudden deep breath. Surely it was Cash who should have died first. It was he who had subjected himself to an extensive catalog of physical abuse. It was doubtful whether he had a bodily organ that hadn't been operated on, an area of skin that hadn't been gashed, or a significant bone that hadn't been cracked. It was he who had overdosed on drugs, been pulled out of car wrecks, and even undergone double-bypass surgery. Even though he was June's junior by two and one-half years, everyone assumed he'd be the first to go. That's the way he wanted it, if they weren't able to go together.

> And when it's all over
> I hope we will go together
> I don't want you to be alone, you know.
>
> ("I Love You Tonight," 1993)

The obvious question on everyone's mind was, "How will he cope now that she's gone?" The couple's mutual devotion was legendary—it had become impossible to

1

imagine one without the other. In the days when Cash was physically tough, the loss of his wife would have been a devastating blow that would probably have sent him straight back on painkillers, so how would he manage now that he was frail and sick? Would he lose his faith? Would he ever record another song? Would he die of a broken heart?

His most recent single, a cover of Trent Reznor's "Hurt," had sounded like the final breath of music by a man admired for his honesty and self-disclosure. Although written about the pain of heroin addiction, Cash had appropriated the song's gritty imagery, masterfully turning it into a melancholy meditation upon his own mortality. The promotional video, directed by Mark Romanek, endorsed this interpretation through selected flashbacks of Cash's public life and lingering shots of the derelict and flood-damaged House of Cash museum where once-prized trophies now lay discarded and broken.

Reznor may well have had junkie squalor in mind when he coined the phrase "my empire of dirt," but Cash's weak and wavering voice imbued new meaning. All empires eventually end in dirt, in dust—even show-business empires. As a Bible-loving Christian, surely Cash recalled the words of Jesus:

> Do not store up for yourselves treasures on earth, where moth and rust destroy, and where thieves break in and steal. But store up for yourselves treasures in heaven, where moth and rust do not destroy, and where thieves do not break in and steal. For where your treasure is, there your heart will be also. (Matthew 6:19–21)

The video frequently cuts from Cash's ravaged features, as he sings and plays guitar, to clips of the swaggering, powerful, dark-haired man he had once been. Here was Cash at San Quentin; Cash waving from the firebox of a steam train; Cash fooling around with June in the back seat of his RV while on tour. The truth of fading beauty, forgotten earthly achievements, and broken human bonds, powerfully and yet wordlessly seeps from the screen. For viewers, "Hurt" lived up to its title, producing at least a lump in the throat, possibly even a tear in the eye. The video peaks emotionally with Cash singing,

> What have I become, my sweetest friend?
> Everyone I know goes away in the end.[1]

As he delivers these lines, the view cuts to June, standing at the foot of a staircase watching him with conflicting emotions of admiration and pity, wonderment and sorrow etched across her face. What indeed had her man become? In actuality, old, gray, feeble, partially sighted, and diabetic. Throughout it all though, she had remained, undoubtedly, his sweetest friend. Her lip quivers, as though she knows that she is watching the man she loves singing his final testament, but it may have been due to her awareness of her own mortality and the prospect that she may precede him. What Mark Romanek didn't know as he filmed this reaction shot was that the day before, October 17, June had been diagnosed with a leaking heart valve.

Death no longer frightened Cash, but loneliness did. As a convinced Christian, he welcomed the imminent separation of soul from body. Cheating death in 1988 initially made him angry. Waking up, he realized, meant a continued life of pain, whereas death meant eternal bliss. The possibility of losing June, though, was an excruciating thought because he found it impossible to contemplate life without her. She was not only his wife but his spiritual companion, his artistic partner, and his caregiver. While maintaining her characteristic optimism and boundless energy, she had nursed him through a series of life-threatening illnesses. She was, as he would often say, his solid rock.

During the early part of 2003, Cash entered the hospital three separate times—his deterioration most noticeable upon his release from Nashville's Baptist Hospital on April 1, 2003, after a three-week stay during which he was on a ventilator for three days. Only seventy-one, he looked *old*. With sunken cheeks and shaking hands, for the first time in his life he had to be pushed in a wheelchair. Once at home, he relied on a walker. Plagued with diabetic abscesses on the bottom of his feet, he needed special oversized shoes with holes in the soles to prevent rubbing. Wearing them made him look slightly Chaplinesque. June fussed over him as best she could, keeping him as comfortable as possible. Although she prided herself on doing everything from cleaning to cooking meals, she and Cash now found themselves in the constant company of two professional caregivers, one of them medically trained.

When Cash returned home in April, it wasn't to the large house on Old Hickory Lake where he and June had lived since marrying in 1968, but to a home nearby that years ago he'd bought for his parents. Though his mother, Carrie Cash, died more than ten years earlier, everyone still referred to the property as "Mama

Cash's house." Since Cash could no longer climb stairs, the ranch house made perfect sense as a place to recuperate while elevator installation continued at the Big House.

Though smaller, Mama Cash's house was comfortable. It forced the couple together. Back home Johnny tended to hide away in his upstairs study, burying himself in books or music. At Mama Cash's he and June would share the gospel and bluegrass CDs his office sent over at his request, or the two would sit and watch television together. Only at bedtime did they separate. Reluctantly, Cash agreed he needed the hospital bed that was put in a single bedroom that led off one end of the living room. June's room was at the other end.

At five o'clock in the morning, two days after arriving home, he woke to the arrival of his younger sister, Reba Hancock, and her daughter Kelly, who worked at the House of Cash. When they stopped by his bedroom door, he knew that trouble had come to the family. "I know that you're the messenger, Reba," he said. "You've been sent to tell me that Louise is gone."

Louise, their oldest sister, had suffered the ills of pancreatic and liver cancer since July 2002. Three hours earlier she had died at her home in Hendersonville at the age of seventy-nine. Hers was the first death in the immediate Cash family for almost ten years. The funeral of Margaret Louise Cash took place at College Heights Baptist Church two days later on Sunday, April 6, and she was buried at Hendersonville Memory Gardens. Cash was too weak to attend.

On the day that Louise died, Ron Keith, a photographer from Madison, Tennessee, was due to shoot a cover photograph of June for her recently recorded solo album, *Wildwood Flower*. June didn't feel well and she called to cancel, but Keith, who'd known June since he was a child, talked her out of it. "You know how these things go," he'd said. "I'll come in and do it very quickly. You can just step outside the house." June relented, although she worried that she looked drained, and Keith came and shot some pictures of her by the house on the lake. A couple of days before, she had showed him round the garden pointing out the various trees that were in bloom. She wanted plenty of flowers in the pictures so the feeling of springtime would come across.

The next day when she accepted an award for "Hurt" on Cash's behalf at the CMT Flameworthy Video Music Awards, it was obvious to onlookers that she was unwell. Not only was she physically bloated as the result of the fluid buildup in her body, but also she was mentally confused due to the lack of oxygen reaching her brain. She looked disheveled and flubbed her lines. The show was broadcast live on television, and Cash watched it at home in the company of his producer, Rick Rubin.

On April 11, 2003, she was admitted to the intensive care unit at Baptist Hospital where she was diagnosed with congestive heart failure, though the doctors were unsure of how best to treat her. She developed a serious cardiac arrhythmia and had to be defibrillated, but she was able to sit up in bed and watch old videos of herself as she recovered. After five days she was considered well enough to return home.

On April 28, she developed acute breathing problems. When her niece Kelly called at the home, the nurse was examining her. The nurse instructed, "Get her straight into the hospital for tests." Kelly called the couple's physician, Dr. Terri Jerkins, at Baptist Hospital and made arrangements for June to be taken in. In retrospect, Kelly believes that June knew she might never come home. Before she left the house, she had a brief conversation with Cash, in which she insisted, "I have to go, and you have to let me go." It was unusual language for June and seemed to have ominous undertones. "Don't worry about me," she continued. "I have to go now. You stay here and take care of yourself."

Over the next three days June underwent a full battery of tests. Doctors established that fluid on the lungs, due to disease in her heart's mitral valve, had caused her breathing difficulties. This inflow valve opens to allow freshly oxygenated blood to flow into the left ventricle of the heart so that blood can be pumped throughout the body. When it fails to open or close completely, blood leaks backward into the lungs, causing buildup. The heart then has to work harder to compensate for the loss of blood, and this leads to heart failure, often recognized by its symptoms of fatigue and shortness of breath.

The only solution was a replacement valve, but because June had taken prescribed blood-thinning medication during her Christmas vacation in Jamaica, surgery would have to wait until she discontinued the medication and her blood had begun to coagulate normally. June was apprehensive about undergoing major surgery at the age of seventy-three, saying she didn't think she had the energy to cope. Cash pleaded with her to go through with it, because it offered the only realistic possibility of extending her life. He told her how much he loved and needed her and said that for him life without her would have no meaning. She eventually agreed, and May 7 was set as the operating date. The day before, her son, John Carter Cash, visited her with the contact sheets from Ron Keith's photo session. She looked over them in her hospital bed, and while Keith had done a good job, she wasn't happy with the way she looked. She looked ill, she thought. She suggested that they go ahead with an alternative cover.

The operation went well. Doctors successfully replaced her damaged mitral valve with one made from an animal's aortic valve. Settled into the intensive care unit (ICU) and attached to a respirator, she surprised her doctors the next day, by recovering enough to breathe unaided. Cash came in and spent six hours at her bedside in his wheelchair. Relieved that they had seemingly weathered the worst, they laughed with each other. June ate a dish of Jell-O. Cash told her that once he got back to the lake house he planned to build up his strength enough to walk again. Rick Rubin had recommended a kinesiologist, Dr. Phil Maffetone, who would wean him off much of his medication and develop a program that would restore the withered muscles in his legs. Then, when they were both recovered, Cash wanted them both to fly to Germany to see their friends Walter and Monica Eschenbach.

But after he left the hospital, June put a call through to Kathy, the second eldest Cash daughter and the only one living in the Nashville area. June still seemed breathless and unable to talk for long. She told her that although she was off the respirator she didn't feel that she was going to make it. "You're gonna be fine, June," Kathy said. "People have that surgery all the time. I'm sure that you're hurting so bad at the moment that you feel you're not going to make it." But June was insistent. "No, honey. I really need you to know that I'm not gonna make it. Please take care of Daddy."

Kathy didn't share the conversation with her father. He had gone home confident in June's recovery and looking forward to her homecoming. He'd even told Kelly that he believed June's speedy recovery had been an answer to prayer because one of the doctors had told him that it was unusual for a patient to come off the respirator so quickly after such a major operation. He'd remarked that she must have the constitution of someone thirty years younger and that it looked like she'd be moved out of ICU into one of the private suites by the weekend.

Early the next morning, at 2:00 a.m., June suffered a massive cardiac arrest. It took twenty minutes for doctors to manually resuscitate her. They couldn't use a defibrillator because of the recent surgery. But the resuscitation was only enough to put her on a life-support machine—she remained in a coma. Cash was called to the hospital immediately, and by early morning on May 9 the family began gathering: June's daughter Rosey, John Carter, Kathy, and Rosanne.

Because they were unsure of exactly how long her brain had been deprived of oxygen, the doctors would have to wait at least three days to see if June responded to any stimuli. If there was no response, they'd carry out tests. Kelly was shocked at the effect this was having on her uncle. To her he had always been a man who was larger than life, a man who stared his own death in the face and didn't flinch, but now he was physically and emotionally broken. He looked defeated and she had never seen him that way before. After the doctors explained the situation, she saw him take a deep breath. "Okay. I'm gonna pray about it," he said. "And I'm gonna go down and see her."

For the next three days the children based themselves in an eighth-floor suite. Every half hour or so Cash would make his way down in the elevator to sit by June's bed. He held her hand. He talked to her. He prayed for her. He sang her songs and read her psalms. He begged her not to leave him. His longtime manager, Lou Robin, put out an appeal for fans to pray for her recovery, something he had done for Cash when he had been in a coma in 1997.

Tests to gauge brain activity were carried out on Monday, May 12, and then the cardiologist came up to the suite where everyone was gathered. The news, he said, was as bad as it could be. There was no brain activity. June was in a vegetative state. No one knew what to do or say, and every eye automatically turned to Cash in his wheelchair. It was the most heartbreaking moment they'd experienced. Kelly was so overcome with emotion that she had to leave the room.

Cash wanted to know what could be done, and the answer was, nothing. The damage was irreversible. He then asked everyone to join hands while they stood in a circle and prayed. "If anyone has anything to say to June," he said, "you should say it now." Then he left the suite and went down to the intensive care unit where he had to give permission for her support system to be switched off. It was expected that her bodily functions would slowly close down and that within three hours she would be dead, but instead she clung to life for three days.

The next day Cash's daughters Tara and Cindy flew in, as did June's oldest daughter, Carlene. Messages of encouragement were coming in from friends. Merle Kilgore and his manager, Kirt Webster, dropped by. John Mellencamp FedExed a letter. Kris

Kristofferson, Al Gore, and Billy Graham made phone calls. Whoopi Goldberg sent food platters for the family. Jessi Colter, widow of Waylon Jennings, flew in from Phoenix, Arizona. Michele Rollins, a close friend, traveled from Delaware. Godson Ted Rollins was there by the family's side.

Cash sat by June's bed with the children as they took turns holding her hand or brushing her hair. Sometimes her eyelids would open and his hopes would be raised. "You know, I think they're wrong," he'd say. "I think she'll be fine. She's opening her eyes." At other times he'd break down, something none of them had seen since his mother died in 1991. Then they'd hold hands and sing the gospel songs and hymns that she loved until they were all crying. The one they sang the most often was "Waitin' on the Far Side Banks of Jordan":

> I'll admit my steps are growing wearier each day
> Still I've got a certain journey on my mind
> Lures of this old world have ceased to make me want to stay
> My one regret is leaving you behind.
>
> If it proves to be His will that I am first to cross
> And somehow I've a feeling it will be
> When it comes your turn to travel likewise don't feel lost
> For I will be the first one you will see.
>
> And I'll be waiting on the far side banks of Jordan
> I'll be sitting drawing pictures in the sand
> And when I see you coming I will rise up with a shout
> And come running through the shallow water reaching for your hand.[2]

Cash would return to the eighth floor to get some sleep, but within minutes he would be restless and making an excuse to leave. "I can't stay," he'd say. "I've got to go back down to see June." On May 15, the signs came that her system was finally shutting down, and the whole family gathered around her bed. At 5:04 p.m. that Thursday the end came.

Cash wanted to go straight home, but his physician, Dr. Jerkins, insisted that he stay. "You need to be in the hospital," she told him. "You're run down." Reluctantly, about eight o'clock that evening, he climbed into a bed. Only Rosanne, Kelly, Karen, and his two caregivers, Betty and Peggy, remained. Cash was adamant that he wasn't going to hang around for long and, true to his word, at 4:00 a.m. he asked Rosanne to drive him home.

The next day he began planning June's funeral. It would take place at First Baptist Church in Hendersonville where they had frequently worshiped since first visiting in November 1967. Her favorite songs would be sung by some of her favorite singers. The gospel that June believed in would be preached. A cross section of friends, family, and fans would share their memories of her. The coffin would be pale blue, June's special color. Then she would be buried in the Hendersonville Memory Gardens alongside her mother, Maybelle, her father, Ezra, and her sister, Anita. Lou Robin told the media that the funeral was going to be a private affair, but when Cash heard this announced on the radio he protested. "Everybody loved June, and everybody should be able to come," he said, and so the invitation was extended to all. Eighteen hundred people attended, and the service was broadcast live on local television.

For those who hadn't seen Johnny Cash in a while, his appearance at the funeral came as a shock. Frail and bespectacled, with rapidly thinning white hair, he had to be assisted from his wheelchair into a front-row seat beside his son, John Carter. He remained stoically impassive throughout most of the service, trying to calm his nerves, but would sometimes turn to his son and whisper. His sight was so bad that he wouldn't have been able to see the extravagant display of flowers on the platform or even his wife's body in the open casket.

The church's pastor, Glenn Weekley, spoke movingly about what he believed was the core of June's Christian faith—a belief in God's love, God's grace, God's presence, God's purpose, and God's promise—and ended by saying that he knew that nothing would have pleased her more than someone coming to faith as a result of her funeral. "There are people here," said Weekley, "who are not ready to die." He warned them against postponing the examination of their souls. "I can guarantee that you'll never run out of excuses. But I can also guarantee you that you'll run out of time."

Courtney Wilson, pastor of First Baptist at the time the Cashes first walked in and sat in the back row of the church in 1967, gave a personal reminiscence of that day and the changes it had brought to their lives. It was June who had brought Cash back to church after a decade or more of wandering. "In this and many other instances," Wilson said, "June was the touching hand of God in someone's life." He didn't want to minimize the pain her loss had brought but, he said, addressing Cash directly, "You know that God is sufficient for all your needs." Cash slowly nodded his head.

Larry Gatlin, who introduced each of the participants in the service, sang "Help Me" with his two brothers. Emmylou Harris and Sheryl Crow joined forces on "Angel Band" and "On the Sea of Galilee." Laura Cash, John Carter's wife, played "How Great Thou Art" on the fiddle. Members of the Carter Family— Janette Carter, Joe Carter, and Dale Jett—from southwestern Virginia sang "Anchored in Love." When the Oak Ridge Boys performed "Loving God, Loving Each Other," Cash took a tissue from his pocket and began wiping his eyes for the first time.

> Loving God, loving each other,
> Making music with my friends;
> Loving God, loving each other,
> And the music never ends.[3]

Spoken tributes were given by people who had known completely different aspects of June's life. A message from the prime minister of Jamaica praised her work with charities in Montego Bay. Film producer James Keach and his actress-wife, Jane Seymour, spoke of her television role on *Dr. Quinn, Medicine Woman*. A Baptist minister came from California to speak of how he owed his salvation to her witness. Tearful fans merely wanted to express their gratitude for her life and music. The overwhelming impression given of June was someone who was utterly selfless, someone whose fulfillment came from serving God and serving others.

The most eloquent and moving tribute came from Rosanne, the only family member to speak. She spoke glowingly of the way June gave to all who came into her life and how she banned the use of the word *stepchildren* in her family. "In her eyes there were two kinds of people in the world: those she knew and loved and those she didn't know and loved," Rosanne said.

> She looked for the best in everyone. It was a way of life for her. If you
> pointed out that a particular person was perhaps not totally deserving of

her love and in fact might be somewhat of a loser she would say, "Well, honey, we just have to lift him up." She was forever lifting people up.

It took a long time for me to understand that what she did when she lifted you up was to mirror the very best part of you back to yourself. She was like a spiritual detective: she saw into all your dark corners and deep recesses, saw your potential and your possible future and the gifts you didn't even know you possessed, and she "lifted them up" for you to see.

She did it for all of us, daily, continuously. But her great mission and passion were lifting up my dad. If being a wife were a corporation, June would have been the CEO. It was her most treasured role. She began every day by saying, "What can I do for *you*, John?" Her love filled up every room he was in, lightened every path he walked, and her devotion created a sacred, exhilarating place for them to live out their married life. My daddy has lost his dearest companion, his musical counterpart, his soulmate and best friend.

Rosanne ended with a story of a family reunion Cash had organized that he called Grandchildren's Week. During it June was honored each day with special tributes and songs from the grandchildren, and on one of the days she sent everyone on a canoe trip down the Holston River. She continued,

It was a gorgeous, magical day. Some of the more urban members of the family had never even been in a canoe. We drifted for a couple of hours and as we rounded the last bend in the river to the place where we would dock, there was June, standing on the shore in the little clearing between the trees. She had gone ahead in a car to surprise us and welcome us at the end of the journey. She was wearing one of her big flowerered hats and a long white skirt, and she was waving her scarf and calling, "Hellooo!" I have never seen her so happy.

So, today, from a bereft husband, seven grieving children, sixteen grandchildren and three great-grandchildren, we wave to her from *this* shore as she drifts out of our lives. What a legacy she leaves! What a mother she was! I know she has gone ahead of us to the far-side bank. I have faith that when we all round the last bend in the river, she will be standing there on the shore in her big flowered hat and long white skirt, under a June-blue sky, waving her scarf to greet us.

In the days immediately after the funeral, Cash stayed at home. What most struck those who visited him was his loneliness. Since marrying, he and June had spent hardly any time apart. It didn't seem possible to speak of Johnny Cash without adding "and June." Now it was as though part of his being had been amputated. When his children visited, he wanted them to tell him their favorite stories of June, and he'd frequently turn to a framed photograph of her that he kept beside him and start talking to it. "Oh, honey. You look so beautiful. I sure do miss you."

Yet he knew that the only way to minimize the gnawing pain was to start playing music again. He not only needed the sounds to work their healing, he needed a project to give him a new reason for waking up each morning and the fellowship of musicians to distract his mind from the loss. June had told him that she had to go, but she had also said that he had to take care of himself. When he had called Rick Rubin from the hospital to tell him that June had died, he told Rubin that he wanted to record as soon as possible. "I want to work every day," he told him. "I need you to keep me busy." Three days after the funeral Cash called Kelly at the office. "Well, I've thought about it, and I've prayed about it, and June wants me to get to work," he said. "I have a lot I need to do, and so I'm going to work." The next day he was back in the studio recording.

2

The Promised Land

ON THE THIRD FLOOR of the sprawling Hendersonville, Tennessee, home where Johnny Cash spent the second half of his life, a small study was lined with the most treasured of his thousands of books. Here he would closet himself away to read, write, listen to music, or just think. Immediately outside the room, in his dressing area, rested a large black safe in which he kept a cotton boll plucked from the fields of Dyess, Arkansas—the town of his childhood—as a reminder of where he had come from and of how much he had been blessed.

Cash had seemingly always maintained an ambivalent attitude toward his roots—wavering between nostalgia and a desire to forget. Later in life, he became increasingly interested in family history, tracing the origins of his branch of the Cashes back to seventeenth-century Scotland. He held immense pride in the values he'd learned by being brought up the hard way. Yet he had little interest in reunions and rarely returned to Dyess, despite the fact it took less than five hours to drive there from Hendersonville.

Documentary director Robert Elfstrom captured this ambivalence on film in 1968, when together they visited the white clapboard house of Cash's childhood in

Arkansas. Cash walked around the deserted building with June and his sister Louise, but instead of recounting happy times he became unusually pensive. He only stayed a few minutes before wandering alone outside in the cotton field. The visit seemed to have awakened memories that he had long tried to bury. "He walked around and then I saw that it was obviously bringing up other thoughts," says Elfstrom. "I don't know what those thoughts were. Then he left rather abruptly." Asked about the trip in a 1970 interview, Cash mused, "Every room, every window, every wall had a memory. Some almost bring tears."

Cash could never quite bring himself to tell the full story of his early life and the inner conflicts produced during those years. His anger, self-destructive tendencies, and insecurity quite possibly originated with his early relationship with his father, Ray Cash, though in his first autobiography he expressed nothing but admiration for the man. However, he tellingly dedicated that book to June's father, Ezra 'Eck' Carter, "who taught me to love the Word." In his second autobiography, published after his father's death, he questioned the authenticity of his father's Christian conversion and rather pointedly asserted that he didn't visit his father's grave any longer. Yet he stopped short of discussing the full extent of the effect his father's behavior had had on his life.

Like many of his fellow country farmers, Ray Cash loved guns, but, unlike most of them, he seemed to gain an unhealthy pleasure from the process of destruction. He boasted of how he once killed fifty cows with a box of fifty bullets. Cash told his daughter Kathy a story from his teenage years, during which he had a pet dog that gave birth to a litter of puppies, which his father didn't want. "Grandpa put all the puppies in a bag with a rock in it and threw it in the river, and he made Dad come and watch as they drowned. Then he shot the dog."

But, oddly enough, even though such behavior wounded the sensitive Cash deeply as a child and stirred up inner turmoil, Cash almost always maintained that his father never inflicted physical or emotional pain on him. While creating a parent journal, his daughter Tara once asked him, "When you needed punishment as a child, which parent corrected you, and how?" His response: "My mother swatted me with a fly swatter once. I got smart with her. My dad never touched me in his life."

Ray could also be extremely racist and remained that way throughout his life. Though he often talked of the lynchings he witnessed as a child, (there were eighty-two lynchings in Arkansas from the year of his birth until the time he left to go overseas with the army), there was only one in his hometown and that when he was a baby. One of Ray's brothers, a sheriff during the 1920s and a judge during the 1930s, used to boast of his mistreatment of blacks.

Even as an old man living in Hendersonville in the home purchased for him by his now-famous son, Ray held on to his racist views. One afternoon, Cash dropped by with his daughters and a young Jamaican boy named Anthony, who worked on his Caribbean property, Cinnamon Hill. When they stood up to leave, the children naturally called out, "Good-bye, Grandpa!" and Anthony, excited to be in America for the first time, also shouted out, "Goodbye, Grandpa." Ray whirled round and said "No n—'s ever gonna call me Grandpa. In fact, I don't even like having n—s in my house." Mortified, Cash never took Anthony back to his parents' home. "I should have realized that some things will never change about my dad," he said. "He grew up in Arkansas."

AFTER THE FIRST WORLD WAR, Ray met Carrie Rivers in Kingsland, Arkansas. Born in nearby Rison on May 13, 1897, Ray could trace his family back to Strathmiglo, Scotland, where William Cash lived before he left Glasgow in 1677 aboard *Good Intent* to settle in Essex County, Massachusetts. Subsequent generations of Cashes moved south to Virginia, farther south to Georgia, and eventually inland to Arkansas. The first John Cash was born in 1757 and fought in the Revolutionary War. His grandson Reuben Moses Cash served in the Confederate army. Reuben's son William Henry Cash, a farmer and then a Baptist preacher, fathered Ray Cash.

Ray had eleven brothers and sisters, although only seven of them reached adulthood. Raised on the farm, they left school at fourteen, after a rudimentary education, to pick cotton. By the time Ray joined the army, just shy of twenty, both of his parents had died. He went first to New Mexico with the Second Arkansas Infantry, where he helped protect border towns from Pancho Villa's bandits, and then, in August 1918, he received orders to report for duty in France. Fortunately by the time he was fully combat trained, the Armistice had been signed, and he found himself reassigned to low-key convoy duties.

Carrie Rivers's ancestors likewise came from Britain. It was said that five Rivers brothers left Hampshire, England, in the eighteenth century, one settling in

Virginia and four in South Carolina. Two of the South Carolina settlers established themselves in Chesterfield, close to the North Carolina border, where Carrie's father, John Lewis Rivers, was born in 1866. At twenty-six he left Chesterfield with two other families and took the train to Kingsland, Arkansas. Once settled, he married Rosanna Lee Hurst, the daughter of one of those families, and Carrie Rivers was born on March 13, 1904. Recognized as a "godly man," John Lewis Rivers also had an ear for music, leading the singing at Crossroads Methodist Church in Kingsland for forty years.

When Ray Cash received his discharge from the army on July 1, 1919, he returned home to Rison. He soon found work with a brother felling oak and cypress trees near Kingsland to build a bridge over the Saline River. For a dollar a day they lodged and ate with John and Rosanna Rivers, who lived in the nearby Crossroads community. Ray struck up a relationship with their daughter Carrie. He was twenty-two and she was fifteen. A year later, on August 18, 1920, they married, and in 1921 Carrie gave birth to their first child, Roy. Three years later came their first daughter, Margaret Louise (always known as Louise), followed by Jack in 1929.

In almost every way, Ray and Carrie were opposites. She was cheerful and outgoing, self-controlled and consistent. He tended to be sullen and withdrawn, always harboring a wild streak of unpredictability. Carrie, a lifelong devoted Methodist, was a teetotaler. Ray, a backsliding Baptist, enjoyed his spirits—to excess. Even physically they clashed: she tall and slim, he short and broad.

While winter snow still covered the ground, Carrie, with the help of a local midwife, gave birth to their third son, J. R. Cash, at home on February 26, 1932. Time would show that this boy would literally embody all of his parents' extremes. He was a man who had his mother's height and his father's breadth. One minute he could have her cheerful and friendly disposition, and then, suddenly, plunge into the harder, more rigid moods of his father. He could keep the faith like his mother but would just as easily backslide like his father. And while he could display Carrie's respect for discipline, he would often reproduce Ray's wild and uncontrollable behavior.

Even choosing his name pulled his parents in different directions. His mother wanted to call him John after John Lewis Rivers, but his father wanted to call him Ray after himself. *Ray John Cash* didn't suit Carrie, and *John Ray Cash* didn't suit Ray, so they compromised by naming him J. R. Cash. "Did you ever have an imaginary friend?" Tara asked, in another question for her parent journal. "Yes," he told her. "Sometimes I am two people. Johnny is the nice one. Cash causes all the trouble. They fight."

The 1930s were difficult days for Southern sharecroppers like Ray Cash. Bank foreclosures had brought mass unemployment and the price of cotton had dropped more than 80 percent. A five-hundred-pound bale that was worth $125 in 1928 would only raise twenty-five dollars in 1932. Ray took any work available to provide for his expanding family. He walked miles to cut wood in a sawmill, drove cattle, worked his brother's farm, and even hopped freight trains to Charleston, Mississippi, to dismantle a chemical plant.

Because the railroad ran close to their home in Kingsland, one of Cash's earliest memories was the sound of the train whistle and the sight of migrant families huddled in boxcars. Sometimes his father would take the leftovers from their family meals and offer them to the hungry travelers. The mystery of the railroad and the symbol of hope it represented would remain with Cash throughout his life.

In 1934 Ray heard about an experimental community being set up in northeast Arkansas. Part of Roosevelt's Federal Emergency Relief Administration (FERA) provided resettlement for the families worst hit by the Depression. Sixteen thousand acres of reclaimed swampland in Mississippi County was bought in order to build a model farming community. Each family would receive a newly built house, twenty acres of land to clear and cultivate, a barn, a mule, a milk cow, and a hen coop. The town center would have a town hall, cinema, cotton mill, cannery, school, hospital, churches, cotton mill, and shops. To ensure the best market price, all the cotton picked would be collected by the colony and sold in bulk, with proceeds divided equally among the residents.

Initially known as Colonization Project Number One, and later named Dyess after Arkansas's Emergency Relief Administrator W. R. Dyess, the colony offered Ray Cash the chance he needed. His family, now seven strong with the arrival of baby Reba in January 1934, would have a new start. The project also offered the added incentive of eventual property ownership. FERA maintained a strict selection criteria. Applicants, besides having to prove their genuine need, needed a strong work ethic, outstanding moral character, and the skills to clear and farm their own land.

Ray was one of only five people chosen from Cleveland County. His experience in cotton picking and forest clearance stood him in good stead. On March 23, 1935, a pickup truck came to collect the family from Kingsland and drive them to their new home. Carrie, Louise, and baby Reba sat beside the driver. Ray and the three boys rode beneath the tarpaulin in the back, along with the few family possessions. Though a mere 250 miles, the journey down narrow icy gravel tracks and dirt roads took a day and a half. Carrie lifted their spirits by singing hymns— the most memorable to Cash being "I Am Bound for the Promised Land," probably because the heavenly hope chimed so perfectly with their earthly aspirations.

> O the transporting, rapturous scene,
> That rises to my sight!
> Sweet fields arrayed in living green,
> And rivers of delight!
>
> I am bound for the Promised Land,
> I am bound for the Promised Land;
> Oh, who will come and go with me?
> I am bound for the Promised Land.[1]

The landscape was flat and uninteresting, the soil rich and dark, and freshly painted white clapboard houses with porches at the front dotted the roads that led out like spokes from the town center. Ninety miles of ditches drained away the rainwater to prevent the land from turning back to swamp.

When the Cash family pulled up to House 266 on Road Three, the paint cans still littered the living room floor and the yard was waterlogged, but this two-bedroom home was the biggest and best they'd ever lived in. No matter that the road was little more than a dirt track, or that it was a two-mile walk into the town, or even that they had neither electricity nor running water. To Ray and Carrie it was paradise.

In Dyess everyone was on equal footing. There was no division between rich and poor, native and newcomer, or manager and worker. All of the five hundred families arrived around the same time and in the same economic condition. Each family had the same style of house on the same amount of land and shared the same opportunity to improve their situation. Cash would later remark, "I grew up under socialism."

Dyess families were expected to be essentially self-sufficient. Every household had a cow for milk, hens for eggs, a mule to pull the plough, and hogs to kill for ham and bacon. They grew corn for bread and biscuits, and alfalfa to feed the livestock. They collected rain in barrels and firewood from fallen trees. Government home economists showed the women how to can their fruit and vegetables for the winter months. Besides clothes, oil, matches, sugar, coffee, and flour, little else came from the store. "We had plenty to eat," says Joy Cox Gower, who grew up a near neighbor to the Cashes. "It might not have been what we wanted, but there was plenty of it. We didn't want for the necessities of life."

Each colonist began by clearing the land and preparing it for planting. Having never been cultivated, the land, though full of useful nutrients, was also choked with trees and thick undergrowth. Ray and thirteen-year-old Roy started by chopping trees and tearing up the undergrowth. By the end of the year they'd managed to clear and plant three of their twenty acres. They cleared more during 1936, but early in 1937 heavy rains flooded the Tyronza River and one of the main drainage ditches, putting the whole area under water. Carrie and the young children evacuated to Kingsland. Ray and Roy stayed at the house, but after a week they also had to leave. Only one family held out. Armed deputies in boats patrolled the area to prevent looting while radio broadcasts from Memphis kept the now-scattered residents informed of the water levels. For a while it seemed that the whole dream of a new life would literally be washed out.

When the Cashes returned home on February 16, they found the inside of the house covered in silt and their land dotted with driftwood. All things considered, they'd gotten off lightly. The worst things they faced were the snakes who'd taken refuge in the barn and the hens who'd laid eggs on the living room sofa. Ray reckoned that the deluge had made the soil even better for cotton, and he was soon harvesting two bales per acre as well as soybeans and corn.

By the time he was six years old, J. R., when not at school, was helping out in the cotton field. He started as the water boy, but when he got older he carried his own six-foot-long canvas sack to fill with cotton. The work was tiring and tedious. The increasing weight of the sack hurt his back, and the sharp spikes on the cotton heads cut his hands. Yet, when he looked back on his cotton-picking days, he didn't remember the pain, but only the love he learned for the land and respect for diligence.

Music provided both a relief from the hardship of work and an escape to places beyond the limited horizons of this perfectly designed community. Farmers sang hymns in the fields to pass the time and take their minds off their aching backs and bleeding hands. Inside, music on the radio brought a magical world from down the railroad, where the lights were brighter and the buildings were taller. "Nothing in the world was as important to me as hearing those songs on that radio," Cash remembered. "The music carried me up above the mud, the work, and the hot sun."

If correct, Cash's reminiscences reveal that, from an early age, he had almost a mystical connection with music. He realized that music did things to him, that it could create states of consciousness like nothing else. When he thought of beauty, the most beautiful thing he could picture was a song like "Vacation in Heaven." When he thought of God he thought of songs like "I'll Fly Away," which, to him, were prayers. "These songs carried me away," he once wrote. "They gave me a taste of heavenly things."

The first song Cash recalled hearing on the radio was "Hobo Bill's Last Ride," a ballad that told the sad tale of a railroad bum who dies of neglect. It contained many of the elements that would characterize Cash's future: storytelling, the railroad, loneliness, poverty, a marginalized character, and death. Perhaps unsurprisingly, his favorite book at the time was a 1918 Western titled *Lone Bull's Mistake* by James Willard Schultz.

Ray Cash thought his son was wasting time by listening to the *Grand Ole Opry* on WSM from Nashville or the *Wheeling Jamboree* on WWVA from Wheeling, West Virginia. He took the view that popular music kept people's minds off what was important and filled their heads with escapist rubbish. It wasn't a view that Carrie shared. She played piano at church and sang to her children in the evenings, and she wondered if her son might follow in the footsteps of her singing-instructor father.

By 1939 Roy Cash was playing in an amateur band with four classmates. They called themselves the Delta Rhythm Ramblers. The fact that his brother performed and had been on KCLN in Blythesville made a deep impression on the seven-year-old J. R. Cash. Though they never made any recordings, the *Dyess Eagle* in April 1939 reported that they won first place in a local talent contest held in Portia and would consequently be competing in a statewide contest in Little Rock on May 15. Unfortunately, the band broke up when World War II drafted all the members. Only two survived the war.

Meanwhile, the births of Joanne in 1938 and Tommy in 1940 completed the

Cash family. With Roy away in the navy, Jack became J. R.'s biggest influence. Named after the former World Heavyweight Champion boxer Jack Dempsey, Jack Cash was tall, strong, cheerful, hardworking, and passionate about his faith. He read his Bible assiduously at home, tried to base all actions on Christian principles, and wasn't afraid to defend his beliefs in front of others. To J. R. he was everything a boy should be.

The Baptist church stood on the corner of Ash Street and Third. A three-story white building with a pitched roof rather than a steeple, it could seat up to four hundred people. It was here that Cash first heard the Bible stories that would exercise a hold on his imagination for the rest of his life, where he fell in love with the words and music of hymns, and where he first felt challenged by the message of the gospel. Although his understanding and appreciation deepened over the years, the lessons that he learned at First Baptist and the example of the simple Christian cotton farmers and their wives remained a constant reference point for Cash.

Two of his closest friends while growing up in Dyess were A. J. Henson and J. E. Huff. "We were like the Three Musketeers," says J. E. "We were three distinctly different personalities, but we never had an argument." A. J.'s father was Baptist and his mother was a member of the Church of Christ, so he had a choice of where to worship on a Sunday. Mostly he would go to the Church of Christ, because the altar calls at the Baptist church scared him. J. E. though would go with Cash, not only to both Sunday services but to the Wednesday night Bible study. He reckons that from the age of eight onward they went seven straight years without missing a single meeting.

With that kind of record, it seemed almost inevitable that Cash would respond to an altar call one Sunday. Being "saved" was a cultural rite of passage in rural Southern communities of the period. If someone hadn't "made a decision" by their early teenage years, the adults would wonder why. There were no open atheists in Dyess—only good Christians and backsliders. The pressure to conform made it difficult to differentiate between those who claimed conversion simply because it was expected of them and those who'd made a genuine commitment.

At age twelve, Cash answered the call during a revival in 1944. This was the age that many Southern Baptists regarded as the "age of accountability," when children were considered morally developed enough to choose or refuse. This was the age, according to the Gospel of Luke, that Jesus went to Jerusalem with his parents for the Passover and, with a clear sense of his divinity, debated with the rabbis in the temple.

If Cash remembered who preached the night of his conversion he never mentioned it. It's unlikely that he heard anything that he hadn't heard before. It was just the right night. He'd always known that someday he would have to choose one way or another, and he'd tried to put it off, but this night, for a reason he couldn't explain, he felt that postponing the decision would, in itself, be a decision. How many times could a person put off salvation? If Jesus Christ was "the way, the truth and the life," what possible benefits were there in keeping him waiting?

Cash believed in the reality of heaven. He also believed in the reality of hell. Heaven was like the sound of sweet music working on your soul at the end of a hard day's work. Hell was like the red glow of burning fields in the still of an Arkansas night. The fear of hell was one of the instruments God used to make us hunger after heaven. When the preacher called for those who wanted their sins forgiven to make their way to the front, Cash got out of his seat as the congregation sang "Just as I Am":

> Just as I am, without one plea,
> But that Thy blood was shed for me,
> And that Thou biddest me come to Thee,
> O Lamb of God, I come, I come![2]

Cash would never regret or renounce this decision. And though he would go through long periods of disobedience, he never lost the conviction that Christ had accepted him, just as he was, and that nothing could reverse that acceptance. The church's thirty-five-year-old pastor, Hal Gallop, baptized him soon afterward in the Blue Hole, a large pond used by all the local churches. J. E. Huff experienced a similar call around the same time. "When I was saved I didn't want to come down because I felt so light," he says. "I'm sure J. R. felt the same."

Cash's conversion made him feel even closer to Jack. They'd always been brothers by blood; now they were spiritual brothers too. They were on the same road and headed for the same destination. Jack had even told those close to him that he wanted to become a preacher. Then, in May 1944, when Jack was fourteen, he was killed. Jack's death, more than any other single event, would shape Cash's life.

Many times Cash would tell the story of how Jack went off one Saturday to cut fence poles on the circular saw in the school's agricultural building, and how he tried to persuade Jack to go fishing instead, but Jack declined because he needed the money. Cash would then recount how later, when coming back from the river, he met his father carrying Jack's blood-soaked clothes and learned that there'd been an accident and that Jack might not make it. Seven days later, with his family around the hospital bed, Jack passed away.

What Cash never said in interviews or in his books, but confided to close friends and some of his children, was that his father had blamed him for Jack's death. This contributed to Cash's lifelong feeling that he didn't deserve the happiness and success that came his way. Ray told him bluntly that he should have died rather than his faithful brother, that he had no business going fishing while Jack was out working for the family.

It's impossible to imagine what these accusations did to Cash's tender psyche. To lose the brother he idolized and loved, only to then be blamed for the death, had to be almost too much to bear. It perhaps explains why, in 1995, he told journalist Nick Tosches that while he had always referred to Jack's death as an accident, he actually believed something more sinister. "There was a neighbor that went down to the shop with him that day and disappeared after the accident. We couldn't prove anything, but I always thought of it as murder. My mother and daddy didn't. They never mentioned that boy. Nothin' was ever done about it."

Many believe the neighbor in question was Everett Strawn, who as a twelve-year-old, happened to meet Jack on his way into the school and asked to join him in his morning activity. He stood to the side as Jack cut the fence posts on the machine. He was watching when the circular blade suddenly lurched toward Jack. "It was one of those saws that you pull toward you," he recalls. "It hit a snag or something. It jumped and came on out and got him." [A rumor also emerged that a wrangler passing through the colony had somehow been responsible for the death, but no evidence has ever emerged to prove that anyone but Strawn was present at the time or that the death was anything but a terrible accident.]

The majority of fatal accidents involving circular saws occur when the guard is not in place, causing the wood to jump, or when the machinist reaches over the saw to clear away waste and comes into contact with the revolving teeth. In Jack's case, the blade ripped through his clothing and into his stomach. Blood splashed onto the sawdust on the floor, yet Strawn remembers that Jack didn't fall down. He walked calmly out of the building and lay down beneath a tree, holding his stomach to prevent his intestines from falling out. "I saw it happen," Strawn says. "But there wasn't much I could do except to raise the alarm."

He ran to the home of the school custodian, Mr. Matlock, who called an ambulance. Dr Hollingsworth, the community's all-purpose physician, operated but couldn't repair the extensive damage and didn't expect Jack to last the night. With the pain controlled by morphine, Jack clung to life. On May 17, the midweek Bible study at First Baptist turned into a prayer meeting for Jack Cash, and the next day he seemed to rally. He read letters and spoke to his mother. When he began hallucinating the next day, Dr. Hollingsworth, realizing his patient was near death, suggested that the whole family spend the night at the hospital.

On the morning of May 20, J. R. came to see his brother—ashen and swollen with gangrene—for the last time. He brought his cheek down next to Jack's and told him good-bye. Jack began to ramble. What he actually said has varied depending on the teller and the passage of time, but the consistent memory has been that he asked his mother whether she could hear the angels singing. Jack said that he could hear them and that was where he was going. Then, with all his family gathered around him, Jack Cash passed away.

The next day the body lay in an open coffin in the living room of the Cash home while those who knew Jack came by to pay their respects. Joy Gower was fourteen at the time and went with her mother. "The adults would talk to the family and offer their condolences. I can particularly remember Tommy, who was only just four years old at the time, pulling himself up to the coffin and looking in. He was obviously wondering why his big brother was laying in a box like that."

After a funeral at First Baptist, Jack was buried in the cemetery twelve miles away in Bassett. A group of his fellow Boy Scouts filled in the grave after the coffin had been lowered. A marble headstone later erected bore the Boy Scout crest, "Jack D. Cash 1929–44," and the question "Will You Meet Me in Heaven?" Unsure whether his father was truly a Christian, Jack may well have asked him this question in the hospital. "His dad didn't go to church at the time," remembers Joy Gower. "The rest of the family was real strong, but his dad wouldn't go. I was told that either the day before he died or a few hours before he died Jack told his dad that he felt he could go on if he knew for sure that he [his dad] was a Christian. That played a great part in the family's life."

The question apparently had a dramatic effect on Ray Cash. "I think that's why God allowed Jack to last those few days," says Joanne, who saw her brother die. "Daddy got down on his knees and gave his heart to the Lord." He started attending church more often, tried to control his drinking, and apparently stopped his violence. But it was always a struggle for Ray. His addictive personality and his sometimes brutal tongue would frequently hamper his progress.

The memory of Jack inspired and guided Cash. In his adult imagination Jack grew old with him and when faced with a moral dilemma Cash would ask himself what Jack would do in such a situation. "He was a very devout Christian who studied his Bible every day," he said in 1988. "He was a very wise person. He gave me advice on a lot of things. We were very close. When he died I felt a really great loss, but his memory has always been an inspiration to me."

Jack's death and the ensuing guilt made Cash more introspective. Although he enjoyed his fun, he also had a reputation for being quiet and thoughtful. He avoided competitive sports. In class photographs he always wore the slightly worried face while all those around him looked blissfully cheerful. It can be no coincidence that he always marked the age of twelve as the start of his creative life, the age at which he began writing stories and poems, the age at which he first learned the rudiments of guitar playing.

"It's when I really started writing," he later said. "I was trying to put down what I was feeling . . . I'd never known death either in the family or among friends, and suddenly I realized that I wasn't immortal, that I too could die someday. The poems and songs reflected the despair and grief of Jack being killed. I guess it told me a whole lot about life early on."

His mother had bought a guitar from the Sears & Roebuck catalog, but around the time of Jack's death it disappeared without mention. Years later Cash realized that they must have sold it to get the family through some hard times. So when he wanted to learn guitar, he visited a boy named Jesse Barnhill, who was a year ahead of him at school. Despite a withered right hand—the result of childhood polio—Barnhill impressed Cash with his ability to create chords on his Gibson flat top with his left hand and beat a rhythm on the strings with his right hand. He would play songs by Hank Snow, Ernest Tubb, and Jimmie Rodgers while they both sang along. Years later, writing of his guitar technique, Cash referenced that early influence: "Sometimes it's magic and I just believe that when it all comes together it's the right way for me to do it. Like Jesse Barnhill did it. Like Mama did it."

Although his grades in English didn't show it (he regularly got Cs and Ds), Cash began to build a reputation as a writer. Cohen Cox, who graduated three years ahead of Cash, can remember him reciting one of his poems in front of the whole school. "It was like a talk given in rhyme," he said. "I thought it was really unusual for a guy like him to be doing at his age. I can't recall what it was about, but I do remember him doing a real good job."

Both A. J. and J. E. remember Cash as the one people would turn to if they were stuck with creative writing assignments or book reports. Once the class had to write a poem on a western theme and A. J. was stumped. Cash ended up writing it for him. A. J. can still remember eight lines of it:

> The top hand mounted his trusty steed
> And rode across the plain.
> He said, "I'll ride until setting sun
> Unless I lose my rein."
> The horse gave a jump and then a jerk
> And Bob drew up the slack.
> He rode his trail until setting sun
> Then rode a freight train back.

The young Cash was always moderate in his way of life. The church's teachings and the model of his mother profoundly influenced him, and his father's preconversion behavior only made him appreciate peace and sobriety all the more. He had no intention of following his father's example, and he pitied his mother for having to put up with him. When a boy who drank started to hang around with his gang, Cash informed him that he wouldn't be welcome until he quit drinking. "He was dreamy," says A. J. "He was kind of off on another planet, but not in a bad way. He always seemed to have some view of where he was going, but I don't think at that time he would have envisaged a musical career."

There wasn't a lot for young people to do in Dyess. On weekends the teenagers (over 180 attended Dyess High School) hung out around the Circle, where the main attractions were the movie theater, a roller rink, and a café with a jukebox. When Tara asked her father about his first date for her parent book, he replied: "I was sixteen. My dad let me have the car (a 1935 Ford) and I took Evelyn Shaddix to the movies and got her back by 9:30 p.m." Asked about his first kiss, he added: "Evelyn Shaddix in the car, first date. She immediately said, 'Take me home.' And I did!" To the question, "Who was your first girlfriend?" he said, "Louise Nichols. But she didn't know it."

Louise was a girl in his class, and she admits that they "claimed each other" during their junior year in high school. "It was the way kids do these things," she says. "We were always big buddies. We were always together walking to class and doing all that stuff. I tell you, he was something special! He really was. He was just so comical and everybody loved him. Everybody. He asked me out on a date but we didn't have places to go. There was only the theater or church! So I didn't go out with him at first, but I did later. I just had to give in!"

In his senior year Cash dated fifteen-year-old Sue Moore, who'd been A. J.'s girlfriend until he joined the army at the end of eleventh grade. Innocent and uncomplicated, their relationship mostly consisted of hanging around at the café or the movie theater, usually in the company of others. "I thought he was a hunk," she says, "but at that time I don't think you could have said that he was wild about girls. He was just a kind of laid-back person. A nice, lovable guy." The relationship ended after about three months when Sue moved to Atkins, Arkansas. Cash was apparently brokenhearted, and his sister Reba wrote Sue a letter saying that he wanted her to come back. She didn't, and they never saw each other again.

Cash's only other girlfriend during his senior year was Nadine Johnson, who lived in the nearby community of Marie and went to school in Wilson. Her best friend, Joye Leta Wells, was in Cash's class and would ask Nadine to walk her home in the dark on the nights she had to stay late to rehearse school plays. It was during one of these rehearsals that she first met Cash in the school hall.

"He came in and sat in a straight-backed chair that was leaning against the wall," she remembers. "Everybody was laughing and having fun. He was carrying on and acting silly and, suddenly, the chair flew out from under him and he fell. And I thought, 'Oh my! How cute!' We got to know each other, and the night he graduated from high school he asked me for my first date."

Nadine went to the May 19, 1950, graduation as a guest of Joye Leta. Cash sang "The Whiffenpoof Song." Afterward they all went to the café at the Circle, and it was there that Cash asked her out. "When he came to get me for that first date, he had a blanket or quilt on the seat of his father's car," she said. "The car had no side windows and the seat was wet with rain."

To Nadine, Cash seemed well adjusted and popular. He was polite and never cursed or drank. Although they were both churchgoers (she belonged to the Church of Christ), they didn't discuss religion, and she even felt that Cash's mother viewed her with suspicion because she wasn't a Baptist. When Cash was in the car with her he liked to sing. In particular, she remembers him singing songs by the Inkspots and, between the lines, he would shout out invocations such as "Do you hear me, girl?" and "Say, Nadine, do you hear me?"

"I think what attracted me to him was that he was so well liked," she says. "Everywhere he went it was, 'Hey J. R. How you doing? You okay?' He had the most absolutely gorgeous brown eyes I have ever seen. That's one thing I do remember. And he was so tall and slim. He was quite attractive. An eye-catcher."

At the end of a typical date he would drive her back to Marie. "When he gave me a good-night kiss, he'd stand on the ground and I'd have to stand on the porch to make us level. I'd always be scared to death that my daddy was going to open the door. Dads were pretty strict in those days with their girls. I was a good girl though. I know that. There was never any intimacy. We just stole a few kisses."

After graduating, Cash had no idea of what to do with his life. He always claimed that he had never wanted to do anything other than be a musician, and his mother had impressed on him that he'd been given "the gift" by God, but in 1950 he was ill qualified to earn money that way. He could only pick a couple of chords on a guitar, had taken a few singing lessons in 1948 with LaVanda Mae Fielder of Lepanto, and had sung at church and at school. His only experience of commercial performances consisted of a Louvin Brothers concert and a visit to the Grand Ole Opry during a school trip in 1950.

He started by taking casual day labor. He hitchhiked to Bald Knob, Arkansas, and picked strawberries for three days; spent three weeks in Pontiac, Michigan, working at the Fisher Body Plant; and then did a two-week stint at Procter & Gamble's oleomargarine factory in nearby Evadale. On June 25, 1950, North Korea invaded South Korea and, within days, American troops were involved in their first military conflict since the end of Word War II. In July, Cash drove to Blythesville, Arkansas, and signed up for four years with the United States Air Force. He'd received his registration certificate shortly after his eighteenth birthday. He had to give a first and middle name—initials were not acceptable. He filled in "John Ray."

Joining the air force was a big change from the life he'd known thus far, but Cash always knew that someday he would have to leave his home town. There was no future for young people in Dyess. "When we were young," he once said, "it was taken for granted that we wouldn't live in Dyess when we were grown. It was the aim of every person to get a better job." As his classmate Billy Shaddix (who joined the army) says, "When we was growing up, all we was thinking about was getting out of them cotton fields. All we was thinking about was getting off the farm and doing something different."

3

Leaving Home

CASH'S MILITARY YEARS helped him grow from a boy into a man. He left Dyess a callow, naive teenager with no clear idea of what he wanted to do with his life. He returned in 1954 as a self-assured and well-traveled man with a definite vision of becoming a professional musician. The USAF had given him pride in his abilities—something he'd never had at school and had certainly never gotten from his father. Military life introduced him to a diverse range of fellow Americans and gave him the opportunity to explore the cultural centers of Europe.

After finishing his paperwork in Blythesville, Cash returned to Dyess, packed a small canvas bag, and took a train from Wilson to Little Rock, where he was inducted on July 7, 1950. From Little Rock he was sent to Lackland Air Force Base in San Antonio, Texas, for seven weeks of basic training and then on to Keesler AFB in Biloxi, Mississippi, for a special intercept operator course. While at Lackland his tests indicated he had an aptitude for typing and for distinguishing sounds. Intercept operators were trained to eavesdrop on enemy radio communications in order to transcribe the Morse code signals.

At Keesler Cash met men like Bob Moodie, Ben Perea, and Bob Whitacre, who would later serve with him in Europe. They remember him as a clean-living, affable boy who distinguished himself in his classes. He was quiet, but this wasn't because he had nothing to say, merely that he never spoke before thinking. "He was a very smart guy," says Ben Perea. "When we were learning the international Morse code, he picked it up quite a bit faster than anyone else. He had a sharp mind. He was able to learn things very quickly."

The best students on the radio intercept course were approached by the USAF Security Service, which was recruiting men for the newly formed Twelfth Radio Squadron Mobile (RSM) to be based in Landsberg, West Germany, at the forefront of cold war radio surveillance operations. Those chosen would undergo further intensive training at Brooks AFB in Texas and be subjected to rigorous background checks for top-secret security clearance. Cash, who graduated from Keesler on April 27, 1951, received one of the coveted positions.

During his eight weeks of training at Brooks AFB, he met Vivian Liberto. One Friday night, after a month of training, he and a friend went to St. Mary's roller rink on North St. Mary's Street in San Antonio and saw her skating. He was attracted, he later said, by Vivian's dark eyes and broad smile. Cash's friend bet him that he couldn't walk her home that night. He began talking with Vivian, and when it was time to leave he joined her on the bus ride home. Though she wouldn't let him kiss her or walk her to the door, she did give him her telephone number.

They dated for the rest of his stay in San Antonio. She was seventeen and from a very strict Italian American family. Her father, Tom, owned an insurance company and was an amateur magician. Her uncle, Vincent, was a Roman Catholic priest. They worried about Vivian dating a Southern Baptist and were probably relieved to learn that he was being shipped to Germany for three years of service.

Cash returned to Dyess for a month before leaving by train from Memphis. From there he went on to Trenton, New Jersey, and finally to McGuire AFB, where he met the rest of the Twelfth RSM for embarkation. Bob Moodie, who was from Rhode Island, invited him back to his family home for a weekend. On the way they stopped off in New York City. While having a coffee during the afternoon, they were approached by a man giving away two theater tickets he couldn't use. They were sixth-row orchestra tickets for the Mark Hellinger Theater on West Fifty-First Street, where a new musical titled *Two on the Aisle* was playing.

With music by Jule Styne and lyrics by Betty Comden and Adolph Green, *Two on the Aisle* gave Cash his first taste of Broadway theater. "I think we were given the tickets simply because we were young men in uniform," says Bob Moodie. "I remember we had a great view, and it was a huge theater with probably fifteen hundred seats. The stars of the show were Bert Lahr and Dolores Gray. Afterward we went to Rhode Island to meet my family, and then I had a date with my girlfriend at the time and he had a date with someone."

They left New Brunswick for Bremerhaven, Germany, in September 1951 on the USNS *General W. G. Haan,* a decommissioned warship now run by the Military Sea Transportation Service. The 10,654-ton ship could carry over forty-seven hundred troops and was capable of a speed of eighteen knots. The twelve men bound for the Twelfth RSM were kept together in an undesirable forward hold. Cash shared a cabin with four of them, including Ben Perea, a Catholic boy from New Mexico who loved to sing. Elsewhere on the ship, in a more comfortable cabin, was the singer Vic Damone, who was serving with the infantry.

"When I first saw Johnny Cash, I don't think we liked each other, because he reminded me of John Wayne, and I didn't like John Wayne," says Perea. "But then we started talking and found that we had a lot of things in common. Neither of us liked going out and getting drunk and picking up girls. We liked to write letters home and talk about our families. He'd just met Vivian and he liked to talk about her, and I'd talk about my girlfriend. He'd talk about his mom as well. He loved her very much. That's when we started singing and harmonizing together."

Landsberg AFB lay just outside Landsberg am Lech, a small town thirty miles west of Munich in the Bavarian region of Germany, with a population close to ten thousand. The town's prison had once hosted Adolph Hitler during his incarceration for treason in 1924, and it was there that he composed his book *Mein Kampf,* dictating to Rudolph Hess his theories of the supremacy of the Aryan race and the benefits of a Nazi state. In the same prison, three months before Cash arrived, four concentration camp commanders had been executed for war crimes after being tried and found guilty by a U.S. military tribunal in Nuremburg.

Originally built for the Luftwaffe for early bombing raids against France, Landsberg AFB dated back to 1935. Hit four times by the Allies, American forces commandeered the base in 1945 and used it for ammunition storage until they completed repairs. By the time the Twelfth RSM arrived in 1951, it had been upgraded into a fully modernized airbase, complete with tennis courts, a golf course, a gymnasium, and a bowling alley.

The Twelfth RSM couldn't have asked for a more beautiful setting on the *Romantische Strasse* (Romantic Route), within easy reach of rivers, streams, lakes, and mountains. They had access to sailing on Lake Ammersee, skiing at Innsbruck, and relaxing in the resort town of Garmisch-Partenkirchen in the foothills of the Alps. Neuschwanstein Castle, used by Walt Disney as the model for the castle in the animated movie *Cinderella,* was a little less than twenty miles away.

The sensitive nature of the Twelfth RSM's mission required that they function as a self-contained unit within their own quadrangle on the edge of the base. Mixing socially with other men at the base was awkward because they couldn't discuss their work. Colonel Glen E. Pennywitt, then a thirty-five-year-old major and commanding officer of the Twelfth RSM in Landsberg, remembers, "We were isolated. We lived in our own barracks and worked upstairs in the attic. We couldn't talk about what we were doing with anyone else. As a matter of fact, there was a base commander who was desperate to see what we did, but he couldn't get up my stairs. We couldn't let him in. People depended on us."

The buildings consisted of four levels. There was a basement for laundry and washing; a ground-floor leisure and eating area; upstairs dormitories; and then, tucked under the eaves, the nerve center—a cramped space where the men worked in three eight-hour shifts a day. "There were no windows," remembers Leo Ard. "The only doors were an entrance and an exit. If there was a fire [you were] gone." The work space contained little more than chairs and desks. On each desk stood an MC88 typewriter and a one-hundred-pound Hammarlund SP600-JX receiver that could cover 540 kHz to 54 MHz in six bands. Between forty and fifty men comprised a shift, known as a "trick."

The operators each wore a set of headphones, tuned in to Soviet broadcasts from both ground and air, and typed what they heard. Because they listened for Morse code signals rather than speech, they earned the nicknames "ditty bops" or "ditty chasers." The hardest part of their job, which required great patience, was calibrating the frequency, or "digging hard." Those who dug the hardest made the best operators.

"Part of the skill was being able to listen to the signal you wanted and to ignore the signals you didn't want," says Rich Collins, who worked the same trick as

Cash. "When you got the signal you wanted, what you typed out was the actual letters corresponding to the Morse code. You had no idea what you were writing. Then what we wrote was encoded and passed on to trained analysts. They were better trained than we were. They understood cryptographic techniques and had equipment to help them decode. If we heard actual voices we could record, but we couldn't translate. None of us had any knowledge of those languages."

Cash excelled at this work and gained a reputation within the Twelfth RSM both for his diligence and his speed. Despite a persistent ear infection from swimming in the Tyronza River as a boy, his hearing was acute enough to isolate sounds in the ether. He also had the ability to transcribe quickly. In high school he'd learned to type, and by the time he was in Germany he could type forty words a minute. Impressed by Cash's ability and with the fact that he was "appreciated by and liked by all his companions," Colonel Pennywitt recommended him for promotion to staff sergeant, which put Cash in charge of his forty-man trick. The promotion also meant he could be assigned top-priority work elsewhere. In June 1953 the USAF dispatched him to Foggia, Italy.

The nervous energy that would later characterize his life onstage had already begun to emerge. Cash couldn't sit or stand still. It seemed that he always had to be on the move. "I worked right next to him for a number of months, and the thing that struck me about him was that when you watched him he was always kind of agitated," says Rich Collins. "He smoked and drank coffee excessively, and his legs were always going. It was like he was impatient, nervous, or overmedicated as they would say today. On the night shift a lot of guys would get sleepy, but John was always hyper. I would remember that about him even if nothing else had happened in his life."

Years later, when remembering his youth, Cash would often paint a picture of himself as someone who became morally lax while away from the strictures of home and church. "Once I knew how to drink beer and look for a girl, it was no big thing learning how to drink the hard stuff and look for a fight," he wrote in *Cash: The Autobiography* (1997).[1] In *Man in Black* (1975) he spoke of "graduating" from beer to cognac and having "wild times" in which he would see "how good I could curse."[2] He suggested that he had become violent, claiming that his nose had been broken during a fight with a paratrooper. In 1971 he told Christopher Wren, author of his first biography, *Winners Got Scars Too,* that at Landsberg AFB he had attacked two security guards who attempted to confiscate boxes of cigarettes he was smuggling out to sell on the black market. "I invited them both out at once, and I knocked them down a fifty-foot embankment," he told Wren. "I knocked out one's teeth and I broke the other's nose. They ran off."[3]

None of these stories rings true with any of the men who served with him. This latter tale even contradicts his later claim in *Cash: The Autobiography* that, "I've done no direct physical violence to people." An assault on two military policemen would have resulted in a serious investigation followed by demotion or a dishonorable discharge if found guilty. The story of brawling with a paratrooper seems out of character for a man chiefly distinguished for abstemiousness and a peace-loving nature. Everyone who knew Cash points out that whereas it was almost expected that red-blooded American teenagers would go wild on their nights off, Cash distinguished himself with his self-control. "We would all go to German guest houses and have a few beers," remembers Chuck Riley. "If we were drinking in Landsberg, John would come with us. He would joke and do what the rest of us were doing, but if any of us felt like chasing ladies, John would just sit at the table and have another beer."

Similarly, no one can remember Cash's threatening to pistol-whip a lieutenant in Italy—another act of subordination that would have seen him court-martialed—or hurling his typewriter through a window when he got frustrated during a particularly difficult shift at Landsberg. The absence of windows in the work area makes this story difficult to believe.

Many times in his writing Cash appears to embellish basic facts to make his story more compelling. For instance, he told Christopher Wren that a school friend had put a pencil in his left ear, which caused his abnormally acute hearing. Four years later, in *Man in Black*, he suggests the incident occurred while in the service, the "school friend" morphs into "a German girl," and instead of "abnormally acute" his hearing becomes "temporarily impaired." Rather than showing signs of a bad memory, the embellishments suggest a tendency to add danger and intrigue to otherwise mundane events. As one of his producers would later say of him, "John never let the truth get in the way of a good story."

While he was, in fact, at Landsberg on March 5, 1953, the day Joseph Stalin died, his comment in *Cash: The Autobiography* that "I was who they called when the hardest jobs came up. I copied the first news of Stalin's death"[4] brings a wry smile to the faces of those who worked with him. "That's nonsense," says one. "He didn't understand Russian, and if it came in code we wouldn't have been able to decipher it anyway. It created a certain aura about his skill that in my view was directly related to his celebrity."

"I don't know if something like the fight could have happened, but if it had it would have [caused] a lot more rumor, discussion, and discipline," says Rich Collins. "You don't ever hit an air policeman. I don't even remember him having a reputation that way. He wasn't a renegade. He never tested the limits."

A controversial incident that really would have brought Cash shame was either forgotten or left out. One weekend he was in the town of Ausburg on a weekend pass. He and a couple of friends got "blasted" on German beer and cognac and went to a strip club. The colleague he went with says only, "I have a couple of good stories about what happened in Ausburg, but I wouldn't want to tell them to you." The story he doesn't want to tell is well known among others who served in the Twelfth RSM. "John was walking down the sidewalk with this friend of mine," says one of them, "and he saw a black soldier with a white German girl. He was so incensed that he used profanity to say that a black guy was trying to have sex with a white woman and that this wasn't the way it should be. The guy who was with [Cash] had to pacify and restrain him, and in the end MPs came and calmed him down. They told him that while this might not go on where he lived back home. He had to lay off or else he would be in big trouble. That was an incident that stuck with me. I had never seen him being racist back on the base. Ours was an integrated unit. There was probably a black guy for every four white guys."

Probably, a combination of the drink and Cash's cultural heritage led to the incident. Not only did he hail from what was then one of the most racist states in America, but he came from a town where the only African American anyone can remember worked as a janitor. What he saw in Germany—black GIs dating white German girls—was a totally new and shocking experience for him.

His old school friend A. J. Henson says that they were all racist at the time. They considered African Americans to be "almost a different breed" to themselves and never knew any as friends. Henson can recall stepping aside to let an African American pass by on a sidewalk in Memphis, when the friend he was with from Dyess rebuked him for doing such a thing for anyone who was only a "n—."

Throughout his books, Cash claimed that his level of religious commitment decreased during his time in Germany, but his friends remember him regularly attending the Protestant chapel on the base. They allow that he may eventually have changed his habits, but more likely because of the nature of the shifts and the days off. "I can't remember hardly a Sunday that John was not in church," says Bob Whitacre, one of his roommates. "In basic training he was in church all the time. As far as I knew it never tapered off. He was someone who didn't get carried away with his beliefs, but I don't think he had any doubt as to where he stood. He was very obviously a Christian." Says Rich Collins, "He was fundamental, decent, and Baptist. I assumed that there was a moral code behind the fact that he didn't go whoring and drinking like the other guys."

Ben Perea, who roomed with Cash at Landsberg, remembers that he would pray each day and lay on his bunk reading his Bible. "He would always express his faith," he says. "I would do my prayers, and he would do his meditation. He would meditate for what seemed like a lot longer than my prayers. He would just close his eyes and be very quiet. I can still picture him meditating very deeply, and then he would go back to his guitar and start singing."

Music had asserted its place in Cash's life almost as soon as he arrived at the base in Germany. He didn't have a record player but would listen to the Armed Forces Network and, late at night, could even tune a high-powered receiver into American domestic radio stations to listen to the *Grand Ole Opry* broadcast live from Nashville.

Very few men of the Twelfth RSM in the early 1950s liked all types of popular music. Those from the cities of the North and East liked cool jazz and swing and considered artists like Hank Snow too crude, simple, and sentimental. On the flip side, those from Southern towns and farming communities liked country and gospel and found Stan Kenton too complicated and disorganized.

Cash fell in with a group of fellow country boys whose idea of a good time was to hang out in the basement with their musical instruments for picking sessions. Rich Collins thought of them as "footlocker guys"; "the kind of guys who, if they weren't working, would play cards, do music, or socialize in small groups" as opposed to the "traveling types," who looked for pleasure in the cities or the "jocks," who played competitive sports. Ben Perea, Ted Freeman from West Virginia, Orville Rigdon from Louisiana, and Reid Cummins from Arkansas made up the original core of pickers. When Ben Perea left the Twelfth RSM in 1953, he was replaced by Bill Carnahan from Missouri.

Except for Perea, who only sang, they were all more accomplished musicians than Cash. Freeman played a mean mandolin, but he could also play fiddle and banjo and had perfect vocal pitch. Carnahan boasted the best voice and could finger-pick beautifully on guitar. Eventually, Rigdon accompanied Cash into Landsberg and helped him choose a twenty-five-Deutsche Marks guitar. Returning to the basement, he and Carnahan then had to teach John the rudiments that he'd last been taught by Jesse Barnhill. "I had to show him basic chords," remembers Rigdon. "Then he would start to sing. His key was usually E or A."

This informal group is frequently referred to as the Landsberg Barbarians, but if Orville Rigdon's memory is right, they only once played outside the barracks as part of a fund-raiser on the base for United Way, and it's unlikely that they ever formally adopted a name. If they were known as the Landsberg Barbarians, then it wasn't, as some commentators have speculated, because they acted wildly in the local bars and taverns, but as a playful reference to the biweekly base newspaper, the *Landsberg Bavarian.*

The picking sessions gave Cash the stimulus he needed to learn to play guitar and even to begin to write songs. The fact that they didn't perform in public— other than for interested onlookers from the Twelfth RSM—meant that Cash's music education took place in the context of friendship, respect, and a mutual love of music. "The other guys had been brought up playing music and they taught him," says Bob Whitacre. "Like anything else it takes practice and hard work."

The music they played was a combination of the popular songs of the time and old favorites that they'd grown up singing on farms, ranches, and cotton fields. Bill Carnahan remembers Cash singing the cowboy song "One More Ride," written by Bob Nolan of the Sons of the Pioneers. Ben Perea remembers harmonizing with Cash on the bluegrass classic "Beautiful, Beautiful Brown Eyes" and the spiritual "Were You There When They Crucified My Lord?" Their collective musical heroes included Jimmie Rodgers, Hank Snow, Roy Acuff, Ernest Tubb, and, inevitably, Hank Williams.

Hank Williams's music combined elements of folk, blues, and gospel, and the story he told usually involved someone who could be alternately hard-living and repentant. Hank sang with a poignant sadness in his voice, and yet at the same time the listener sensed that he enjoyed the misery for the dangerous edge it gave his life. He drank to drown his sorrows and then felt sorry that he'd been drunk. During Cash's time in Germany, Hank was at the peak of his recording career. In 1951 he released "Cold, Cold Heart" and "Hey, Good Looking." In 1952 he released "Honky Tonk Blues," "Half As Much," "Jambalaya," and "Setting the Woods on Fire."

The papers widely reported Williams's errant lifestyle, which would become the template for the postwar country music star. Country stars came from poor backgrounds, and as they acquired wealth they would often use it ostentatiously. Once they'd reached the top of the charts, they'd become addicted to alcohol or drugs and carry on a series of tempestuous relationships. Hank Williams died in the back of a car while being driven to a gig on New Year's Day 1953. "AFN had the story right away," remembers Jack Matheson. "That was the hardest moment of John's life in Germany. He went into a depression for the rest of the day."

Cash started writing songs while at Landsberg. Ben Perea remembers him writing "Hey! Porter" and that the military paper *Stars and Stripes* published the words. He wrote "Belshazzar," his earliest gospel song, while there, and Orville Rigdon asserts that he started writing "Don't Take Your Guns to Town" at the barracks. Certainly the song's protagonist, Billy Joe, was named after Billy Joe Carnahan. Also while in Germany, Cash saw Crane Wilbur's 1951 film *Inside the Walls of Folsom Prison,* which inspired him to begin writing almost immediately. "He liked that film quite a bit," remembers Ben Perea. "It was shown in the recreation hall on the base, and he wanted it to be shown again."

Cash also claimed that the musical inspiration for "I Walk the Line" came when someone inadvertently twisted a rehearsal tape in the Wilcox-Gay tape recorder that he'd bought from the base PX. When he hit play, it sounded like religious music, but what he was actually hearing were backward chords. "The drone and those weird chord changes stayed with me," he said. In 1956 he added the words.

The first time they heard themselves on tape was when Paul E. Smith arrived in January 1953 and spent eight weeks, with Cash as his Morse code instructor. Smith had a reel-to-reel recorder that he'd had sent to him by Allied Radio in Chicago, and he joined the boys in the basement to tape their efforts. "They would pick and sing and John would write little ditties and songs, and so I would record these," he says. "Later I was shipped to Scotland, and I sold the recorder to a GI in Kirknewton, and I let the tapes go with it."

"When we were playing in Germany I knew there was something special about John," says Carnahan. "He was kind of a charismatic character. He was always telling stories. He had the wildest imagination you ever came across in your entire life. It was a very wild imagination. He also seemed to have this uncanny ability to know which way things were going to develop in the future. He was able to anticipate trends."

Besides telling stories, Cash was writing stories. He told a friend that he had published some under the pen name "Johnny Dollar" (a popular radio detective) either in a magazine for men or in a literary journal. One of his stories from 1953, a science fiction piece titled "The Holografik Danser," was kept in his drawer until 2001, when his daughter Rosanne published it as part of the collection *Songs without Rhyme: Prose by Celebrated Songwriters.*

For a twenty-one-year-old Arkansas farm boy who'd never taken a course in literature, "The Holografik Danser" was an imaginative piece of writing. It portrayed a twenty-first-century America that had been conquered by Russia— major cities had been razed by nuclear attacks, and entertainment was paid for in kiosks and then piped into homes via phone lines. Partly inspired by the news of the explosion in television broadcasting, he envisaged a time when live holographic entertainment would be beamed into living rooms for twelve dollars a show. He further imagined the possibility of a man projecting himself into the hologram.

The story illustrates his growing preoccupation with words. One of the first things the Soviets did, he wrote in his story, "was to desecrate the English language." In order to speed up integration, the niceties of grammar and spelling were forsaken, and everyone wrote words phonetically. His friends at Landsberg remember his fascination with unusual words and new coinages. Jack Matheson has never forgotten Cash informing him that the longest word in the English language was *antidisestablishmentarianism.* With Chuck Riley he used to pass time during breaks by organizing word-making competitions. "We each had to make up a word which would stump the other," he says. "John would always beat me. I remember one time he came up with *crematearatlatax.* I gave up and asked him what it meant. He said that it was the art of burning rattails. *Latax* was Latin for the tail of an animal, *cremate* was to burn, and then there was the *rat*, obviously!"

Cash also liked to draw. Bob Moodie recalls that he loved the cartoons of Rube Goldberg and often made sketches of mechanical devices. Well remembered by those who lived in the Landsberg barracks, Cash's drawing of a saguaro cactus surrounded by sand and bleached bones hung framed on the wall beside his bed. He titled it *Custer's Last Stand*. A closer look at the drawing revealed a hidden genius—a thinly disguised finger raised as a symbol of insult. "It was giving the bird," says Jack Matheson. 'The guy was a total talent."

One of the great advantages of serving with the Twelfth RSM in Germany was the three-day break that followed every six days on duty. Men could take their passes and travel to major European cities. If transport was available they could even save money by hitching rides on military aircraft. For the more hedonistically inclined this presented a grand opportunity to sample the beer and brothels of places like Amsterdam and Copenhagen. The sporting types looked forward to skiing in the Austrian Alps or swimming on the French Riviera. To Cash, these breaks brought the chance to follow country pursuits, such as trout fishing at Gross Kitscherkoffen or exploring the art and architecture of major cultural centers. As Rich Collins observes, "It was a great opportunity for those of us who were young and who had seen nothing more than our local towns to go to Europe and see this remarkable variety of cultures. For most of us it was a tremendously opening experience."

Cash most preferred traveling with Ted Freeman and Ben Perea. The red-headed Freeman grew up on a farm in Nicholas County, West Virginia, and Cash nicknamed him Fenrod, both in honor of his given name, Fenton, and the eponymous twelve-year-old hero of Booth Tarkington's novel *Penrod*. They took the train down to Venice, where they played together in a sidewalk café, and to Oberammergau, where the renowned passion play is produced once every decade. The last production had been in 1950, when General Eisenhower had attended a show. With Perea Cash went to Zurich, London (where they saw the newly crowned Queen Elizabeth arriving for the premiere of the film *The Conquest of Everest* at a cinema near Piccadilly Circus), Munich, Salzburg, Amsterdam, and Berlin.

What struck Perea was the way in which Cash would become quietly absorbed in all he saw. In Holland the sight of the old windmills with their huge wooden sails transfixed him. "He looked at them, and once he saw something he really liked he would stop. He would gaze at it and just stand there thinking. I'd just stay beside him until he was done. That's the way he was."

When they went to Paris in October 1953, Cash wanted to drink in everything. "He wanted to see the Sorbonne. He wanted to see Notre Dame. He wanted to visit the Louvre and see the *Mona Lisa.* Oh, how he wanted to see that! We saw the Pigalle district and the Arc de Triomphe. We did a lot of walking in Paris. He wanted to walk and to see. He didn't really like organized tours. He wanted to walk and see, to look at everything. He actually wanted to touch the things. To see and to touch."

Cash's jottings made on the trip reveal how little sophistication he had at the time. A country kid who grew up surrounded by flat, dark earth, cotton, and single-story, white buildings now stood before some of civilization's greatest artistic and cultural achievements. He had no points of comparison, no vocabulary adequate enough to analyze his responses. It was all so awe-inspiring.

Upon first impression, October 18, 1953, Cash found Paris "a poor, dirty place," but after cleaning up back at the hotel and putting on civvies he found it "didn't look so bad." He saw the Arc de Triomphe: "It was really a beautiful thing. About three times as big as I thought it would be and a lot prettier. We walked around there taking pictures and then went on to the Eiffel Tower. That was something else. That was different than I'd imagined. It didn't seem so high but was probably higher than it looked. We couldn't see it from very far off because of the fog, and we didn't go to the top because we were plenty cold on the ground where we were, and it sure looked a lot colder up there."

Privately Cash began to focus on the idea of making music his career, a bold step for an unskilled instrumentalist who could count on his fingers the total number of his public performances, including those at school. Based on sheer musical ability, the best bets in Landsberg would have been on Ted Freeman and Bill Carnahan, both of whom possessed skill and versatility. Cash's primitive playing style and limited voice range still needed a lot of work. "I thought he had great potential as a performer," says Orville Rigdon. "I just didn't care much for his singing ability. His voice wavered and was unstable. His forte was his charisma and his ability to write. He was never an accomplished guitar player, but he did have a knack for writing story-type songs."

Though Cash's religion and upbringing may have contributed to his restraint from any wild passions he might have had during his tour of duty, an even more significant influence keeping him on the straight and narrow was Vivian Liberto. Everyone who knew Cash knew about Vivian. He had her picture in his locker, talked about her to anyone who was willing to listen, and wrote to her every single day. For example, between May 2 through 18, 1952, he posted a total of twelve letters. On May 9 alone he posted three.

Cash thought he was in love with Vivian, and she thought she was in love with him. He wanted her to come to Germany and marry him and proposed to her through the post. He even rented a hard-to-come-by apartment in Landsberg for her, but Vivian's father wouldn't entertain the idea. He wasn't going to let his precious daughter go off to Europe to marry a man she'd only dated for thirty days. When he realized that she wouldn't be coming, Cash passed the apartment on to Bill Carnahan, who was himself newly married.

Cash's utter faithfulness to this girl he barely knew astonished most of his colleagues who thought that military service was synonymous with excess and wild oats. Some of them felt that his devotion to Vivian contributed to his feeling of restlessness. "He was in love," says Rich Collins. "He saw faithfulness to her as a big factor in his life. If you put together his music, his love of socializing in small groups back at the barracks rather than drinking and picking up girls, and his loyalty to this woman, you can see why he probably didn't see the military as opportunity-making as a lot of us did. He was marking time until he could come back home and marry."

Cash flew back to America from Germany and went to Camp Kilmer, New Jersey, where he received his honorable discharge on July 3, 1954. This was the same day that a guitarist in Memphis, Scotty Moore, called a hopeful young singer, Elvis Aaron Presley, and invited him to audition for Sam Phillips at Sun Records. Musical revolution was in the air.

4

Walking the Line

ACCORDING TO HIS BIOGRAPHER Christopher Wren, after his discharge Cash took an American Airlines flight back to Memphis, where he was met by his family and Vivian Liberto. According to Marshall Grant, who was working at the time as a mechanic at Automobile Sales at 309 Union, Cash arrived home by Greyhound bus and was met only by his brother Roy. Marshall, who worked alongside Roy, can remember that the bus was delayed by two hours.

"When they came back I looked up and saw them coming through this big overhead door," says Marshall. "I had a car up on a lift and was working on the back of it. They walked straight to me down the aisle and Roy said, 'Marshall, this is my brother J. R. that I told you about. J. R., this is Marshall Grant.' He said, 'Hi,' we shook hands and his next words were, 'I hear you do a little pickin'?' I said, 'Very little.' He sort of laughed and said, 'Me too!'"

Marshall found Cash very easy to talk to and attributed this to the fact that he was so much like Roy, who he'd now known for three years. He also knew Ray and Carrie Cash and had become a close family friend. After talking for a bit, Marshall took him across the shop to meet another mechanic who enjoyed locker-room pickin'—Luther

Perkins, a poker-faced preacher's kid from Mississippi. The three men spoke for about fifteen minutes, promising to get together soon with their guitars.

Whichever way he traveled back from New Jersey, Cash undisputedly met Marshall and Luther when he got to Memphis. They delayed the pickin' session a few weeks though, because Cash was due to marry Vivian on August 7, 1954. Tom Liberto had finally relented and agreed—with a few conditions—to give Cash his daughter's hand. Not only would the couple have to wait at least four weeks before walking down the aisle, but Cash would undergo Catholic instruction, to guarantee that any future children would be raised in the Catholic faith. Had Cash not complied, Vivian would have been excommunicated.

That gave Cash four weeks to find a job and a suitable apartment. He wrote to Orville Rigdon, inviting him to be his best man. "I was broke at the time," remembers Rigdon. "I couldn't go." He then tried Ben Perea, but he had already enrolled in a college course and couldn't get the time off. In the end, the role went to his brother Roy.

Roy introduced his brother to a friend in the Memphis Police Department, thinking that Cash's work in the USAF Security Service would qualify him for police work. Cash discussed the possibility but soon realized that law enforcement wasn't his calling. The police officer in turn referred him to George Bates, president of the Home Equipment Company at 2529 Summer Avenue. Cash went to see Bates and was offered a job selling washing machines, refrigerators, and ornamental irons door-to-door.

While Cash knew this job wasn't a calling, it would pay the rent. He didn't have the slick false cheerfulness so often associated with the profession and, even worse, once he realized that a prospective client clearly didn't need or couldn't afford what he was offering, he would politely pack his catalogues and move on. The only good things about the job were that he set his own hours and traveling by car meant he could listen to all the latest record releases on the radio. The profusion of experimental music coming out of Memphis in July 1954 revolutionized twentieth-century popular music. People schooled in white church music, country, and pop were blending their sounds with the blues and gospel, creating a new hybrid called rock-'n'-roll. The day after Cash arrived back in Memphis, Elvis had recorded his first single, "That's All Right (Mama)" in a studio a few yards away from Automobile Sales with Scotty Moore and bass player Bill Black. Three days later it was being played on Dewey Phillips's late-night radio show *Red Hot and Blue*. Anyone living in Memphis at this time was getting a foretaste of a music style that would very soon sweep the world.

One of Cash's service buddies, Tom Weaver, had worked as an announcer on WMCA, a radio station in Corinth, Mississippi, and suggested Cash look up his former boss, John Bell, when he returned to the States. Because of their technical skills, radio operators often found it easy to get work in electronics, radio, and television. Since Corinth was only eighty miles due east of Memphis, one morning Cash decided to drive over to cold call on Bell, hoping for the offer of a position.

"So one day this big, tall, gangly kid comes in," recalls Bell. "He was very inarticulate, but he wanted me to give him a job as an announcer, maybe as an apprentice. I had to be as kind as I could, but I told him that he'd never make it in this business as an announcer. Back in those days radio was quite straitlaced. It wasn't as relaxed and down-home as it is now, and you had to be able to work controls as you spoke. He talked in a *patois*. He didn't use good English. I told him that he should go to a school where he could be trained. I suggested that he go to Keegan's in Memphis."

Keegan's School of Broadcasting, at 207 Madison Avenue, offered basic instruction in radio production, complete with a certificate at the end of the course. The curriculum focused on scripting commercials, developing a presence at the microphone, and managing the desk. Students learned how to operate on air in the mock studio. Taking advantage of the GI Bill, Cash signed up for a part-time course, studying two mornings a week for ten months.

Being a radio presenter, especially a disc jockey, was a recognized way of getting into the music industry. It was a small step from playing other people's songs on disc to performing your own. Jim Reeves, for example, started as a news reader on KGRI in Henderson, Texas, then became an announcer on KWKH in Shreveport, Louisiana, before starting his recording career. The best known disc jockeys in Memphis became local celebrities who went on to write newspaper columns, promote concerts, manage artists, and cut records.

"His first priority though was to get married to Vivian Liberto," says Marshall Grant. "And he did it. He didn't have any money so I loaned him fifty dollars and he went off to San Antonio." Cash married Vivian at St. Ann's Catholic Church on August 7, 1954, in the midst of a Texas heat wave. She wore traditional white lace, and, with sweat popping off his brow, he stood beside her in his military uniform (he couldn't afford a suit). Her uncle, the priest from New Orleans, officiated. Following the reception on the Cascade Terrace of the St. Anthony Hotel, the couple headed back through the Ozarks to Memphis, stopping to spend their honeymoon night at a hotel in Palestine, Texas.

By September 1954 the Cashes had set up house in a small, two-bedroom apartment on the second floor of a building on Eastmoreland Avenue. They had a private bathroom but shared the third-floor kitchen with the other tenants. The rent was fifty-five dollars a month. Cash's lingering memory of it was only as "hot and horrible," with no space for musical gatherings. Any guitar pull would either have to be at Luther and Birdie Perkins's home on Nathan Avenue or Marshall and Etta Grant's on Nakomis Avenue.

Though both four years older than Cash, Luther and Marshall shared with him a country upbringing, an enjoyment of music, and a love of practical jokes. Marshall, raised in Flats, North Carolina, grew up picking cotton. Although born in Memphis, Luther had grown up in Como, Mississippi. And like Cash they were both Southern Baptists whose first choice of songs invariably included the gospel numbers of Ira and Charlie Louvin, the Statesmen Quartet, and the Blackwood Brothers, all of whom coincidentally lived in Memphis.

"When we started playing, most of what we did was gospel," says Marshall. "That's what we all liked. John would sing and I would sing harmony with him. Luther didn't sing very much. Even though John has said that he wrote a song or two in Germany, he didn't bring any of them along with him. The only other stuff we did was some Ernest Tubb and some Hank Snow. In fact, when Roy had told me about his brother, he had said that he sang just like Hank Snow."

The three musicians jelled right from the start, and within weeks they dropped the three-rhythm-guitar line in favor of lead guitar, rhythm, and bass. Thinking ahead about playing on the radio or even making a record, they reasoned that three acoustic guitars all playing rhythm would not impress a producer. They needed more depth and breadth to their sound and elected Luther to play lead on a borrowed electric Fender. They also agreed that Cash should stick with rhythm guitar since he did most of the singing. Marshall bought a secondhand stand-up bass for twenty-five dollars.

This division of labor and their limited playing ability produced a unique group sound. Luther's caution on the lead guitar led him to play slowly, one note at a time. To eliminate the ringing made when playing too loud, he removed the metal plate and would deaden the strings with the palm of his right hand. Cash fed paper through his strings to make his rhythm playing sound like brushes on a snare drum. Marshall, meanwhile, didn't know how to tune a bass fiddle. He asked Gene Steele, a friend who played in a band, to find out from his bass player how to do it. Steele came back from a gig with a crude pencil drawing of a guitar neck and handwritten instructions.

"The bass didn't have frets, so when we had tuned it, we still didn't know the position of the notes," says Marshall. "So I had to ask Luther to give me an A, and I'd go up and down all four strings until I'd found every A note, and where I found them I'd stick a piece of tape. Then I did the same thing for B, C, E, F, and G. My bass was full of tape when we got through and we all just stood there and laughed and laughed!"

"Then, jokingly, I suggested that we play something. Luther said, 'In what key?' I said, 'I don't know. Let me look at this thing a minute. E looks pretty good but . . . don't change no chords on me!' So they started a rhythm in E, and I started slapping the strings. So there was Luther with the palm of his hand laying on his strings and John with his old awkward style of guitar playing and me hitting the same notes as Luther. We didn't necessarily like the way we sounded because we wanted to sound like people with records."

Missing documentary evidence and fading fifty-year-old memories make it hard to pin down the precise chronology of what happened next. Everyone agrees that after about four months of these informal picking sessions, they played their first public performance in a Memphis church. Marshall can't remember how the invitation came to them, but Cash once said that neighbors of either Marshall or Luther heard them practicing and asked if they would be willing to play at their church.

Marshall is sure that the church was on the corner of Cooper Street and Young Avenue. In a 1970 interview, he specifically mentioned Galloway United Methodist Church, which was (and still is) at this junction south of Union Avenue. They disagree, however, on the nature of the concert. In his books, Cash claimed that they played as part of a Sunday evening service, but Marshall remembers it as a midweek event, not in the main church itself, and attended only by a few elderly ladies.

Two parishioners, still members of the church, claim to remember the event. Gerry Stewart says they played in the nave of the church and probably drew over seventy people. Allen Caldwell, on the other hand, recalls a basement performance that attracted no more than forty. They agree that it was part of a church fund drive. "I was the one who asked him to come," says Caldwell. "We had a good time. There were a lot of young people in attendance and several adults from the class. I remember that he was kind of bashful in those days. We thanked him for what he'd done and he said, 'It's nothing. I'm glad to do something for Galloway.'"

Marshall agrees they played in the basement but reckons that the audience had ten old ladies at most. "We set up in a little room that was maybe sixteen feet square. The ladies had the chairs circled about in the back of the room and we set up close to a place where Luther could plug his amplifier in. It took us no more than three our four minutes to set up and then we played everything we knew for them. It lasted for about twenty minutes I guess."

Their next public performance was a fund-raiser held at a Bob's Barbecue on Summer Avenue for Ralph Johnson, a local powerboat racer and friend of Marshall who'd been injured in a collision while racing at Hot Springs, Arkansas. A group of Johnson's racing buddies organized the event to help him pay the hospital bills he couldn't afford.

The band actually got paid for their third public showing. The Hurst Motor Company, situated next to Automobile Sales, gave them fifty dollars to spend a Saturday afternoon cruising Union Avenue on the back of a flatbed truck. "We didn't have a current for Luther, and so both he and John played rhythm while I played bass," says Marshall. "We were on the move all the time. Nobody paid any attention to us. Nobody knew who we were. We laughed about it. But we got paid."

Cash had his mind set on making a record. He had heard of Sun Records on Union Avenue, whose owner, Sam Phillips, had recently been getting a lot of publicity as Elvis Presley's producer. On September 9, 1954, he'd even seen Elvis perform on the back of a truck for the grand opening of Katz Drug Store on Lamar Avenue and spoke with him after the show. Elvis invited Cash to the Eagle's Nest, a ballroom on Highway 78, where WHHM D. J. Sleepy-Eyed John promoted rock-'n'-roll nights. That night, Cash later said, he spoke to Scotty Moore, who suggested that he give Sun Records a call.

Either way, by late 1954 Cash had contacted Sam Phillips at the studio and asked for an audition. The stories vary about the way in which he approached Phillips. In one version he phoned Phillips to tell him that he was a gospel singer and was told that Sun had no place for him since they'd always failed with gospel. In another, he got the same response but only after arriving at the studio with Luther and Marshall and playing a gospel selection. In *Cash: The Autobiography* he goes solo to the first audition, where he played songs by Hank Snow and Jimmie Rodgers along with his own compositions "Belshazar" and "Hey! Porter." In *Man in Black,* Marshall and Luther play together songs by Hank Snow, Jimmie Rodgers, and Ernest Tubb, as well as Cash's compositions "Belshazar," "Hey! Porter," and "Folsom Prison Blues."

The archives of Sun Records detail two early sessions and, significantly, the first, dated only as "late 1954," features Cash alone. During it he recorded "Wide Open Road," "You're My Baby," "My Treasure," and "Show Me the Green"—the first three songs his own compositions and the last one unattributed. The second session, dated March 22, 1955, features Cash with Luther and Marshall playing "Hey! Porter," "Folsom Prison Blues," "Wide Open Road," and Clarence Snow's "My Two Timin' Woman."

All the accounts agree that Cash, Luther, and Marshall played for Phillips either in late 1954 or early 1955 and that at least part of the session was taped. To boost their sound, they took along with them A. W. "Red" Kernodle, another mechanic from Automobile Sales who sometimes sat in with them on steel guitar. Already in his midthirties and unconfident as a musician, Kernodle panicked and couldn't tune his guitar. "He was shaking all over," remembers Marshall. "He was sitting in a chair with this little guitar on his lap and both he and Luther were plugged into this amplifier. He stood up, laid his guitar down in the chair, and said, 'I'm going back to work. I can't do nothing but hold you guys up. You might make something, but I'm too nervous.' I told him that he should hang around a bit and get over it, but he wouldn't listen. So he just turned and walked out."

They did manage, though, to impress Phillips. He could see that Cash was someone who would only sing songs that he believed in. He had integrity. "The mere fact that he never sang one song (at the audition) that was written by another person gave me a clue that this was a man who had a message," Phillips later said. (Though it should be noted that Cash had, in fact, performed songs written by others.) He felt that Cash had chosen the basic musical lineup "so that the fundamentals of his message would ring forth without being inundated with pretty music."

Marshall recalls that the trio's unusual, ragged sound intrigued Phillips. "Thank God we didn't achieve a polished sound before we went to see Sam Phillips because, if we had gone up there and been real professional and had sounded like those people in Nashville, he would have sent us home. We just played the only way we knew how, and he later said that he had never heard anything like it. With the blend of John's voice everything fell into place. It wasn't that we put it there. It just happened."

"Hey! Porter" was the first of Cash's songs that Phillips thought had potential as a single. Although written in Germany, he hadn't rehearsed it with Marshall and Luther, and it required a lot of shaping. The lyrics focused on returning to the South and contained hints of themes that would preoccupy Cash throughout his career: home, trains, movement, America. "We had to work that one up," says Marshall. "You have to remember that we were two mechanics and an appliance salesman at the time and we were not professional musicians. So it took us some time to work this thing up, to get it to a point where we felt it was the way we wanted it to be."

When they recorded it, they seemed unsure whether to sound like Elvis or Hank Williams, and the guitars sound tentative and indistinct. By July 30, 1955, Cash had found his natural bass-baritone voice and the elements of the boom-chicka-boom sound had fallen into place—with Luther's flat-handed muting of the strings adding the "chicka" and Marshall's heavily slapped bass supplying the "boom." When Phillips asked for a flip side, they suggested the 1920s hymn "I Was There When It Happened," but Phillips didn't want gospel tunes tucked away on the backs of his singles. He told them to write a new song—something that would contrast with "Hey! Porter"—a love song or a tearjerker.

Cash, by now, had moved into a bigger apartment at 2553 Tutwiler Avenue, and Vivian was heavily pregnant. Over a period of two weeks he wrote "Cry, Cry, Cry" based on a catchphrase he'd heard used by D. J. Eddie Hill: "We've got some good songs, love songs, sweet songs, happy songs, and sad songs that'll make you cry, cry, cry." He took a copy of the handwritten lyrics to Phillips, who then booked a session for a Thursday evening in May. In a letter typed during work time on Home Equipment Company letterhead he told ex-Landsberg Barbarian Ted Freeman about the session:

> We finally made the other side of my record. We worked two and a half
> hours on it Thursday night. Finally got it perfected. Sounds like hell. No,

I believe it'll be purty good. The name of it is "You're Gonna Cry, Cry, Cry." It's a flat romping dob. That ole' clickety-clack rhythm. Other side is "Hey! Porter."

The name of us on the record is "Johnny Cash and the Tennessee Two." When you write in to all the stations requesting it, request it. OK? It's gonna be out in two to three weeks. Can't say when 'cause I don't know. It all depends on when the market is right.

When they start making the record here, I'll send you a copy.

He signed the letter, "Johnny Cash of Johnny Cash and the Tennessee Two."

Cash originally suggested the Tennessee Three, but Marshall thought they should use John Cash and the Tennessee Two since Cash did all the singing. Sam Phillips suggested he change his first name to Johnny because *John* sounded old and boring whereas *Johnny* sounded young and rebellious. Marlon Brando had played a character called Johnny in *The Wild Ones; Johnny Guitar* was a recent movie directed by Nick Ray; and the R&B singer Johnny Ace had killed himself on New Year's Day in a backstage game of Russian roulette. Cash thought that at twenty-three he was too old to be a Johnny, but Phillips persuaded him otherwise and the name went on the label.

The Cashes' first child, a daughter Rosanne, arrived May 24, 1955, exactly a month before the release of "Hey! Porter." Cash picked up an advance copy the day before and rushed it over to disc jockey Bob Neal at WMPS, who, after approvingly playing both sides, accidentally broke it. Desperate to get radio play and unsure how long it would take to get a replacement, Cash panicked.

"I think that our biggest ambition when we started was just to hear ourselves on the radio," says Marshall. "I know that's how I felt about it. So when I was going to work early one morning alone in the car and heard Sleepy-Eyed John play our record, it was almost more than I could stand. It was unbelievable. I thought that was *it*. The next day about five stations in Memphis played it. The day after that, all of them were playing it. By the end of the week, they were all playing both sides. Within a month, every station that it had been sent to across the South was playing this record. A lot of these weren't *Billboard* reporting stations, but even so the record got to number fourteen in the [country music] charts."

A late July letter to Ted Freeman captures the excitement of that spring:

I'm not too happy about writing this letter because I wrote you one and it came back to me because you left no forwarding address [Freeman was still serving in the USAF]. I don't know about a guy that won't leave a forwarding address. Of all things, I say! And another thing. I'm getting to be such a big shot [that] I don't know if I should write to you at all.

But before I go any further, I want to kind of chew you out a little. As soon as my record was off the press I *rushed* down and got you a copy of it and mailed it to you. Well, you didn't say one dad blamed word about it except that you got it and it was warped. Now if you had said the things that Carnahan said, I don't give a rat's rear end whether you say a thing about it or not. He seemed to think the music is too shallow and I have no business being on that label. But since "Cry, Cry, Cry" has been on top in Memphis and vicinity for the first two weeks, I don't give another rat's rear end.

Guess who your friend John is going to be playing with next Friday night? Just *Webb Pierce, Sonny James, Bud Deckleman* and about fifteen more. Yep, next Friday night at the Overton Park Shell here in Memphis will be the biggest thrill in my life. And *they asked me* to be on the show. I didn't ask them. Friend I tell you, it just don't seem real. It seems like a big cherry pink and apple blossom white dream.

Do you hear my record out there? My brother just got back from Alabama and he says they're wearing it out all over Alabama and Mississippi. I've had a lot of good reports on it from Kansas, Oklahoma, Arkansas and Virginia. Viv and I went to Texas last week and it's getting a good start down there.

I've got several bookings already three weeks after next in towns around here. Then the week after next my potential manager says he can book me solid five or six nights a week from then on through the winter. I believe I can make a pretty good living at it. This guy says he'll guarantee me I'll never make less than $20 a night and lots of nights I'll make $30 or more when we play the bigger towns. There'll be myself and another boy on Sun and Bud Deckleman on MGM on the tour.

This time he signed himself "Johnny Cash" and added underneath "(the most promising young artist Memphis, Tennessee, has ever produced)."

The "towns around here" that he was playing were places like Etowa, Lepanto, Osceola, and Helena in Arkansas or Henderson in Tennessee. In search of bookings, Cash would drive around approaching theaters, cinemas, and schools, as well as clubs with names like Junior's Dew Drop Inn and Pearl's Howdy Club, telling anyone who would listen that he was Johnny Cash and he had a hit on the Sun Records label. The boys would travel to the venues after work with Marshall's bass strapped to the roof of the car. At the shows they'd play both sides of the new single, some gospel songs, a couple of current hits like Dean Martin's "Memories Are Made of This," and some old favorites like Hank Snow's "Moving On" and Leadbelly's "Rock Island Line." As their fame spread and the shows got bigger, they began to supplement their income by selling photographs of Cash for twenty-five cents during the intermission.

The "boy on Sun" whom Cash mentions in his letter to Freeman will tour with him, was Elvis Presley. Cash probably didn't refer to him by name simply because, although Elvis had become a sensation in Memphis, his name meant very little to those who revered the older singers like Ernest Tubb. In the year he'd been recording, only one of Elvis's four singles had made an impression on the national country charts, and his limited tour had only taken him to a dozen or so Southern states. Though three releases and several months of touring behind Elvis, Cash had every reason to think of himself as someone with the same opportunities. Of all the artists appearing with him at the Overton Park Shell, Cash had the most esteem for headliner Webb Pierce, who'd been recording since the early 1950s. His hit songs, such as "That Heart Belongs to Me" and "The Last Waltz," were among those that a young Cash had listened to while in Germany.

—

WHEREAS CASH WOULD BECOME CLOSE FRIENDS with some fellow recording artists at Sun—most notably Roy Orbison and Carl Perkins—his relationship with Elvis was always one of rivalry. Never less than courteous to each other, they always each had an eye on the others' record sales and successes in concert. In his show Elvis would frequently mimic Cash, and Cash in turn perfected an Elvis parody that involved hip swiveling, lip pouting, and a comb that needed to be shot after slicking back his greasy hair. The Overton Park Shell concert, which took place on August 5, 1955, proved to be a turning point for both Sun artists. For

Elvis it was a homecoming. He'd only given two Memphis shows that year (in February and July). The last time he'd played the Shell, he'd taken bottom billing for a Slim Whitman show. For Johnny Cash and the Tennessee Two it was a debut. Not only had they never played a concert in Memphis before, they'd never shared a bill with a major artist. Now they were part of a Bob Neal promotion featuring twenty-two acts that would draw more than four thousand fans. No wonder it seemed like "a big cherry pink and apple blossom white dream."

Cash, Marshall, and Luther played both sides of the single that night and were called back for more. As an encore they premiered "Folsom Prison Blues," the song they'd recently recorded. All Cash's friends and family came to witness his triumph. The next day the only two photos of the show included in the *Memphis Press-Scimitar* beneath the headline "4000 Jam Shell, Hundreds Turned Away—Country Rhythm Fills a Country Park" were of Elvis Presley and Johnny Cash. He'd only been stateside a year and two days, and already he was making his dream come true.

Yet this concert, which he frequently regarded as marking the birth of his career, also marked the beginning of Cash's marital troubles. Vivian looked, uneasily, over the sea of girls screaming for Elvis. This scene, she realized, could one day greet her husband, and that wouldn't bode well for a happy home. Where Cash saw only fame, success, and financial stability, Vivian envisioned temptation, loss of privacy, and loneliness.

Vivian held the very traditional idea of marriage in which the husband worked and a wife cooked, cleaned, and reared children. When he first spoke to her about a career in music, she never anticipated the screaming women or weeks of separation that went along with a tour.

In September Cash wrote Ted Freeman of the latest touring activity—guest spots on *Barnyard Frolics* at Little Rock, the *Big D Jamboree* in Dallas, a concert in San Antonio with Eddy Arnold, and then a trip through West Texas with Elvis, Jean Sheppard, and the Louvin Brothers. It would be, he said, "a heap of picking and grinning."

The West Texas tour of places like Abilene, Midland, Amarillo, and Lubbock, would pay the group one hundred dollars a night between them, which, as he pointed out, didn't leave much after deducting travel and accommodation expenses. They only agreed to the rate because they'd been promised a return engagement within six months for two hundred fifty dollars a night.

Cash wrote about the tour:

> It'll take a while for me to get the good money, but if my next record does
> as well as "Cry, Cry, Cry" I've got it made. We cut one side of my next
> record Monday night. It's by far the best song I ever wrote, has a nice tune
> to it and sounds a lot more professional than the first one. The name is "I
> Get So Doggone Lonesome."

Emboldened by the success of "Cry, Cry, Cry," Cash mocked the conventions
of mid-1950s country music, seeing his sound as something new and radical.

> It ["I Get So Doggone Lonesome"] probably won't sell over three or four
> copies because I don't have a steel guitar in the band. Heck, people don't
> want anything different. They want the same old stuff. If you ain't got a
> steel guitar, you're hurtin' for certain. That steel guitar is it. Try to sound
> like Jerry Byrd.
>
> Shoot! Those teenage girls don't care about catchy rhythm. They want
> to hear a pretty steel guitar. Cause *everybody* has a steel guitar. Guess I'm
> just wasting my time. My music is so shallow and simple. Country people
> don't like it. Although Webb Pierce told me my style was versatile and that
> I'd go far in country music because I have the honest country flavor that
> everyone likes, I might as well quit. What does Webb Pierce know about
> country music? Heck.

Ted Freeman must have failed to detect Johnny's ironic tone. He wrote to Cash
and asked him if he was anticipating such failure, why didn't he just add a steel
guitar to his sound? Cash responded in his next letter:

> You just ain't got no sense. You're just nuts. I used to think you had some
> sense but now you ain't got no sense. You're just nuts. I didn't put a steel
> guitar in the band because everybody has a steel guitar in their band. My
> little ole record still tops in this part of the country, so as the little boy in *Mad*
> comics says [a reference to cartoon character Alfred E. Neuman]: 'What, me
> worry?' . . . Don't listen to the music on the record. Listen to the rhythm.

A week before setting off on the West Texas tour, he again wrote to Ted Freeman, who had obviously asked him why "Cry, Cry, Cry" was not yet a national hit. Cash listed the cities where it had been a hit: number one in Memphis, Little Rock, Shreveport, Texarkana, Richmond, and Jackson; number two in Miami; number three in Cincinnati; number four in Florence and Baton Rouge; and so on down to number nine in New Orleans.

> Now you're asking why it didn't make the Top Ten charts coast to coast?
> Reason #1—New artist.
> Reason #2—Small label.
> Reason #3—No financial backing.
> Reason #4—(Which could be #1) It's only hot in a few places at once because the disc jockeys in some areas didn't start to play it until they noticed it was a hit elsewhere.

Elvis was now on the cusp of national fame, and until now, he and Cash shared the same manager, Bob Neal. But Colonel Tom Parker had already made himself Elvis's "special adviser" and he was luring him away from Sun Records. "Mystery Train," Elvis's current single when he and Cash toured West Texas together, would be the last produced by Sam Phillips. Parker called the tour the Elvis Presley Jamboree. Charlie Louvin of the Louvin Brothers remembers the tour as the beginning of the orchestrated hysteria around Elvis. "The colonel and his entourage would give away tickets to little girls in Woolworth's and all the dime stores," he says. "They were told that the tickets were free, but the one thing they had to do was to holler 'WE WANT ELVIS' every few minutes. This was very disturbing for the rest of us. By the time Elvis came on, it was pandemonium."

One of Cash's new friends was Sun recording artist Carl Perkins, whom he'd met in February when Carl was cutting his second single "Let the Jukebox Keep on Playing" backed with "Gone, Gone, Gone." The two men had a lot in common. They were born in the same year, grew up on cotton farms in Mississippi, faced poverty as children, and were now married with families. Carl was a smart songwriter as well as one of the most distinctive young guitarists in the business. His playing style would eventually have a profound effect on the Beatles.

On November 19, 1955, Carl and Cash were booked on a show in Gladewater, Texas, where Elvis topped the bill. In the dressing room before the show started, Cash ran through the riff that he'd heard on his twisted tape in Germany. He told Carl that he wanted to write a song about being true—about being true to himself, true to Vivian, and true to God. He thought he might call it "I'm Still Being True" or "I'm Walking the Line." Carl pounced on the idea. He said it should be called "I Walk the Line." Cash wrote the song in twenty minutes. He later said that it was one of those songs just waiting to be written.

Cash returned the favor less than a month later when the same package show stopped in Amory, Mississippi. After seeing Carl onstage, Cash was convinced he should record what he described as a "bop" song, and he began telling Carl a story about C. V. White, a black serviceman who'd been with the Twelfth RSM in Landsberg. White, a cool dresser, had a way with the local women. He also had a way with words and often amused Cash with particular phrases. As Jack Matheson remembers the incident that Cash related to Carl that night, "Bill Carnahan and I were with John on the chow line and some guy backed up and stood on C. V.'s toes. What he actually said was, 'Hey man! I don't care what you do with my fraulein or what you do with whatever, but don't step on my blue suede shoes.'" The joke was that C. V., like the rest of the guys, was wearing his regulation-issue black shoes, but at the time, blue suedes were in fashion for leisure wear.

Carl took the phrase and fashioned it into "Blue Suede Shoes," a song that would not only become a hit for him but for Elvis. Later he would claim that he wrote it about a boy he'd seen dancing in front of the stage in Jackson, Mississippi, who had told his girlfriend to be careful with her footwork lest she tread on his blue suede shoes. In that version of the story, Carl recalled that he woke in the middle of the night, December 17, 1955, wrote the words out on a paper potato sack and recorded it two days later.

However, Cash was telling his own version of the story at least as early as January 1957, when he told the *Memphis Press-Scimitar* that he'd given Perkins the original idea. Both Bill Carnahan and Jack Matheson clearly remember the incident with C. V. White. Marshall Grant backs this version of the story, although he sets it two months earlier at a September 6 concert in Bono, Arkansas: "John told Carl this story about his friend in the service and told him that he should write a song about blue suede shoes," he says. "Carl was in the dressing room while someone else was onstage and then he came out for his set and played it live. Of all the stories that you'll hear, that's what actually happened. I was standing there when it took place."

Amazingly Cash was still combining his work as a salesman with all of the touring. Signing autographs for adoring fans at night, he would knock on doors trying to sell refrigerators the next morning. He kept his day job mostly because, despite the huge sales of "Cry, Cry, Cry" (it would eventually sell over one hundred thousand copies), his first royalty check wasn't due until the accounts settled at the end of the year.

In late November he wrote to Ted Freeman:

> I don't know when I'll quit the Home Equipment Company. I've got three personal appearances this week—in Ripley, Bolivar and Henderson [towns in Tennessee]—and four next week, but I don't yet know where. One of the local disc jockeys is managing me and booking me. I suppose I'll hang on at selling awhile and pick up a few bucks when I can.
>
> I haven't the faintest idea how much my record has sold, and I won't know till they check the records and do all the tabulations at the end of this year. On the hit parade here Saturday night one of the local disc jockeys played my record as #16 coast-to-coast. I don't know if he was lying or not. I'm anxious to check this week's Cashbox magazine. [It was actually #14 on the country charts of November 26th].
>
> Do you hear my record there [in West Virginia]? My sister said it's hot in Norfolk.

Cash released his second single, "Folsom Prison Blues," on December 15. Written from the perspective of a prisoner, it contrasted the restrictions and crushed hopes of jail with the unlimited freedom and hope of someone riding a train. It contained what must be one of the most cruelly dispassionate lines in popular song: "I shot a man in Reno just to watch him die," a line he said he made up after asking himself what the most evil reason for killing someone could be.

There were precedents in country music. In "Blue Yodel #1," sometimes known as "'T' For Texas," Jimmie Rodgers had written: "I'm gonna buy me a shotgun / Just as long as I am tall / I'm gonna shoot poor Thelma / Just to see her jump and fall."

But in light of Cash's background and the demons that dogged him, it's not difficult to see a connection between the imagined brutality and the real violence he had seen. His father had forced him to watch puppies drown. His uncle had apparently shown him the body of a lynch victim. His brother Jack's body had lain in their house for two days while neighbors came calling. The idea that people got pleasure from watching the dead or the dying was not foreign to him.

Although no one knew it at the time, the melody of "Folsom Prison Blues" and much of its imagery had been lifted from part of a song on a 1953 album by composer Gordon Jenkins. Cash likely heard the album, *Seven Dreams,* when he was in Germany, perhaps played by one of his more sophisticated urban friends. In the second dream of the album, singer Beverly Mahr (Jenkins's wife) sings about how she wants to leave Crescent City:

> If I owned that lonesome whistle
> If that railroad train was mine
> I'll bet I'd find a man a little farther down the line
> Far from Crescent City is where I'd like to stay
> And I'd let that lonesome whistle blow my blues away.[1]

Cash's version differed very little:

> Well, if they freed me from this prison
> If that railroad train was mine
> I'd bet I'd move on over a little farther down the line
> Far from Folsom Prison that's where I want to stay
> And I'd let that lonesome whistle blow my blues away.

Jenkins either didn't hear "Folsom Prison Blues" at the time or heard it and decided not to act. But thirteen years later when it was recorded live for the best-selling *Johnny Cash at Folsom Prison* album, Jenkins filed a lawsuit. The claim was eventually settled out of court.

On December 3, Cash made his first appearance on the *Louisiana Hayride*—a live radio show with an audience, which KWKH broadcast every Saturday night from the Municipal Auditorium in Shreveport, Louisiana. Having started in April

1948, it became known as a stepping stone to the *Grand Ole Opry*. *Louisiana Hayride* had launched the careers of several country stars whom Cash admired, including Faron Young, Webb Pierce, and Hank Williams.

Cash gave his all that day in two separate performances, both of which drew encores. Leaving the stage, sweat pouring off his face, he experienced, for the first time, the sheer intoxication of performing. He finally tasted that rare combination of the audience energy, the thrill of being in the spotlight, the recognition of his peers, and the congenial backstage atmosphere where he mixed easily with stars, agents, and attractive women.

The next morning, traveling back to Memphis, Cash saw people driving to church and felt a twinge of conscience knowing that, if he wasn't to be seduced by stardom, he should maintain his church connection. When he first returned from Germany, he'd accompany Vivian to a Catholic mass at 9:00 a.m. each Sunday and later, alone, attended a Baptist service at 10:30, but work began to interfere. The best paid concerts took place on Saturday nights, which meant they traveled Sunday mornings.

Ted Freeman came to see him on the *Louisiana Hayride* tour, but because of a mix-up they didn't meet. In his Christmas letter, Cash apologized for not catching Ted in Shreveport and included a copy of an advertisement they'd paid three hundred and ten dollars to run in *Billboard,* hoping to generate more national attention:

I was on the *Big D [Jamboree]* in Dallas two weeks ago. I went over as good as I did the night you were at the *[Louisiana] Hayride.* They wanted me permanent on the *Big D* with one week a month on the *Ozark Jubilee* but they'd already made the deal to put me on the *Hayride* permanent. I told them, didn't I? But they didn't listen. I said, "Wait." But they didn't wait.

I've got a year contract with the *Hayride* with nights off for guest spots on the *Big D*, the *Jubilee* and the *Opry* I hope. I think I can take the top spot on the *Hayride* away from E. Presley. I got five encores Saturday night and he didn't get any. That's counting both times I was on Saturday.

Say, I'm fixin' to buy me a big Martin [guitar], nearly new with a heavy leather case both for $90. That's a right nice deal and see if it is. That's durn good for a newcomer like me. Right? I hope it's so.

Cash must have given up his job at the Home Equipment Company in January 1956 when he received his first full royalty check from Sun. With the six thousand dollars, he outearned his brother Roy's annual salary as a field service representative for the Chrysler Corporation, making more than his father had ever earned in a year. As he approached his twenty-fourth birthday, Johnny Cash was indeed doing "durn good" for a newcomer.

5

Amphetamine Blues

THE PURCHASE OF Elvis Presley's recording contract by RCA in November 1955 brought national and then international attention to the music scene in Memphis. Until then the emerging young musicians had largely remained a Southern secret—the singles put out by Sun hit the charts below the Mason-Dixon Line as Sun artists stuck to touring Texas, Florida, Mississippi, Tennessee, Arkansas, and Louisiana. Elvis had no network TV coverage until January 1956, and it would be another year before Cash made his television debut on the *Jackie Gleason Show.*

Both Elvis and Carl Perkins burst onto the national scene in early 1956. Carl's "Blue Suede Shoes," released January 1, was the fourth-best-selling single in March. Elvis's "Heartbreak Hotel," released by RCA on January 27, reached the number one spot in April. A new generation of mainstream, white teenagers had caught on to the music previously considered rural, regional, or racial. Until "Heartbreak Hotel," the industry considered Elvis a country artist, so his singles registered only on the country charts. Carl's "Blue Suede Shoes" broke all the norms and became the first song to simultaneously hit the pop, country, and R&B charts.

If Carl had looked like Elvis, he would probably have become the king of rock-'n'-roll. Unfortunately he was losing his hair fast at the age of twenty-three. Just as "Blue Suede Shoes" climbed the charts, a car crash on the way to a recording of the *Ed Sullivan Show* put Carl out of action for six months. Twelve days after the accident, while recuperating in bed, he saw Elvis announce on the *Milton Berle Show* that "Blue Suede Shoes" would be his next single. "Elvis had the looks on me," he told journalist Michael Lydon in 1968. "The girls were going for him for more reasons than music. Elvis was hitting them with sideburns, flashy clothes, and no ring on that finger. I had three kids. There was no way of keeping Elvis from being the man in that music."

Johnny Cash wasn't far behind. "Folsom Prison Blues" had been a huge country hit, and on April 2, 1956, he recorded four tracks for potential follow-up, including "I Walk the Line." Phillips thought the song was too slow and asked him to record a faster version for comparison. While driving back from a show later that month, Cash heard his new single played for the first time on Eddie Hill's late-night show on WSM. Upset to discover that Sam had pressed the fast version rather than the slow ballad that he'd wanted, he returned to Memphis to plead his case with Phillips. Though he politely promised to "think about" switching the versions, Phillips had no intention of distributing the ballad.

Phillips instinctively knew what would sell. "I Walk the Line" was the first Johnny Cash single to reach the pop charts, selling more than two million copies in the process. With his first big check, Cash moved out of the duplex on Tutwiler to a two-bedroom house at 4492 Sandy Cove in the more upscale Berclair district of Memphis. He also upgraded his car. He gave his 1954 Portsmouth to Vivian's father and bought a maroon Lincoln with only eleven thousand miles on the speedometer from country singer Ferlin Huskey. Vacations, until then, meant visiting his parents in Dyess. He now ventured farther from home—trips to New Orleans and Mexico with Vivian and to the coast of Florida for deep-sea fishing.

Cash's success and the publicity that accompanied it not only affected him and Vivian but his family back in Dyess. Suddenly they too were in the spotlight, and people began to treat them differently. "We couldn't believe what was happening," says Tommy Cash, who was sixteen at the time and still in high school. "It changed all of our lives. Instead of being the Cash family from Arkansas, we were Johnny

Cash's family. Instead of people asking me how my basketball was going, or asking daddy how much cotton he was picking this summer, it was, 'How's Johnny? When's his new record coming out?' It was a total switch."

Back on April 2, Cash also recorded "Get Rhythm." Inspired by a conversation while having his shoes polished at the Memphis bus station, Cash wrote this song about a shoe-shine boy with Elvis in mind. However, he always managed to strike a false note when he wrote rock-'n'-roll. The words of "I Walk the Line" had conviction. The words to songs like "Rock & Roll Ruby" (later cut by Warren Smith) and "You're My Baby" (which he gave to fellow Sun artist Roy Orbison) were merely exercises in generic writing. As he said in his 1978 song "I Will Rock and Roll with You":

> I didn't ever play much rock and roll
> Cause I got so much country in my soul.

On July 7, 1956 he achieved one of his life's ambitions by appearing on the *Grand Ole Opry*—country music's best known and most prestigious showcase. He wore a white jacket with blue trim (made by his mother), a black shirt, black trousers (with a white stripe on the outside seams), and white shoes. Thirty-one-year-old country star Carl Smith introduced "the brightest rising star" of country music, not only to the thirty-eight hundred people in the crowd at Nashville's Ryman Auditorium, but to the tens of thousands in the radio audience beyond.

Journalist Ben A. Green witnessed the one-song debut (a prelude to being invited to join the Opry), reported in the *Nashville Banner:*

> He had a quiver in his voice, but it wasn't stage fright. The haunting words of "I Walk the Line" began to swell through the building. And a veritable tornado of applause rolled back. The boy had struck home, where the heart is, with his song that is Number 2 in the nation today. As his words filtered into the farthermost corners, many in the crowd were on their feet, cheering and clapping. They too had taken a new member into the family.[1]

Speaking after the show, Cash said that he was "grateful, happy, and humble" to have been invited to the show. "It's the ambition of every hillbilly singer to reach the Opry in his lifetime."

The Carter Sisters and Mother Maybelle—who'd joined the Opry in 1950—
appeared that night as well. Maybelle Carter, then forty-seven, started her career
as an original member of the Carter Family, whose 1927 recordings for the Victor
label jump-started the country music explosion. The Carter Family, who were from
southwestern Virginia, hadn't created a new form of music—they merely
performed (and therefore helped preserve) the ballads, hymns, and mountain
songs that had been handed down from parents to children for generations. As a
great collector with a knack for embellishment, A. P. Carter, (married to
Maybelle's cousin Sara), helped the Carter Family preserve, on record, a rich
heritage of American song.

When A. P. and Sara retired, Maybelle carried on with her three daughters,
Helen, June, and Anita. They performed a mixture of novelty numbers, gospel, and
the old songs associated with the Carter Family, including "Will the Circle Be
Unbroken?" "Wildwood Flower," and "Will You Miss Me When I'm Gone?" June
and Anita, both with long, dark hair and fetching smiles, set hearts aflutter in the
Opry. In July 1952, June married Carl Smith—then one of the most successful
recording artists in country music—but within six months the marriage faced problems as Smith took extended and unexplained trips away from home. By September
1955, when June had their first child, Rebecca Carlene, the couple had already
separated. Both Hank Williams and Elvis were smitten with Anita, who is described
by a male contemporary as having been "the quintessential Southern belle."

Like any man of his age, Cash was delighted to meet June backstage after the
show. She had apparently heard about him from Elvis, whom she knew very well.
They exchanged small talk, and Cash promised to bring her copies of "Folsom
Prison Blues" and "I Walk the Line" when he returned to the Opry on July 28 for
his first show as a member. She later wrote that even then he "seemed like a special
person." As the story goes, Cash jokingly told June that one day he would marry
her. In a photograph of the meeting, June, in a low-cut dress, is sitting on a chair in
front of a radiator while Cash squats at her feet, holding on to a circular pillar.

On July 24 he wrote to Ted Freeman to tell him about the Opry and the success
of "I Walk the Line":

> I have been on the *Grand Ole Opry*. I was on the P. A. show three weeks
> ago. Didn't you hear me? I'll be there this Saturday, so dig. No, I don't care

[about] Hogjaw Hawkins stealing my sound [a reference to "It Would Be A Doggone Lie" by Hawkshaw Hawkins]. I'm always proud when someone tries to imitate. I've just come off a week tour in Florida with Hawkshaw, Jean Sheppard and Jim Reeves. Hawkshaw says he's sorry he put that record out because everybody knows he's imitating me. But ole Hogjaw is a fine feller and I like him. [Hawkshaw Hawkins later died in the 1963 plane crash that also killed Patsy Cline.]

Friend, if you ain't heard my record you don't listen to the radio because last week it was the #2 [record] played by disc jockeys and this week it's #3. It's also #3 best seller and #2 on the juke boxes. Ole Ray Price got #1 in all three charts this week. "Crazy Arms" is fine. I'm picking Sunday up at Roy Acuff's Dunbar Cave in Tennessee. In October I'm making a tour with Faron Young in Florida, Georgia, the Carolinas and Virginia. I don't know how close we'll come to your house but I'll let you know.

Johnny Cash and the Tennessee Two had a busy touring year in 1955, made more difficult because of their commitment to the *Louisiana Hayride*. Almost every Saturday night they had to be in Shreveport, Louisiana—a seven-hundred-mile round trip from Memphis. In his first two years of touring Cash clocked over one hundred thousand miles of road travel.

At the *Hayride*, Cash befriended Johnny Horton, another regular on the show. Like Cash, Horton had a keen intellect and loved outdoor pursuits. Before turning professional he'd studied at the University of Seattle and had worked as a fisherman in Alaska. He was such an expert at casting with a rod and reel that the Fred Abergast Company paid him to do demonstrations. His favorite trick, one that greatly impressed Cash, was to attach a sugar lump to his line and cast it into a cup of coffee fifteen yards away.

Although by 1956 Horton had only had one hit, "Honky Tonk Man," he considerably raised his profile by marrying Billie Jean, the extraordinarily beautiful dark-haired widow of Hank Williams. Hank, divorced by his wife Audrey in May 1952, had taken up with the then nineteen-year-old Billie Jean Jones Eshlimar. Already married and separated once, she was dating country star Faron Young when Hank met her backstage at the Opry. Though she'd come to see Young's debut, Hank reportedly told her, "If you ain't married, ole Hank's gonna marry you. You're about the purtiest thing I ever saw." On October 19, 1952, he did just that, in a lavish public ceremony onstage at the New Orleans Municipal Auditorium. Three months later Hank was dead and she was the widow of a legend.

In September 1953, Billie Jean married Horton, guaranteeing him the spotlight. "She had Johnny Horton wrapped around her finger," says Marshall Grant. "She was a gorgeous, gorgeous woman who knew how to dress the part. Johnny Horton was a very plain, straightforward type of guy and you could say that they were mismatched. What held the marriage together, I have no earthly idea. Absolutely none."

Horton believed in the powers of the supernatural. Although raised in a fundamentalist Christian home in Tyler, Texas, Horton's curiosity about the paranormal had led him to investigate hypnosis, mind reading, dream analysis, automatic writing, and spiritualism. Some people dismissed him as a charlatan, while others were frightened by his claims to be able to predict events, move objects though mind control, and see spirits. Horton's favorite party trick while on the road was hypnotizing band members and coaxing them into uncharacteristic behaviors. He once put Cash into a trance and urged him to explore childhood memories. When he came to, he had the words of a new song.

Horton had been drawn into spiritualism by J. Bernard Ricks, a local postal worker who came to the Hayride offering to enhance the creativity of the performers by unleashing spiritual power. Merle Kilgore, a songwriter (he wrote Webb Pierce's 1954 hit "More and More") and neighbor of Horton's, believes that Horton influenced Cash in this area. "He called me one day when Johnny Horton was out of town and came over to see me and my wife," he says. "We went into my music room that had album covers on the walls and he said it felt so relaxed. My wife brought him coffee and he said, 'If you don't mind I'm going to close my eyes and meditate.' Then we heard this tremendous POP! The ceiling had split. My wife and I just looked up and he said, 'Oh. I'm sorry. I've just ruined your new music room.' I said, 'How did you do that?' He joked, 'Just meditating. I got the power too strong.'"

The national success of "I Walk the Line" increased the demand for Cash to play concerts outside the South, so he found himself traveling to Colorado and Arizona, Pennsylvania, Ohio, and Minnesota. In December 1956 he toured California and in April 1957 took a twenty-four-day tour of Canada—his first time onstage outside the U.S., except for shows in Landsberg, Germany. In the smaller venues, Johnny Cash and the Tennessee Two appeared alone, but on the concert tours they played with many of the top names in country entertainment—legends like George Jones, Jim Reeves, Faron Young, Patsy Cline, and Ray Price.

Cash's manager Bob Neal ran a Memphis-based agency called Stars Incorporated, which represented many Sun artists. Although he'd lost Elvis to Colonel Tom Parker in 1957, he still counted Jerry Lee Lewis, Carl Perkins, Roy Orbison, Sonny James, and Warren Smith among his clients. If a tour promoter wanted to book Johnny Cash or Carl Perkins, Neal could put together an attractive package by including other artists on his books.

The California tour, which started in Salinas, was booked by a young Santa Barbara–based promoter named Stew Carnall, who'd become interested in Cash after hearing "Hey! Porter" playing on a jukebox in Phoenix, Arizona. Carnall came from a wealthy family and had been educated in the best schools. Well spoken, Carnall had cultivated tastes and drove an El Dorado convertible. He believed that there was an untapped market for country music in the central farm-lands of California, which were filled with Midwesterners who'd migrated west-ward in the 1930s and 1940s.

The California dates were unlike anything Cash had played in the South. Instead of concert halls, he and the Tennessee Two performed in large ballrooms in towns like Modesto, Vallejo, and Niles, where the opening act usually consisted of a country band playing dance music. Ralph J. Gleason, the most perceptive pop cultural commentator of the period and later the inspiration behind the founding of *Rolling Stone* magazine, attended one of the California shows. An early cham-pion of the beat poets, Bob Dylan, and San Francisco psychedelic rock, Gleason was one of the first critics to treat popular music as an art form rather than as "mere entertainment." In the December 16, 1956, edition of the *San Francisco Chronicle* he wrote: "During the past week, Cash has been playing one-nighters in California . . . and if the reaction of the crowd at the performances is any indica-tion, Presley has a rival. Like Elvis, Johnny Cash sings and strums a guitar, but unlike Presley there are no bumps and grinds in his routine. He is a fair-to-middling country guitar player himself and composed the words and music to the first four tunes he recorded."[2]

Although the California tour lasted for only ten dates, Carnall liked Johnny's act so much that he negotiated with Bob Neal to buy 50 percent of his management contract for five thousand dollars, plus 7 percent of Cash's next annual gross. Neal would continue to manage the business side from his base in Memphis and Carnall would, in effect, become tour manager, handling the day-to-day business on the road.

Naturally, as Cash's popularity grew, the touring intensified. He also appeared on TV shows such as *Country Style USA* and *Ranch Party,* and made a ten-show commitment to the *Jackie Gleason Show.* After returning from his twenty-four-day tour of Canada in May 1957, he complained to Ted Freeman about the stress of his schedule: "I'm twenty-six pounds lighter and ten years older. We averaged four hundred and twenty miles per day, and *I am tired* and sick."

There were no tour buses, personal assistants, road crews, or short-hop flights for touring artists in those days. All travel was by road, and since the interstate network hadn't yet been constructed this meant slow driving down two-lane black-tops. Because of the many long distances between gigs, they often drove at night, taking turns at the wheel. If they were lucky, they'd arrive at the motel early enough to catch a nap.

In July 1957 while touring Florida with Patsy Cline, Ray Price, Ferlin Husky, Faron Young, and Hank Thompson, Cash first encountered the overworked travel-ing performers' panacea: the drug amphetamine. The small tablets, which immedi-ately increased alertness, could be obtained legitimately with a prescription. Not only could the drug sharpen the senses while banishing tiredness, but it could sustain an all-night song-writing session or add some sparkle to an after-show party. To many country stars of the 1950s, amphetamine seemed like a blessing.

During World War II, soldiers used Benzedrine tablets to combat fatigue, heighten endurance, and elevate their mood. After the war, amphetamines became particularly popular with long-distance truck drivers, students studying for exams and people trying to lose weight. A simple complaint about anxiety, excessive tiredness, or obesity to a GP usually resulted in a prescription. The short-acting tablets created effects that lasted for four hours. The long-acting capsules worked for up to twelve hours.

Although the drug seemed to produce energy out of nothing, it in fact created a fast track to the body's natural stores by overstimulating the central nervous system. It initiated an emotional roller-coaster ride that began with sudden elation and a rise of confidence, progressed through a period of euphoria, and then ended with restlessness followed by fatigue. The choice, then, was whether to fall into a deep sleep that could last for as long as seventeen hours or to take another pill and repeat the cycle.

Gordon Terry, a fiddle player then working with Faron Young, gave Cash his first tablet. They had just finished a show in Miami and had 340 miles to cover before the next day's date in Jacksonville. That night, Terry was driving Young's limousine just ahead of Luther Perkins, who was driving Cash's car. In the early hours of the morning both vehicles pulled over to take a break, and Terry walked over to Luther and offered him a small, white pill that he said would keep him awake and alert for the rest of the journey. Cash asked if they were dangerous. Terry told him that he'd never suffered any side effects—a view shared with the medical community at that time. One country singer received his supply from his father-in-law, a leading surgeon in California who believed that amphetamine was a wonder drug. Merle Kilgore remembers a Nashville doctor who would visit clubs in Printers Alley and reward musicians whose performances had drawn particularly rapturous applause by thrusting a prescription for Obedrin in their hands.

Cash swallowed a pill and settled back in the car. Within half an hour his fatigue had given way to wide-eyed verbosity, and when they arrived in Jacksonville he was in no mood to take his customary nap. The next night he found Terry and got another pill to help him through the show, and he eventually came down the night after that. While he felt exhausted, Cash nevertheless believed that he'd discovered something that could only enhance his career. "I thought God had sent them to me to help me," he later admitted.

By nature a shy, reflective man who hated small talk and the false bonhomie of show business parties, Cash suddenly found himself becoming garrulous and entertaining in company. Amphetamines sped up his thoughts, and he found himself making bizarre mental associations that even affected his performances. Gone were the preshow nerves, replaced by a stage presence that emitted an almost superhuman power. His previously halting delivery of lines between songs eased into a smooth patter. He began his habit of sometimes picking his strings high up on the neck and slinging the guitar over his shoulder like a guerilla's rifle when not playing. There was an electricity in his performance that mesmerized audiences. Marshall Grant, who usually chewed gum on stage, bobbed up and down as he slapped his bass, and Luther Perkins stood bolted to the spot looking nervously to his right as if in need of approval for every note he played.

Though he was not breaking any laws, and at that time had no reason to believe he was sustaining long-term damage, Cash kept his amphetamine consumption private. Vivian didn't know to blame the drug for the long nights he spent in the den alone rather than in bed with her. Sam Phillips didn't detect any change in Cash's behavior during his recording sessions at Sun. But Marshall Grant, who didn't smoke or drink alcohol, was well aware that something was amiss. Cash's timekeeping became erratic, his conversation often veered suddenly toward the surreal, his vocals suffered, and his weight dropped, leaving him looking permanently drawn.

"By the later part of 1957 I knew that something was wrong," says Marshall. "I didn't know what it was. I didn't know anything about drugs. It was bad and getting even worse and one night we were backstage and I was looking for him to go on when I went through the door into his dressing room and found him with his head tipped back and a handful of pills. He dropped one and it rolled across the floor. That's when I knew that it was drugs."

Despite the dried-up mucous membranes, occasional concert cancellation, or lapse into incoherence, "the going up," as Kris Kristofferson would later put it, seemed "worth the coming down" during the first two years of Cash's amphetamine affair. Lying in the back of the car with his notebook or prowling the corridors, guitar in hand, before showtime he was getting ideas for more and more original material. He wrote "Give My Love to Rose"—about an escaped prisoner's last wishes for his family—after meeting a former San Quentin inmate who asked him to pass on a message to his wife the next time he was in Shreveport. In a dressing room in White Plains, New York, after reading a story about himself titled "Johnny Cash Has the Big River Blues in His Voice," he had the idea for "Big River," which tells the tale of someone pursuing a woman down the length of the Mississippi.

Although the songs contained the familiar themes of loss and longing that permeated Cash's country music and the blues, Cash's simple, direct delivery often disguised a poetic depth. He had an ability to effortlessly incorporate assonance, alliteration, and internal rhymes without drawing attention to his technique. He also had no problem incorporating his ideas into an overarching metaphor rather than settling for the plain description of emotion. Lines such as "I taught the weeping willow how to cry / And I showed the clouds how to cover up a clear blue sky" ("Big

River") showed a lyrical richness that preceded folk rock by at least eight years.

Indeed, his songs contributed indirectly to the folk rock movement. Bob Dylan heard Cash's songs on his radio in Hibbing, Minnesota, as a high school teenager and they became his early inspiration. He loved the primal imagery of "Big River," later describing it as "words turned into bone." In 2002, when asked to contribute a track to the Johnny Cash tribute album *Kindred Spirits,* Dylan chose "Train of Love," saying by way of introduction, "I used to sing this song before I ever wrote a song."

Though Sam Phillips produced "Big River," "Train of Love," and "Give My Love to Rose," Cash felt that Phillips had lost interest in him and wanted to concentrate on his latest discovery, Jerry Lee Lewis, who'd had hits with "High School Confidential," "Whole Lot of Shakin' Going On," and "Great Balls of Fire." When Phillips's newly hired trainee engineer Jack Clement took over the April 1957 session to record "Next in Line" and "Don't Make Me Go," Cash knew for sure. His comment on the listless "Next in Line," made in a letter to Ted Freeman, summed up his feeling about the new direction. "I don't particularly care for it," he said, "but it's getting good radio play."

Jack Clement was a local boy who'd done a four-year stint in the army before his discharge in 1952. He played music in the evenings and on weekends, taught dance for six months, spent two years at Memphis State University thinking he might become a journalist, and then started work with a building supply firm. As a sideline, he produced demo tapes in a friend's garage. When he took one of these tapes to Sam Phillips in June 1956 to have it mastered, the producer offered him a job. At that time the label employed only three other people—an office manager, a secretary, and an engineer from a radio station also owned by Phillips.

"It was a pretty crude setup when I went to work there," says Clement. "The desk was a basic audio console made for radio stations by RCA. It wasn't fancy, but it was good. If you wanted echo you had to have a separate microphone and run it through a separate tape machine. We only had six microphone inputs, so if you wanted echo on the voice that used two of them and if you wanted echo on something else that would use up two more. The sound could be balanced but it all had to be done live. You could add things, like we often did with vocal groups, but you couldn't take things away."

Albums had little importance in the 1950s and typically included some recent singles plus filler tracks. Cash's debut album, *Johnny Cash with His Hot and Blue Guitar,* which was also the first album Sun had ever produced, had four previously released sides and was bulked out with eight sides recorded by Clement, only one of which, "Country Boy," was a Cash original. He recorded two gospel songs, "I Was There When It Happened" and his own "Belshazar," which was later dropped.

Even though Cash's church attendance had waned, he still used church teachings as a guide. In particular, the Christian tradition of tithing influenced him to tithe 10 percent of his musical output by making one in ten of his releases a gospel song. Had "Belshazar" remained on the album, he'd have been up to date on his tithing—for by now he'd released twenty tracks for Sun.

"He did put out this gospel song, but he didn't do a whole album of them because Sam didn't want him to," says Clement. "Sam knew that it wouldn't sell. He wanted to keep the momentum going and he knew that a gospel album would divert sales. Gospel wasn't what Johnny Cash was known for. Starting to do gospel would have diluted his impact. I don't think Johnny Cash understood that. I did."

Almost everyone at Sun had a strong fundamentalist church background. Elvis had been raised in the Assembly of God, and one of his earliest professional ambitions was to join the Songfellows, a junior gospel quartet designed to feed the long-established Blackwood Brothers. Carl Perkins grew up reading the Bible and singing gospel. Sam Philips liked to pontificate on theological matters, especially after a drink or two, and his language at times seemed to come straight from the King James "Authorized" Version of the Old Testament.

The artist most tortured by the apparent conflict between rock-'n'-roll and religion was Jerry Lee Lewis, who had been raised in the Assembly of God and had attended Bible College for a brief time. He sometimes argued that by playing rock-'n'-roll he was "dragging people to hell." Jack Clement remembers engineering the session that produced "Great Balls of Fire," when the singer had such an attack of conscience that he threatened to abandon the session. "Great Balls of Fire," filled with sexual innuendo, also alluded to the coming of the Holy Spirit on the Day of Pentecost.

A theological argument between Lewis, Sam Phillips, and visiting singer Billy Lee Riley broke out in the control room—all of it preserved for posterity on tape by Clement. Phillips argued that rock-'n'-roll, by bringing pleasure to people, continued the healing ministry begun by Jesus Christ. Lewis considered the sound "devil's music" and said he would only bring damnation on himself by playing it.

In the end though, despite his apparently strong theological objections, Lewis finished the session, probably with an added edge coming from his convictions that he was demon possessed.

Most of these men still considered themselves Christians because they hadn't denied any key doctrines, but the teachings of the Bible no longer shaped their behavior. As Lewis once said, they thought religiously but they didn't walk religiously. They still recognized the importance of church, but few of them went to services. Regular Bible reading and prayer got lost somewhere between the traveling and recording. Elvis once went to his pastor and said, "Everything you told me to do, I haven't done. Everything you told me not to do, I have done. And I'm an unhappy man."

Religion for these men shifted from a way of life to a largely sentimental or nostalgic feeling. It reminded them of better, less complicated times and enduring values. When they were troubled they'd think back to their times at church. When they were touched by remorse they'd make vows to God to walk the straight and narrow. Hank Williams, the prototypical Southern backslider, gloried openly in the sins of the flesh and then wrote songs like "When God Comes to Gather His Jewels" and "I Saw the Light." Ira Louvin of the Louvin Brothers wrote guilt-inducing gospel songs even though he was a wife-beating alcoholic. Cash was different. He never had a crisis of conscience over recording secular music and his affection for the message of gospel music remained genuine.

On August 13, 1957, at a party in California following a TV appearance, Cash met Don Law, a British-born producer, who invited him to consider signing with Columbia Records when his contract with Sun expired at the end of July 1958. Law, a highly respected music-industry veteran, had started back in the 1920s when recording was done directly onto hot wax. Law recorded the now-legendary sessions with blues musician Robert Johnson in 1936 and 1937 that captured such classics as "Ramblin' on My Mind," "Crossroad Blues," and "Hell Hound on My Trail." He also recorded Bob Wills and Gene Autry. He appreciated the direct and uncomplicated nature of Cash's voice and his openness to new ideas.

Cash didn't need a lot of persuading. He knew that his recording career was stagnating at Sun, and he didn't appreciate the fact that Sam Phillips wanted Clement to "freshen up his sound" for the teenage market. He'd also still harbored resentment toward Phillips for not allowing him to record an album of gospel songs. Then there was the question of money. Columbia offered to pay 5 percent of the retail price of a record in mechanical royalties rather than the 3 percent of 90 percent of retail that Sun offered. In addition, being a major company guaranteed that Columbia would be more rigorous in its accounting than a small independent.

"Sam was stealing us blind," says Marshall Grant. "We couldn't get the royalties from him. Another thing was that Sun was still more or less a regional label. After Elvis left and we left, it got a lot of recognition nationwide and finally world wide, but that wasn't the case when we were there. It went to Texas, Louisiana, Mississippi, Arkansas, Tennessee, and Kentucky. That was about as far as it went."

When Phillips got wind that Cash was thinking of leaving, he took it as a personal snub. He didn't know that Cash had already struck a secret deal with Columbia in November 1957 that would become effective immediately upon termination of his Sun contract in July 1958. Nothing Phillips could now offer him would make him stay. "Sam Phillips loved Johnny Cash," says Jack Clement. "He respected him a lot more than the other characters because he was a real gentleman. Sam was always raving about how easy he was to work with. He loved his singing. He would talk about the authority he had in his voice and how people trusted him. I was really surprised when he left. I think it was based on a misunderstanding. He thought that Sam no longer had time for him."

The remaining singles Cash recorded for Sun only convinced him that he'd made the right decision in leaving. Although commercially successful, they compromised his vision. His raw sound was being padded out with drums, piano, and overdubbed background vocals. Instead of the stark and unusual points of view in songs like "Folsom Prison Blues" or "I Walk the Line," he was being given lyrics about dating and young romance. Thirty years later, Cash still complained about its overdubbed vocals: "All that junk on it. That ruined it for me." However, Cash would develop a working partnership with "Cowboy" Jack Clement that would last for the rest of his life.

The fact that only three years into his career Cash was recording singles written by other people illustrated just how unhappy he had become. For his farewell Sun single, he cut "You're the Nearest Thing to Heaven," which he'd written with Hoyt Johnson and Jimmy Atkins, backed by "The Ways of a Woman in Love" by

Charlie Rich and Bill Justis.

After getting a letter from Phillips reminding Cash of his contractual obligation to record sixty-five songs, he laid down over twenty tracks (only three of which he'd cowritten) between May 15 and July 17. "He didn't want to record," remembers Jack Clement. "He was annoyed that he had to. It became my job to get him to do it. There was a Hank Williams songbook in the studio and I said, 'Why don't you cut five Hank Williams songs in forty-five minutes? You sing, let the guys play, and I'll add overdubs.' He said okay, and so that's what we did. It took care of a certain number of tracks." The five songs recorded were "You Win Again," "I Could Never Be Ashamed of You," "Cold, Cold Heart," "Hey, Good Lookin," and "I Can't Help It."

Cash's contract with Sun expired on the last day of July, so on August 1, 1958, his secretly negotiated contract with Columbia took effect. Two weeks later he performed at Columbia Records' national sales convention in Estes Park, Colorado, where he received a standing ovation from the gathered reps. It felt like a new beginning. And while Elvis, drafted into the army, would leave for Germany in September, Cash had Hollywood beckoning him with talk of movie offers.

Stew Carnall managed to persuade Cash that his future lay in California. He suggested that his contacts in the film and television industry would be helpful. Bob Neal didn't object because he'd fallen out with Sam Phillips and had lost his connection with the Sun artists. Luther and Marshall, on the other hand, opposed the move because they could see no advantage for them other than when they toured California or Western Canada.

This time marked the end of the really close relationship between the three men. First the social life they had established in Memphis would go and then the attention to rehearsals. When, after a short time, Marshall and Luther moved back to Tennessee, they would only reunite to play on stage or in the studio.

"Johnny wanted to go out and try it but I always thought it was a ridiculous move," says Marshall. "It was supposed to be a move for the better but it wasn't a move for the better. We kept touring all over the country and the driving back and forth nearly killed Luther. It would eventually get to a point where we couldn't do it anymore."

6

Going Down, Down, Down

NEVERTHELESS, THE CASHES MOVED to California in August 1958, driving the eighteen hundred miles with three-year-old Rosanne, two-year-old Kathy, and the newly born Cynthia (Cindy). Initially they rented an apartment on Coldwater Canyon Avenue in North Hollywood, where Cindy's bed had to be made up in a drawer. A few months later they moved into a seventy-five-thousand-dollar ranch house with a swimming pool on Havenhurst Avenue in Encino, bought from TV host Johnny Carson, who had moved to New York to start a new show for NBC. They became near neighbors to John Wayne and Clark Gable. Shortly afterwards, Marshall and Luther moved to the San Fernando Valley.

At the time, most recording stars considered acting the next big career step once they had a few hit singles under their belts. Bob Neal, who'd folded his Stars Incorporated agency in June, had been led to believe that Cash had a good shot at hosting a regular music show on TV. With these and other opportunities in mind, Johnny Cash Enterprises established itself at the Crossroads of the World, a prestigious Spanish-style building on Sunset Boulevard. "Johnny and I both felt we could storm Hollywood," Neal later said.

Recording for Columbia took place at the Owen Bradley Studios in Nashville, and after cutting enough tracks for his first album with Don Law, boldly titled *The Fabulous Johnny Cash,* he started work on his first collection of gospel songs, *Hymns by Johnny Cash.* Half of the songs were published hymns, and half were new songs either written or arranged by Cash. The liner notes stated, "Johnny Cash turns his attention from the popular songs that have made him one of the brightest stars of today to the simpler songs of faith and devotion, presenting a program that combines religious feeling with music in splendid fashion."[1]

One of the first new friends Cash made in California was Johnny Western, a twenty-three-year-old recording artist introduced to him at the office by Gordon Terry. Western (his real name) was a singing cowboy who had performed with the legendary Sons of the Pioneers and had once been Gene Autry's featured singer and guitarist. His recording "The Ballad of Paladin" was currently the theme song of *Have Gun—Will Travel,* a popular CBS series in which he had also acted.

Cash invited him to play on some guitar transcriptions at McGregor Studios in Hollywood for discs that were distributed to the armed forces and after that, to open for him on a tour of California. Then came some shows in the Midwest that featured Gordon Terry. From these beginnings grew what would become the *Johnny Cash Show.* The only changing feature was the female vocalists. For the first year Rose Maddox had a spot and the next year Patsy Cline. "Then we took Barbara Mandrell on her first tour when she was only thirteen years old," remembers Western. "That was a tour in 1962 and Patsy took care of her."

Even though Cash now headlined a showcase he had put together himself, the rigors of touring differed little from his days as a support act. Now he had a trailer packed with suitcases and instruments to tow behind the car. Western always tuned two identical Martin guitars for him because Cash's escalating drug habit meant that he would often accidentally drop his instruments. Some guests didn't trust Cash's driving ability and so a second car was brought along. "He was the world's worst driver," says Western. "Patsy Cline wouldn't ride if he was driving. She would only ride with Gordon Terry or me, and she was the best road buddy in the world."

Touring was one part ecstasy to three parts monotony. The excitement of being away from home and on the move soon paled—particularly when visiting towns for the second or third time. In order to quell the inevitable boredom, the Cash entourage developed the art of hotel destruction, something that fell somewhere between outright vandalism and an elaborate practical joke.

Each member developed a specific role. Marshall Grant's areas of expertise included cutting up furniture and setting off explosions. As Johnny Western explains: "He would carry a small Black & Decker circle saw. What he would then do is cut the legs off the furniture in his hotel room and then put them back in place so that everything looked perfectly all right. When the maid walked in the whole room would fall apart as soon as she touched something with her duster."

Marshall usually arranged the explosions in open spaces late at night, purely for amusement. He started with firecrackers and small amounts of gunpowder but eventually only found satisfaction with sticks of dynamite that he would pack around with yards of string. One of his most exciting discoveries was a signal cannon that he would sometimes fire down hotel corridors. He even managed to adapt it for shooting gravel at neon signs on the highway.

Gordon Terry specialized in painting and decorating. He would carefully paint everything in the room—not only the furniture, but also the walls and ceiling. Sometimes even the mirrors and television would get a quick coat. The result was even more surreal because it was so professionally executed. "We didn't mess up the room," says Marshall Grant. "We did a good job on it. It was a bizarre thing to do and if you did it today you'd probably get sent to jail. We always used to pay for the damage. We'd say that we'd had a party and someone had got a bit overexcited. The manager would ask for fifty dollars or one hundred dollars and that's what would happen. Looking back it seems quite ridiculous and it's not something that I'm too proud of."

Cash and Western often did something appropriately cowboyish, like setting up shootouts with replica Colt .45s in hotel lobbies or arranging for someone in the party to be publicly "kidnapped" and bundled into a waiting car in front of gawking pedestrians. More out of frustration than as a stunt, Cash once stuck a Bowie knife into a *Mona Lisa* reproduction in a hotel room that didn't measure up to his standards. One of their most elaborate jokes took place during a stay at the Waldorf Astoria in New York. Cash and Stew Carnall procured bales of hay and buckets of manure from a riding stable in Central Park and smuggled them into their room via a service elevator. They then proceeded to carefully spread the straw across every available inch of floor space before checking out. "It had a beautiful rug in this room," remembers Western, "but by the time they'd finished it looked as though Trigger had been living there for a week."

Some of the stunts had a touch of comic genius. In Scottsbluff, Nebraska, they removed all the furniture from a hotel room and placed it outside the elevator with two of the troupe tucked up in single beds. They then called for room service. When the waiter came up with the food he immediately went back down to fetch the manager. By the time the manager arrived on the scene, the hall was completely clear. The routine was then repeated with another call to the waiter.

Other stunts were inexcusably destructive and foreshadowed the hotel vandalism by bands like the Who and Led Zeppelin by at least ten years. Johnny Cash and the Tennessee Two must have been the first traveling band to fill a bathtub with Jell-O, create a connecting doorway with a fire ax, explode cherry bombs in a toilet, smear fish paste on radiators, and toss light fixtures out of windows just to hear the sound they made on impact. As their reputation as pranksters and vandals increased, they found themselves banned from certain hotels, and country artists in general became viewed with suspicion by hoteliers.

Although Cash had guest appearances in four TV Westerns—*Tales of Wells Fargo, Shotgun Slade, Wagon Train,* and *The Rebel* (for which he sang the theme)—his only big-screen appearance was as a drugged-up killer in the film noir *Five Minutes to Live* (later marketed as *Door-to-Door Maniac*). "Part of the reason he came to California was to be an actor," says Johnny Western. "He knew that he couldn't do that while living in Memphis. But then he was touring so much that he often wasn't around when offers came up. When studios call you, they want you today. They're not going to hang around and wait until you come back to town."

Cash was now away from home 80 percent of the time, traveling three hundred thousand miles a year. It would be easy to say that his marriage to Vivian fell apart simply because he was absent too often, that he wanted a wife who traveled, and she wanted a husband who stayed at home. The truth is that they were never really suited to each other, having completely different backgrounds, beliefs, life experiences, interests, and expectations. They'd each married some sort of projection of their youthful desires, fueled by three years of passionate letter writing.

No one would have guessed the Cashes were having marital troubles from the publicity of the time. Cash was always portrayed as the contented family man who liked nothing more than being at home with his "charming wife and three little daughters." Vivian perpetuated the image of domestic tranquility through her letters in Cash's fan magazine in which she'd talk about him planting rose bushes and hosting barbecues for friends while she looked after the children and played in the local bowling league.

Vivian didn't like the music business, and not just because it had taken her husband away from her. She didn't feel comfortable around music-business people. Rare photographs of her taken backstage show a painfully shy woman obviously feeling out of place. Because music was so important to Cash, he interpreted Vivian's discomfort as a rejection of who he was.

Out on the road, Cash was meeting sassy women who loved music and the music business as much as he did. They were often forthright, wickedly funny, and sexually alluring—quite unlike the simple country girls he had dated in Dyess. Most importantly, they made him feel good about himself.

In 1957 Cash toured with the Collins Kids, a brother-and-sister duo originally from Oklahoma that was part frenetic rock-'n'-roll and part novelty act. Larry was the crazy and annoying kid brother. Lorrie was the older and more restrained sister. They both played guitars and had built up a reputation by appearing regularly on *Town Hall Party,* a *Grand Ole Opry*–style show televised weekly from the Compton district of Los Angeles. Within months of arriving in California, Cash and the Tennessee Two played on the show with Merle Travis, Bob Luman, Jeannie Sterling, Johnny Bond, and Joe Maphis. That day, the Collins Kids performed Elvis's "I Got Stung," the Big Bopper's "Chantilly Lace" and a blues medley.

Although Cash had vowed to "walk the line," his resolve was faltering, particularly when the now sixteen-year-old Lorrie Collins caught his eye. Over the next several months as the Collins Kids played dates with them they spent a lot of time together and he became infatuated with her despite the fact that she was dating teen idol Ricky Nelson. She became aware of his feelings for her but, despite rumors to the contrary, insists that nothing transpired. "It was a long time ago and I have no idea why he felt that way about me," she says. "It must have been the fact that I was young and the association with music, that sort of thing. It was just something that happened but nothing ever took place between us."

For the increasingly burdened Cash, the sexual chemistry was powerful and confusing. "It was one of those things that just swept him off his feet," says Johnny Western. "She'd just blossomed into womanhood and he was attracted. Sometimes he and I would get into my Jaguar and drive fifty or sixty miles into the desert and he'd tell me things that he hadn't told anybody else. His marriage was falling apart, his daughters were small, and he felt trapped. He didn't know what to do about his feelings for Lorrie because she was so young. He'd say, 'What am I going to do?'

I said, 'Johnny. You love cowboy movies?' He said, 'Yes. I do.' So I said, 'Well, you've got to step in the saddle and ride into the sunset on this one. This isn't going to work. You know it's not. It's going to cost you an arm and a leg and people are going to blame this young girl for being a home wrecker.' He said he still didn't know what to do." The problem went away when Stew Carnall began dating Lorrie and married her in 1959, when he was thirty and she seventeen.

The problem went away when Stew Carnall began dating Lorrie and married her in 1959, when he was thirty and she seventeen. A rumor circulated that the marriage had been staged to prevent the exposure of Cash's liaison, but Western denies it. "Stew was desperately in love with her. They stayed married for quite a while and had two children."

Cash always returned home restless. He couldn't settle into the ordinary routines of suburban home life and craved the excitement and stimulation of the road. "He'd be home and tired for a couple of days and he'd play by his pool with the kids, but by the third day he'd be ready to move off," says Western. "He got itchy feet. Work was his main hobby and he absolutely adored being up onstage. If he wasn't playing for a few days he'd be on the phone finding out about the next tour."

Consequently, Cash stopped returning to Encino even when his tours ended. Instead, he often headed down to Shreveport to stay at Johnny Horton's home at 1610 Audubon Drive. He would hang out there for days, hunting, fishing, and playing music with Horton and Billie Jean. Sometimes the two men would disappear to another part of the house to discuss the ideas of the psychic Edgar Cayce, who claimed to be able to access special knowledge after putting himself into a self-induced sleep state and to answer questions impenetrable by reason and logic.

Billie Jean made a huge impression on Cash. Besides being the gorgeous former wife of Hank Williams, she was a forthright and amusing conversationalist, an excellent shot with a rifle, and an accomplished angler. She loved the company of men and delighted in the knowledge that when she arrived at a country music convention or sat close to the stage for a concert, she would turn heads. "If she was in the room, you'd know she was in the room," says Horton's former guitarist Reggie Young. "She had huge hair and she dressed provocatively. She was the total opposite of the sort of person you thought Johnny Horton would be with."

Horton, with good reason, was jealous of the attention his wife got. Tillman Franks, Horton's bass player as well as his manager, felt that the way she dressed when she attended concerts detracted from her husband. She was conscious, as was Horton, that Cash was paying her more attention than was usual from a family friend.

Unsurprisingly, as someone who spent a fair amount of time trying to contact the other world, Horton was given to premonitions. The most persistent vision convinced him that he would die an early death. Specifically, he thought his death would somehow relate to alcohol. As a teetotaler, he concluded that most likely he'd die at the hands of a drunkard, perhaps after one of his concerts, and he became wary of playing in clubs and bars. Convinced of the inevitability of his premature death, he talked Cash into making a pact with him: if one of them died, the one remaining would look after the widow and children of the other, until they regained their stability.

The annual D. J. convention of 1960 took place at the Hermitage Hotel in Nashville, and Cash attended with Vivian. One of the rare times they traveled together without the children, she wanted to enjoy some private time together, but he wanted to hang out with the musicians and songwriters in their rooms. Later that Friday night, November 4, they had what he later described as "one of our worst fights." Vivian went to bed while Cash scoured the corridors looking for action.

Early the next morning he received the news that Johnny Horton was dead. The night before, he'd done two shows at the Skyline Club, north of Austin, and while driving back to Shreveport in his 1959 Fleetwood Cadillac with Tillman Franks and guitarist Tommy Tomlinson, his car was struck head-on by a Ford Ranchero outside Milano, Texas. Tomlinson and Franks survived, but Horton was pronounced dead on arrival at the hospital in Cameron, thirteen miles away. The Ranchero driver, a young student, survived. He had, in fact, been drinking.

Cash couldn't leave for Shreveport right away because he had a session booked at Owen Bradley Studios to cut the title track of his movie *Five Minutes to Live*, but later that day he flew down to console Billie Jean. Horton's death seemed to unhinge Cash—those close to him thought that he began acting "weird"—and may have exacerbated his addiction to the amphetamines.

The funeral was held five days later at the Rose-Neath Chapel in Bossier City, Louisiana. Tillman Franks's brother, Billy Franks, preached the sermon, The Plainsmen Quartet sang a gospel song, and Johnny Cash read from John 20—a passage chosen randomly by Billie Jean, by flipping open the Bible. "It was a glass-covered casket and Johnny stood beside it as if he was talking to a friend," remembers Tillman Franks. "He read the Bible with a catch of emotionalism in his voice. He was very quiet, but he never faltered."

None of Cash's friends fully realized the depth of his feelings for Billie Jean. They interpreted his desire to be with her at this traumatic time solely as the actions of a man who had promised to take care of his best friend's widow. "Johnny's marriage was unraveling and everybody knew it," says Johnny Western. "Billie Jean was very beautiful. She was breathtaking in her day and I'm sure that a lot of guys had romantic intentions toward her. Cash was the biggest thing in the world at the time and he was helping her. I think it was one of those situations where people assume something is going on, whereas there was nothing romantic on Johnny's part."

That said, his friends probably didn't know that immediately following Horton's death Cash escorted the widow to New York for a three-week shopping spree, staying at a hotel on Central Park and indulging her every whim. He told at least one person that he eventually intended to marry her. "He spent so much money that it was unreal," says Billie Jean. "He bought me everything he could think of. I'd never been to New York before, and he'd been so many times, so he wanted me to see everything. We were doing something all the time. Because I'd stopped eating when Johnny Horton died, he wanted to introduce me to different kinds of food to try to bring my appetite back."

Taking such an extended break meant canceling concerts, but according to Billie Jean he seemed unconcerned about getting back to work. "Johnny Cash had a habit of doing what he wanted to do," she explains. "How did he explain his absence to Vivian? Johnny didn't do any explaining. He knew that I needed him. I really did need him because losing Horton just about killed me. He was determined to put me back on my feet. By the time we left New York I was doing so much better, and he would call me several times a day to see how I was progressing. Johnny was such a caring person. You really had a friend when you had Johnny Cash."

The relationship continued along the lines established when her husband was alive. Cash essentially divided his time off the road between Encino and Shreveport.

He saw to Billie Jean's finances and arranged for a portion of his royalties to be paid into her account, to tide her over until she received the royalties from Horton's final hit "North to Alaska." He also protected her privacy. If anyone wanted access to Billie Jean Horton now, they knew that they had to go through Johnny Cash.

More than forty years later Billie Jean remains discreet about the precise nature of the relationship. She starts by describing it as the obligation of someone who had promised to care for her in the event of her husband's death. Then she describes him as "my brother in spirit." Finally she admits to a love she believes would have developed further had it not been for his escalating drug consumption. In the weeks before his death, Horton was trying to help Cash go straight.

"I loved Johnny," she says. "I loved him for all of his life. We were so close, but the only thing that put the kibosh on it was the drugs. Had he not been on the pills, trust me, I would have married him because I cared that much about him, and I knew that he loved me. I had to hold back because I didn't know how to handle anyone on drugs or booze because Horton was so clean."

Another obstacle to any long-term relationship was Billie Jean's desire to pursue her own singing career. Cash wanted her waiting at home for him in Shreveport. "Cash did not like me on the road," she says. "He liked me to stay at home with him coming back and forth. That was his idea and, if I'd done that, would probably have led to marriage."

Her refusal to be tamed led to some explosive outbursts. Once, while both performing in Vancouver on the same night—she was part of a showcase at the Queen Elizabeth Theater while he and the Tennessee Two were playing at the Cave—they stayed at the Hotel Georgia and after an argument, Cash stormed down the hallway smashing the hotel's antique chandeliers. Not only did he have to pay for all the damage, but he and his entourage had to check out immediately.

> So you gave up all between us
> For a glamorous career
> And with all your talent
> You should be the big star of the year.
> Then you'll be public property
> So I release my claim to you
> Go on and give 'em all you've got

Sing it pretty, Sue.

I can't take just part of you
And give the world a half
So smile for all the papers
And give 'em autographs.
Go on to all the cities
So your public can see you
But I'll watch on television
So sing it pretty, Sue.

("Sing It Pretty, Sue," 1961)

In April 1961, Cash began work on his second gospel album for Columbia. The Tennessee Two had expanded to become the Tennessee Three with the addition of drummer W. S. 'Fluke' Holland in August. Cash's faith had hit an all-time low, and even he noticed the irony in finally having the opportunity to give voice to his religious feelings. He didn't question the validity of his conversion or the basis of his theology, but he'd grown spiritually sluggish after so many years away from regular worship. And he knew that his behavior went against everything he'd been taught, both by his mother and his church. He'd felt challenged the year before when he'd met Pat Boone at the Steel Pier in Atlantic City, New Jersey, and Cash had been impressed by Boone's "clear-eyed" and "clean-cut" appearance that contrasted so markedly with his own hollowed cheeks and dilated pupils. He knew that Boone's freshness reflected the steadfastness of his faith.

"I was a little ashamed of myself at the time because of the hypocrisy of it all," he said in 1973. "There I was singing the praises of the Lord and singing about the beauty and the peace you find in Him, and I was stoned and miserable. I was climbing the walls."[1]

His first arrest came in November 1961. At 3:30 in the morning, City Police Inspector W. J. Donoho and two traffic officers stopped Cash and Glenn Douglas Tubb (author of "Home of the Blues,") outside a club near Nashville's Printers Alley. Apparently Johnny was kicking down the door of a club he thought was refusing him entry, only to find that it was in fact closed. Both men spent four hours in jail, and, after paying a five-dollar bond, were released. On the police blotter Johnny Cash listed himself as an actor. The next day's story in the *Nashville Banner* was headlined "Johnny Cash Arrested Here on Drunk Charge."

By late 1961, Canadian Saul Holiff, who had started out in the clothing and restaurant businesses, had taken over the managing of Cash's career. In 1959, Bob Neal sold his 50 percent share in Cash's management to Stew Carnall, who acted as his sole manager until July 1961 when Cash realized that no one was managing Johnny Cash Enterprises when he was on tour. The things that had made Carnall a charming sophisticate—his love of gambling, good food, fast cars, and fine wine—made him an inefficient manager. "I think things changed for Johnny Cash," says Lorrie Collins Carnall. "He was having a lot of problems. I'm sure that some of it was Stew's fault too. He loved to party and have a good time. He was a player at the horses. In fact, he talked Johnny into buying a horse that they named Walk the Line, but that's just about all this horse did. He walked. He didn't run."

The end for Carnall came when Cash embarked on a Canadian tour promoted by Saul Holiff. "Stew was a great playboy and a lot of fun to be around, but he just wasn't taking care of business," says Johnny Western. "We were in Ontario and Johnny had been trying to get him all day on the phone, but Stew was on the race-track. He had important business to handle, and he just wasn't around. When Cash finally got through to him and realized where he'd been, he fired him. Marshall suggested that Saul should take over. He said that he'd done more for him on these Canadian dates than Stew had done for him in years. Cash took a good, hard look at that before deciding to hire him."

A sophisticated Canadian, Holiff was the antithesis of a country music manager. He wasn't even a country fan—his music of choice being jazz—but he'd heard "Five Feet High and Rising," Cash's hit song about the 1937 flood at Dyess, on a jukebox and liked it enough to book a few gigs for Johnny Cash and the Tennessee Two. "I'd promoted people like the Everly Brothers, Paul Anka, and Bill Haley, but I really wasn't familiar with Johnny Cash at all," he admits. "In fact, I wasn't familiar with much of anything in country music. I had to become familiar in a hurry when things played out the way they did."

Being an outsider to both the U.S. and to country music affected the way Holiff managed Cash. He marketed him to a broader, more international audience and took him beyond the narrow confines of the country genre. Holiff coined the phrase "America's foremost singing storyteller" to describe Johnny Cash. He first used it in souvenir programs and later in industry advertisements. "He didn't know he was a singing storyteller until I told him," says Holiff. "I wasn't anxious to play up the 'country' label especially. Labeling was a serious thing. If you were lumped into a certain category it meant restricted airplay. I thought that 'singing storyteller' was nebulous enough."

Cash had always had broad musical interests. His repertoire included black gospel, the blues, traditional folk music, spirituals, work chants, mountain music, eighteenth-century hymns, and Irish ballads. He listened to the Louvin Brothers, the Golden Gate Quartet, and the Carter Family. He shopped at the Home of the Blues on Beale Street, where he bought records by people like Pink Anderson, Robert Johnson, and Muddy Waters. He impressed those who knew him with his encyclopedic knowledge of early American music and unique ability to sing something from memory on almost any subject put to him.

When in New York, Cash would visit the folk clubs and record stores of Greenwich Village to keep up with the rising urban folk scene. He befriended up-and-coming musicians such as Joan Baez, Richard Farina, Ramblin' Jack Elliott, Judy Collins, and Phil Ochs and was even paying attention to the more traditional material of the Kingston Trio who, since 1958, had been recording a mixture of ballads, country songs, spirituals, and folk. It was on their 1959 album *The Kingston Trio at Large* that he first heard "Remember the Alamo" and on 1963's *Sunny Side* that he spotted "Jackson." In sponging up these influences he was displaying an openness that was uncommon in Nashville but which would contribute to his eventual longevity.

"He really got into that folk stuff," says Merle Kilgore. "He'd go out and buy all the folk albums that didn't have national distribution, and he'd go back to his hotel room and listen to them. If he found something he really liked, he'd play it over and over again. He'd dissect the song to see what made it work. He'd listen to Odetta, for example, and he'd point out which songs had English roots and which songs had Irish roots. He loved doing that. He had a Leadbelly album and he'd put that on and tell me how Leadbelly got the bones of the song from someone else. Then he'd do the same with Blind Lemon Jefferson. He really studied his craft."

Songs that told the story of the anonymous builders of the nation really interested Cash. He loved material by or about the pioneers and cowboys, slaves and prisoners, farmers and laborers. As he later said, "I love the traditional songs. I like being challenged to do an old railroad ballad that nobody's heard in forty years. I like to keep them alive—gospel, spirituals, Southern blues, cowboy songs like "Oh Bury Me Not." Songs with tragedy and murder are a very strong part of our musical heritage. All the songs I loved as a boy I still love. They come from the same man, the same breath, the same well."

Two records that deeply influenced him in this respect were Merle Travis's *Folk Songs of the Hills* (1947) and the documentary recording *Blues in the Mississippi Night* (1959). On both albums the pain of hard labor and the injustices meted out to workers were explored in songs linked by the spoken word. Travis had recorded eight songs that he'd learned growing up that had been composed by anonymous coal miners and passed through the generations. Possibly influenced by recordings of the poet Carl Sandburg, Travis gave a lively spoken introduction to each song, setting it in its context.

In 1947, Alan Lomax, the renowned musicologist, recorded *Blues in the Mississippi Night* in New York City. It consisted of three anonymous musicians discussing the social conditions that gave rise to the blues, occasionally breaking into songs that illustrated their stories. "Blues is kind of a revenge," says one of them. "You know you wanta say something, you wanta signify like—that's the blues. We all have had a hard time in life, and things we couldn't do or say, so we sing it." They talk about slavery, levee camps, chain gangs, cruel bosses, and racism. In the sleeve notes, Lomax wrote that the recording showed that "people who are virtually illiterate and unschooled can view a complex social problem as a whole; they can analyze it and think about it logically; and can present their views, coherently and powerfully, and with great 'literary' skill."

At the time of the recording, Lomax concealed the identities of the musicians because they feared that they would be hunted down for some of the criticisms they made of their white bosses in Mississippi and Arkansas. Not until 1990, when a CD version of the album was released by Rounder Records, were the names of the by-then-legendary blues musicians Big Bill Broonzy, Memphis Slim, and Sonny Boy Williamson revealed.

Cash's interest in documentary and work songs was most obvious on his albums *Ride This Train* and *Blood, Sweat and Tears. Ride This Train,* which used the analogy of a train journey to link songs about lumberjacks, prisoners, and miners, paid tribute to Merle Travis's style of narration. *Blood, Sweat and Tears,* a concept album about the pains of heavy labor and the brutality of employers, used a song he'd first heard on *Folk Songs from the Hills* ("Nine Pound Hammer") and one from *Blues in the Mississippi Night* ("Another Man Done Gone").

Travis moved from Kentucky to California after the war to act in cowboy films and play in Western swing bands. Cash met him on November 15, 1958, when performing on *Town Hall Party.* Cash was so eager to replicate Travis's sound on *Ride This Train* that, while Travis was sick with an ulcer, Johnny Western borrowed Travis's guitar to play on "Loading Coal" and "Boss Jack."

Holiff worked hard to change the public's perception of Johnny Cash, wanting him to be seen not only as the most popular country singer of his day but as a great American artist as well. Part of this plan involved concerts at Carnegie Hall and the Hollywood Bowl. "The only reason we did them was because they were prestigious venues and that it was unprecedented for an artist like Johnny to appear there," says Holiff. "On the afternoon before the New York concert we had a private reception for him on the top floor of the Time-Life Building. I had fillets of buffalo flown in from Wyoming for appetizers. I thought that these things would redirect people's thinking about him and his stature. They would combine to give him an allure. In fact, it worked."

The Carnegie Hall concert itself, though, was a disaster. Cash had taken so much amphetamine that his throat was dried out and he could barely sing. He dressed in a railroader's cap and jacket that had once belonged to Jimmie Rodgers and everyone involved with the show knew he was flying high. "Columbia was going to record the concert for an album, but they didn't even turn on the machine," says Johnny Western. "He'd been whispering during rehearsals but that's as bad as talking or singing in terms of trying to save your voice because the air is still passing over your vocal chords. He was a sad case, but there was a full house and the people still loved him. He was Johnny Cash and he'd showed up!"

In the fall of 1961, with their fourth child, Tara, only a few weeks old, the Cashes moved a few miles north of Ventura to a new home at 8994 Nye Road in Casitas Springs. Worried about the effect of the Los Angeles smog, they wanted to live where the air was cleaner. Cash bought fifteen acres of land halfway up a steep and virtually barren hill and had his friend Walter "Curly" Lewis, a local contractor, build a five bedroom ranch house. To most people it seemed an odd choice of location. Over sixty miles from Los Angeles International Airport with no surrounding community, it was worryingly isolated for a mother with four young children.

"It was horrible," remembers Rosanne. "I don't know what they were thinking. Dad was on the road all the time, and he moved us up to the top of this mountain in this really poor township. We had the most money and the biggest house in the whole area, and we were perched up there all alone, and it was strange."

But Cash liked the isolation and the arid climate. Going through a desert phase, he loved nothing more than to drive his car out into the lonely spaces and sit there with his own thoughts. He'd already moved his parents from Memphis to nearby Ojai, where he bought them a trailer park to look after. The fan club would be run out of an office in Ventura. Saul Holiff, who'd just bought a home in the province of Ontario, Canada, would live at the house when he was in California.

Cash even returned to church for a brief period, after Curly Lewis introduced him to Floyd Gressett, a Texan-born preacher who presided over the nondenominational Avenue Community Church in Ventura, and worked with inmates in some of California's most notorious prisons. Gressett shared an interest in the same outdoor pursuits. He had a retreat cabin in the Cuyama Valley, ninety miles north of Ventura, and the two men began hunting and fishing together. Sometimes Cash would go to the cabin alone for several days to write songs. He called Gressett "Chief" and Gressett called him "Slick."

After about six months of sporadic church attendance, Cash sent Gressett a note to say that he wanted to be more committed to his faith. "Once I told you that I would join your church when the time is right," he wrote. "Now is the time. Since music is my specialty, you can expect me to have songs played when I am here. . . . Concerning a guitar in the church, near the end of the Psalms there is a chapter saying 'Praise the Lord with *all* stringed instruments and a loud noise' or something to that effect. . . . My 'name' doesn't have any bearing. My heart is a pauper like all men. Only I as a 'soldier' will be judged."

Cash intended to reform, but he found his need for drugs a more powerful force than his determination to change. Amphetamines controlled his sleep pattern, his health, his eating habits, his temper, his sociability, his concentration, and his longings. He began to suffer from muscle spasms. Voices invaded his brain. He found himself embarking on marathon letter-writing sessions simply because he had no other way to rid himself of the artificially released energy.

A poem he wrote at the time, "The Cost in Life," expressed some of these inner tensions:

> When I consider why that I
> Live and love and work and die,
> And know no more than most are told
> Of new things . . . books and stories old.
>
> And why my Maker lets me live
> Why He gives the things he gives
> For I don't follow many rules
> I often walk the way of fools.
>
> I often think, 'Lord, why allow
> Me to live and prosper now?'
> Then I know some time, some way,
> He'll collect what I should pay.
>
> Why does he not snuff me out
> For I don't know what life's about
> The debt I owe for sin is high
> Still he lets me live, love, work and die.

Cash's friends and family found themselves dealing with two people, and from day to day, they never knew which one would appear. "You never knew what he would be like at breakfast time," says Johnny Western, "or even if there would be a breakfast." Saul Holiff remembers wonderful talks he and Cash had while driving back to Casitas Springs from LAX, in which Cash showed a clearheaded approach and a deep understanding of himself, but the next day he'd behave as if the conversation had never happened.

"John R. Cash was one of the greatest human beings who ever walked on the face of this earth," says Marshall Grant, who was often the person left to pick up the pieces. "But Johnny Cash was probably the greatest jerk that ever lived. He had become two different people. That's the way it was. You can't explain it any other way. He was one of the kindest human beings you could imagine and then something would trigger him and he'd come back in the room a totally different person. It would be a 180-degree change."

His relationships with women only added to the confusion in his life. In 1962 the Carter Sisters and Mother Maybelle joined the *Johnny Cash Show* and he found himself attracted to June Carter. "Like anyone at the top in country music or in any other field, he set out to conquer whatever he could conquer. If he had the chances, he took them," says Saul Holiff. "I don't know of very many people either in country or any other field of music who remained chaste."

June took an almost motherly role with Cash, ironing his shirts, pressing his trousers, and making sure he ate properly. She discovered his drug problem when she came in the dressing room after they'd played a show in Macon, Georgia, and caught him with a handful of Dexamyl tablets. She then realized why he was always so intense, why he came offstage in a cold sweat, and why he drank so much liquid. She'd noticed similar behavioral characteristics with Hank Williams when she and the Carter Family had toured with him in the early 1950s. She resolved to stop Cash from going the same way as Hank.

She tried talking to him but to no avail. His determination to change—whether for his faith or his health—always gave way to his need for more drugs. She tried confiscating or hiding his stashes of pills, but somehow he always managed to find other supplies he'd squirreled away. When doctors arrived backstage with the prescription he needed to stay awake during long drives, fight stage fright, or lose excess weight, she tried to head them off, but Cash always found another doctor in another town who'd oblige.

June's partner in this clean-up operation was Marshall Grant. "June and I were the only ones who cared about him as far as keeping him alive," he says. "As far as everyone else was concerned, he was immortal. He wouldn't die. June and I have stayed up many a night just to keep in touch with him, to keep him alive and stop him [from] hurting anybody. She was an ally. We both fought hard. I don't know what we would have done without one another. I couldn't have done it by myself. She couldn't have done it by herself. We could barely do it together."

"When Johnny was on pills all of his closest friends would become his worst enemies, and all his worst enemies would become his closest friends. His worst enemies were the people who supplied him with the drugs. His closest friends were June and I. He came down on us heavier than everyone else combined because he knew that we were going to fight him tooth and nail to keep him off the drugs and keep him alive. Therefore we became his enemies. Now when he got straight, all of a sudden we would be his two best friends. That's the way it was."

Within months of meeting, the relationship between June and Cash became a full-blown affair. Like Billie Jean, June was a woman who was perfectly at ease in the predominantly male world of music and had been married to a leading country performer. Both Johnny and June had as much to lose if news of their affair leaked out, so they were discreet about their movements, never staying in the same hotel rooms or allowing themselves to be photographed in amorous situations.

They both knew that what they were getting into was potentially dangerous. June was married to Edwin "Rip" Nix, a garage and body shop owner from Madison, Tennessee, but they'd drifted apart almost as soon as they were married in 1957. Part of the reason was that she was away from home twenty-five days of each month. Cash had four young children and a wife, who had yet to hear of his extramarital liaisons. Vivian knew that things weren't going well with Cash, and she genuinely wanted to know what was wrong and what she could do to fix things. She poured her heart out in poems that pleaded with God to make things right between them.

June felt her relationship with Cash was becoming too powerful to control. She had started writing songs with Merle Kilgore, who, as a writer, had recently enjoyed a big hit with "Wolverton Mountain," recorded by Claude King. The first song he and June wrote together was "Promised to John: "I'm promised to John / Can't you see that I'm promised to John?" Anita recorded it with Hank Snow on an album called *Together Again*.

"Then one day June came to me and told me that she was torn apart and just didn't know what to do," says Kilgore. "She said, 'That Johnny Cash is spookin' me. I am so in love, I don't know what to do.' I said, 'Well, have you got any ideas for a song today?' She told me that a friend of hers had just got divorced and had written her a letter. She went and got the letter and read it to me. It started 'I never want to fall in love again' blah, blah, blah, and then it said 'I hate love. Love is like a burning ring of fire.'" [Another version of the story says that the phrase was found in a book of Elizabethan love poems.] Kilgore liked the idea of a song that described passion as a ring of fire, especially as a commentary on what June was feeling at the time for Cash, but he knew that the title "Ring of Fire" had already been used by instrumentalist Duane Eddy and his band the Rebels on a 1961 single. Working for a company that owned the original publishing rights, he wanted to avoid any confusion and thus suggested "Love's Burning Ring of Fire" as a title.

While they were writing, Anita Carter was preparing an album, *Folk Songs Old and New,* and asked June if she had any new material. June told her about "Love's Burning Ring of Fire," giving her the impression that they'd completed the song, when the truth was they'd stalled halfway through. "June had put in the word *mire* and I had to ask her what a *mire* was," says Kilgore. "She said, 'You know, Kilgore. It's when you're stuck in the mud. Where I'm from if you're mired, you're stuck.' I said, 'That's not romantic.' I learned right then never to start polishing a song before it's finished because creativity goes right out the window."

Because June had claimed they'd finished the song and Anita was ready to record, they had to complete it in a hurry the next day. "I started working on it," says Kilgore. "And when I got over to her house, we knocked that song out in ten minutes. But the word *mire* was still in it." Anita's version, produced by Jerry Kennedy, was released in November 1962 and Cash immediately liked it. To avoid damaging June's chances of success, he said he would give it four months before he did a cover version. In the meantime, he claimed that he had a dream where he heard himself recording the song with trumpets—an unheard-of arrangement for country music at the time. The dream could have been suggested by something June said, because she based the tune on the swirling sound of music she once heard coming from a *tiovivo* (merry-go-round) in the town square of Villa Acuna, Mexico.

Cash desperately needed a hit. Despite being a remarkably popular touring act and an instantly recognizable name in American pop music, he hadn't had a single in the pop charts in nearly four years. "The Ways of a Woman in Love" made the charts in October 1958. Only two of his last twelve singles had even punctured the Top 100, and of his albums, only *The Fabulous Johnny Cash* made the Top 20. *Blood, Sweat and Tears* never climbed higher than eighty. "His voice was badly affected by his amphetamine use at this time, so he was finding it hard to get the right sound," says Kilgore. "His records weren't selling and he was in bad shape. Columbia was concerned that he'd lost it all. If you don't have hit records then you lose your audience. There's nothing like a hit to bring the people back."

His producer, Don Law, was having an understandably hard time persuading Columbia in New York to keep investing in Cash. His contract, which had been renewed after one year in the middle of 1959, would expire at the end of 1963, and it was clear that if Cash didn't have a breakthrough hit in the next few months, they wouldn't renew him.

One day, Kilgore mentioned over lunch with Jack Clement that Cash was having problems getting the right sound in the studio. "Jack said, 'I can get the sound back.' I said, 'Really? He's doing a song of ours called 'Ring of Fire.' I wish there was a way that you could produce it.' He said, 'There's no way Columbia will let me anywhere near Johnny Cash. Don Law has an iron hand over him.'"

Kilgore repeated this conversation to Cash, who said, "You know what, Merle? I know Jack Clement can get my sound back. When you said that, it put chills all over my body." Clement was living in Beaumont, Texas, where he was doing well for himself as a producer. He'd had a hit with Dickie Lee's "Patches," had the publishing for George Jones's "She Thinks I Still Care," and had written the follow-up "The Girl I Used to Know."

Clement recalls, "I was in the bathtub and Johnny called me and said that he wanted me to come to Nashville and help him produce this song that June Carter and Merle Kilgore had done. He told me he'd had this dream about the song having trumpets on it. So I came to Nashville. We got a studio and hired two trumpet players. Don Law was a nice guy, but he'd just sit around and do what he wanted to do. He was registered as the official producer, but I was the one who ran the session. I came in and told them to change microphones on the drums and told the horn players what to play. I hummed it and they wrote it down. I played my guitar on it and led the band. I thought it all sounded pretty neat, but a few weeks later when I kept hearing it played on the radio all the time I thought, 'Hey! That was good!'"

Though the song was about a relationship, its central image was ambiguous. The "fire" was most obviously the heat of passion but could also have referred to the dangerous nature of the particular liaison or even to the fire of punishment. This latter interpretation gained strength from Cash's intonation of the phrase "down, down, down" which seemed to indicate the fires of hell. The Mexican trumpet sound, unprecedented in country music at the time, added to the impression of heat and passion.

Released in May 1963, "Ring of Fire" reached number seventeen in the singles charts, and two months later a "best of" album, also called *Ring of Fire*, reached number twenty-six in the album charts. For the time being at least, Johnny Cash's recording career with Columbia was safe.

7

Busted

THE PROGRESS OF THE CARTER-CASH RELATIONSHIP could be charted through the music they made together. Just before June and Kilgore wrote "Ring of Fire," she and Cash arranged and adapted "The Legend of John Henry's Hammer," recording it in June 1962. Later that month he cut the first Cash-Carter song, "The Matador," as well as one he wrote with June's father, Ezra, "Who Kept the Sheep?" A month later he was special guest for a day-long Carter Family album session.

Vivian first became aware that something was happening on June 15, 1962, when Cash made his debut at the prestigious Hollywood Bowl in a show that Saul Holiff billed as The First Giant Folk, Western, Bluegrass Spectacular. It featured Cash with the Carter Family, Johnny Western, Merle Travis, Stuart Hamblin, Patsy Cline, Gene Autry, Gordon Terry, Roger Miller, Flatt and Scruggs, and others. Vivian dressed up the girls in their Sunday best and went along with Roy and Carrie Cash. "We all went backstage after the show," says Kathy Cash. "I'll never forget it because Mom had brought it up often since. We were standing there waving good-bye to Dad, and he kissed us all, got into his car, and then June [with Luther and Marshall] jumped into the car right next to him and waved to us. Mom

103

was furious. Her and Grandma were fit to be tied. That was when she started falling apart."

There was naturally a lot of guilt involved in the relationship. June felt guilty that she had already been through two marriages. In fact, she felt so guilty that when she divorced Nix on the grounds of "irreconcilable differences" she waited weeks before she told her parents. Cash felt guilty about his adultery and the fact that he was deserting his children in their formative years. Drugs and drink helped dull his conscience and curb his fretting, but June was already doing her best to stop his drug habit by searching his pockets and relentlessly discussing his problem.

In November 1963 Cash recorded "Understand Your Man," a vitriolic song directed at Vivian and set to a tune borrowed from Bob Dylan's "Don't Think Twice."

> Don't call my name at your window as I'm leavin'
> 'Cos I won't even turn my head.
> And don't send your kinfolks to give me no d— talkin'
> 'Cos I'll be gone like I said.
> You say the same old thing that you've been sayin' all along,
> So just lay there on you bed and keep your mouth shut 'til I'm gone.
> No don't give me that old familiar cryin,' cussin' moan
> Understand your man
> O, understand your man

"I remember lying in bed listening to them fight in the middle of the night," says Kathy, "and I would think, oh boy, this is tiring! Every time he came home I would beg to go and spend the night at Grandma and Grandpa's house. My mother thought it was terrible that my dad would come back and I'd want to leave, but it wasn't because he was around but because I was tired of hearing them fight in the middle of the night and keep me awake."

Cash clearly felt that he was a misunderstood man—that Vivian not only didn't understand the demands of his work but couldn't accept his mercurial artistic temperament. June, on the other hand, he felt loved him for who he was. Being on the road was second nature to her because she had known no other life. She not only knew who all his musical heroes were, but she had met and worked with them, and, most important of all, she tended to be strong in exactly the points where he was weak. She was extroverted, steadfast, and abstemious, whereas Cash was introverted, unstable, and indulgent.

"June was a very basic person," says Harold Reid, who joined the *Johnny Cash Show* as a member of the Statler Brothers in 1964. "She didn't drink. She didn't do drugs. She came from pretty much the same stock that the rest of us came from but she was strong enough, as we were, not to do these things. John saw that strength in her and she was able to help him. In the long run he had to do it himself, but she gave him the strength to stand up on his own feet."

June's roots also appealed to Cash. Through his relationship with her he was connecting with one of American music's most traditional and influential families, and he enjoyed the cachet that came with that. He loved listening to Mother Maybelle's memories of how the Carter Family songs were collected, or discussing history, theology, and literature with June's father, Eck. He reveled in visits to Maces Spring, the small mountain community where A. P. Carter had lived and started his collecting.

Until the urban folk revival, Mother Maybelle and her singing daughters languished in semi-obscurity. Helen and Anita were raising children, and although Mother Maybelle still appeared at the Opry, she had no recording contract and was working as a nurse for the elderly. Badly affected by the success of rock-'n'-roll, country music had undergone a makeover in which the rough and primitive was being supplanted by the smooth and sophisticated. The fiddle and the autoharp were being replaced by the piano, drums, and even orchestral strings. What became known as the Nashville Sound was typified by people like Jim Reeves, Patsy Cline, and Don Gibson, who could take country music and make it sound like pop music.

Educated baby boomers reacted against what they considered to be production-line pop and sought out music that they found more authentic because it had more human fingerprints on it. They wanted music unsullied by commercial considerations and, consequently, more honest about basic emotions and more attuned to universal needs. The Newport Folk Festival, where folk musicians shared stages and workshop areas with gospel, country, and blues musicians, typified this mood. Mother Maybelle made her Newport debut in 1963 at the invitation of the New Lost City Ramblers.

Cash instinctively identified with the folk revival movement. The music that touched his heart most had always been that which was a genuine expression of the joys and travails of life—music composed out of a surfeit of emotion rather than to fulfill the demands of a newly identified market. Little wonder that he responded so enthusiastically to Bob Dylan's album *The Freewheelin' Bob Dylan* on its release in May 1963. Dylan was drawing water from the same well, citing Hank Williams and Leadbelly among his influences. Cash began writing letters of encouragement to Dylan, and Dylan, who'd been a fan of Cash's music since he first heard it on the radio in the 1950s, wrote back.

Through Gene Ferguson, Columbia's promotion man in Nashville, Cash learned of the work of another New York folk musician, Peter La Farge. The son of Oliver La Farge, who was a Pulitzer Prize–winning author and a student of the Navajo people, his songs almost exclusively concerned Native American issues. In fact La Farge barely sang. His songs were more like rhythmic recitations over a backing of acoustic guitar and bongo drums, with titles like "Johnny Half-Breed," "I'm an Indian, I'm an Alien," and "Coyote, My Little Brother."

La Farge played at the Gaslight on MacDougal Street in Greenwich Village and performed at the 1963 Newport Folk Festival. He presented a very exotic background. He said he had left school to work in rodeos, then served on an aircraft carrier during the Korean War, and later spent time as an amateur boxer, radio announcer, painter, actor, poet, and playwright. And though he also claimed to be part Narragansett Indian, neither his father, Oliver La Farge, nor his mother, Wanden, had any Indian blood.

"Johnny wanted more than the hillbilly jangle," said La Farge when trying to explain what had attracted the King of Country to Greenwich Village. "He was hungry for the depth and truth heard only in the folk field . . . the secret is simple. Johnny has the heart of a folksinger in the purest sense, and he has a very lovely soul. He is capable of anything he puts his soul and his Band-Aid heart to, and he is capable of being a folksinger in the very essence of folk truth. He would love to be out from that heavy legend that binds him to Hillbilly Heaven."

In March 1964, Cash recorded "The Ballad of Ira Hayes," a track that La Farge had first recorded in 1961 on a Folkways album *On the Warpath* and re-recorded in 1962 for a Columbia album produced by John Hammond titled *Ira Hayes and Other Ballads.* Ferguson had thought Cash would like it for two reasons. "I knew of John's relationship with the Indians," he says. "I also knew that he had served with the American armed forces. This song put these two things together and I thought John would like it. As it happens, he loved it."

"The Ballad of Ira Hayes" told the story of Ira Hamilton Hayes, the Pima Indian who was one of the six American marines photographed by Joe Rosenthal raising the American flag after the Battle of Iwo Jima. Though feted on his return home, as national interest waned and the speaking engagements and parades stopped, Hayes drifted into a life of poverty, jail, and alcoholism. When found dead from "exposure" in a cotton field on a Pima Indian reservation in Arizona in 1955, Ira Hayes was only thirty-two.

La Farge's song pointed out the irony that despite the personal risks Hayes took for his country, he returned home only to find his tribe's ancestral land lacked adequate water—something which ultimately contributed to his death. The injustice of the tale moved Cash. "I loved it so much," he said of the song. "I had such a feeling for Ira Hayes. I had been to the Apache country. I had seen the old women carrying the big bundle of sticks on their backs for their night's firewood. I had seen the poverty and had a feeling for it."

Cash liked the song immensely and decided to build a concept album around the Native American plight. In June he recorded "Drums" and "White Girl" from La Farge's 1961 debut album, and "As Long as the Grass Shall Grow" (itself the title of a 1940 book written by the senior La Farge) and "Custer" from his most recent album. He added two of his own songs, "Apache Tears" and "The Talking Leaves," and Johnny Horton's "The Vanishing Race."

Although the "protest song" had a long and healthy tradition in folk music circles, such social commentary never made its way into the politically conservative country scene. Native American land rights had yet to become a fashionable cause. Some country music critics thought Cash, by pushing the norms of the genre, was forgetting his humble roots. Others thought he had become tainted by left-wing radicalism. Because country music D. J.s refused to play "The Ballad of Ira Hayes," Cash paid for a full-page ad in *Billboard* that ran August 22.

Addressed to "DJs, station managers, owners, etc.," the ad asked,

> Where are your guts? I'm not afraid to sing the hard, bitter lines that the son of Oliver La Farge wrote. . . . Classify me, categorize me—STIFLE me, but it won't work. . . . I am fighting no particular cause. If I did, it would

soon make me a sluggard. For as time changes, I change, you're right! Teenage girls and Beatle record buyers don't want to hear this sad story of Ira Hayes—but who cries more easily, and who always go to sad movies to cry? Teenage girls . . . Regardless of the trade charts—the categorizing, classifying and restrictions of air play, this is not a country song, not as it is being sold. It is a fine reason though for the gutless to give it thumbs down. "Ballad of Ira Hayes" is strong medicine. So is Rochester—Harlem—Birmingham and Vietnam . . .

The next month, Cash's album of Indian songs, *Bitter Tears,* hit the market. Robert Shelton, the *New York Times* music critic who had given Bob Dylan his first rave review, greeted it as "one of the best LP's to emerge from the 60s folk movement." The album may have alienated Cash from the Nashville scene, but it endeared him to bohemians, students, and intellectuals. Not a complete stranger to this group of fans, Cash had performed "Big River," "Folsom Prison Blues," "I Still Miss Someone," "Rock Island Line," "I Walk the Line," "The Ballad of Ira Hayes," "Keep on the Sunnyside," and Bob Dylan's "Don't Think Twice, It's All Right" to a crowd of seventy thousand at the July 1964 Newport Folk Festival.

Although Dylan once said that he first met Cash at the Gaslight, the two generally agreed that Newport was where they finally came face to face—Cash, the country legend with almost a decade of recording experience behind him and Dylan, the young folk musician who was being hailed as the voice of a generation. Tony Glover, a longtime friend of Dylan's, later recalled the meeting:

That night Cash went on, and that was a groove. He came on like a king country stud, full of humble arrogance, and he lit the night with his own kind of charisma. Dylan came later and instead of all the political material that everybody expected, he did songs from *Another Side* like "Ramona." You could tell the audience was puzzled, but they didn't want to be thought uncool by anybody, so they applauded just as vigorously anyhow. Later, in a motel full of people like Joan Baez, Sandy Bull, Jack Elliott, and some others, Dylan and Cash sat on the floor trading songs. Joan set up a portable machine and that's where Bob gave Johnny "It Ain't Me, Babe" and "Mama, You've Been on My Mind."

"It Ain't Me, Babe" also came from Dylan's soon-to-be-released *Another Side*. The demo of "Mama, You've Been on My Mind" had been made, but the song had not been recorded. Cash went on to record both songs along with "Don't Think Twice, It's All Right" for his *Orange Blossom Special* album. The label released "It Ain't Me, Babe" as a single and advertised it as "A new song from Bob Dylan on a new single sung by Johnny Cash." For Columbia, the championing of one of its new discoveries by one of its established artists provided great cross publicity.

Orange Blossom Special, Cash's most folk-inspired album, contained the three Dylan songs, as well as a version of the Carter Family's "Wildwood Flower," the classically constructed "The Long Black Veil," the Irish ballad "Danny Boy," the 1930s' railroad song "Orange Blossom Special," and his own protest song "All of God's Children Ain't Free."

By 1965, though his marriage was clearly over, Vivian refused to consider divorce because of her strict practice of Roman Catholicism. Cash believed in the family and extolled the virtue of hearth and home in his songs, yet he was no more than an infrequent guest in his own house. His children were growing up outside of his immediate care and control. He was torn because he felt that he had let everyone down.

"He always came home eventually," says Rosanne. "He might be away for long periods and he might come back really messed up, but he would always come home and he would always try. When it was Christmas he would bring back presents and leave footprints through the house so that we'd think Father Christmas had been through. He would get on a tractor and go round the acres of land that we had. He was doing stuff. But he was tortured beyond belief. Even as a little kid I could look at him and see how tortured he was."

To cope with the pain, Cash often drove deep into the desert, usually stoked up on beer, amphetamines, or a combination of both. His interest in the Old West had deepened, and he used these trips to "commune with the cowboy ghosts," as he put it. Sometimes he'd even dress in antique Western clothes with a gun strapped to his leg and spend a few nights in an abandoned ranch near Maricopa, California—with nothing but candles for light and a wood-burning stove for heat—hoping to find inspiration.

He had always enjoyed immersing himself in a subject, reading everything he could lay his hands on, contacting experts, and then projecting himself imaginatively into the situation or historical period. While planning *Bitter Tears* he absorbed himself in Native American studies. Don Law had suggested Cash record an album of Western songs, so for *Ballads of the True West* he investigated cowboys and pioneers. He read books by John Lomax, B. A. Botkin, and J. Frank Dobie; read back issues of *True West* magazine; looked up original newspaper accounts of outlaws and their crimes; and listened to taped interviews with the last of the original pioneers. He quizzed musical friends like Peter La Farge, Ramblin' Jack Elliott, and Tex Ritter about the history of cowboy songs. To write a song about John Wesley Hardin, he read a manuscript of Hardin's original autobiography and, in the end, felt he knew Hardin as well as he knew himself.

Explaining how he prepared for the album Cash said,

> I followed trails in my Jeep and on foot, and I slept under mesquite bushes and in gullies. I heard the timber wolves, looked for golden nuggets in old creek beds, sat for hours beneath a manzanita bush in an ancient Indian burial ground, breathed the west wind and the tales it tells only to those who listen. I replaced a wooden grave marker of some man in Arizona who "never made it." I walked across alkali flats where others had walked before me, but hadn't made it. I ate mesquite beans and squeezed the water from a barrel cactus. I was saved once by a forest ranger, lying flat on my face, starving. I learned how to throw a Bowie knife and kill a jack rabbit at forty yards, not for sport but because I was hungry. I learned of the true West the hard way, *a la* 1965.

Two days after completing the recording of *Ballads of the True West* he smashed June's 1964 Cadillac into a utility pole on South Street in Nashville, causing two thousand dollars of damage to the car. Police came to the scene, and although he didn't have his driver's license with him, he wasn't charged. They did take him to Vanderbilt Hospital, where he was treated for minor injuries. The official reason given for the accident was heavy rain (and a lapse in concentration as he tried to fix a faulty windshield wiper), but as he and everyone around him knew, alcohol and/or drugs were truly to blame.

Permanently hyper and incapable of breaking his amphetamine dependency, thirty-three-year-old Cash looked fifty, with his drawn face, hollow cheeks, and two great furrows scored from his nose down to the outsides of his mouth. His 155

SCHOOL DAYS 1946-'47
Dyess High

Johnny Cash, age 15

Cash's passport photo, early 1960s

THE THINGS WERE
FRIGHTENED AT

WHEN I WAS JUST A LITTLE KID
AND PLAYED ALOT AT NIGHT
BACK IN OUR COUNTRY VILLAGE
WHERE WE DIDNT PAY FOR LIGHT
THEN I COULD SEE BEHIND EACH TREE,
AN INDIAN STANDING THERE
AND SAY, HOW I'D SHAKE AND HOLLER!
IT WOULD FAIRLY RAISE MY HAIR
AND WHEN I GREW TO BE A MAN
I KNEW IT MORE AND MORE
THAT HALF THE FUN WAS KNOWING NOT
WHAT I WAS RUNNING FOR
AND I USED TO GO TO TOWN
EVERY NIGHT FOR PAW
I'D GO DOWN THE ROAD JUST, LICKEDY SPLIT!
UNTIL MY FEET WERE RAW
I HAD A LITTLE COUSIN
(HE WAS SCARY, TOO)
HE'S WORSE THAN I AM
HE'S SCARED OF GHOSTS ARE YOU
ONCE I HEARD MY COUSIN JUST OUTSIDE
A YELLIN'
HE WOULDN'T TELL ME WHAT IT WAS
I SAID THERE AINT NO TELLING

Courtesy of House of Cash
Written by a young J.R. Cash on April 26, 1944

Johnny Cash in Germany, 1952

Johnny Cash in uniform in Texas

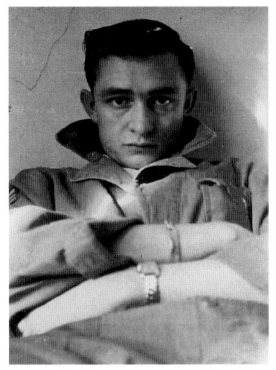

Photos of Johnny Cash in Landsberg, Germany, early 1950s

PNEUMONIA PARTY

DUE TO THE UNREST AMONG OPERATORS, IT HAS BEEN DEEMED NECESSARY TO TAKE MEASURES TO KEEP THE TROOPS HAPPY. SOME MEN WORK TOO HARD. ON SEVERAL OCCASIONS, MEN HAVE BEEN SEEN LEAVING THE OPERATIONS AREA WITH DITS AND DAHS HANGING OUT THEIR EARS, AND THEIR CLOTHES AND HAIR LITERAL SATURATED WITH HAMMARLUND POWDER.

THE ONLY SOLUTION TO THIS IS TO LET THE MEN HAVE MORE TIME OFF. SINC OUR SUPERVISORS THINK THIS IS IMPOSSIBLE, A PLAN HAS BEEN JERKED UP. THIS IS IT:

1. AT 0200 HOURS, NOVEMBER 18TH, ALL MEN, "TRICK A"WILL ASSEMBLE IN A SLOUCHY GROUP DIRECTLY ACROSS FROM THE SWIMMING POOL ON THE HIGH GROUN (DONT COME IS YOU'RE DIT HAPPY)

2. DONT BOTHER TO WEAR CLOTHES. IF YOU'RE MODEST THEN WEAR A PAIR OF SHORTS, BUT YOU'LL NEVER CATCH PNEUMONIA THAT WAY.

3. THE TEMPERATURE SHOULD BE AROUND 20 DEGREES, BUT IF IT'S OUR MIS-FORTUNE FOR THE WEATHER TO BE WARM ARRANGEMENTS HAVE BEEN MADE WITH THE LANDSBERG ICE CO. FOR 1000 LBS. OF ICE WHICH WE WILL CHIP UP TO COVER OU SELVES WITH.

4. AFTER STANDING STILL FOR 30 MINUTES, WE WILL THEN POUR HOT WATER OVER OURSELVES AND SING "HEY GOOD LOOKIN" HANK WILLIAMS STYLE TO INSURE A SORE THROAT.

5. A MEETING WILL THEN BE HELD TO GRIPE. WE WILL ALL LIE ON OUR STOMACH IN THE SNOW(OR ICE) AND DISCUSS OUR SUPERVISORS, USING VILE AND PROFANE LANGUAGE, TELLING WHY WE DONT LIKE WHO.

6. S/SGT DRANE WILL BE REFERRED TO AS "DRAINO". ANYONE CALLING HIM S/SGT DRANE WILL BE GIVEN A COAT AND FORCED TO GO BACK IN WHERE IT'S WA

7. AT THIS TIME WE WILL THEN RUN AROUND THE BASE AT TOP SPEED FOR 30 MINUTES. LATER WE WILL LIE IN THE SNOW (OR ICE) TO MAKE US COLD AGAIN.

8. WE WILL THEN CRAWL ON OUR STOMACH TO THE BILLETS, CLOSE ALL WINDO TURN UP THE RADIATOR, AND STAY SWELTERING HOT ALL NIGHT.

AFTER THIS A FEW OF US WILL PROBABLY CATCH PNEUMONIA. THOSE FAILING TO DO SO WILL HAVE TO FIND A MEANS OF THEIR OWN TO GET OUT OF WORK.

ANY MAN CATCHING DOUBLE PNEUMONIA WILL BE AWARDED (BY THE TROOPS) A ROYAL PURPLE SHAFT WITH TWO BARBED WIRE CLUSTERS.

WE HEREBY FREEZE OUR ##### SEALS:

John Cash

CHAIRMAN OF THE JOINT CHIEFS OF COUGH.

Ted Freeman

SPONSOR OF PNEUMONIA PARTY

Written in the early 1950s while stationed in Landsberg, Germany

Johnny and June, 1960s

Johnny Cash backstage, 1955,
in a jacket made by his mother

1950s press photo of June Carter

JOHNNY CASH
& JUNE CARTER

MANAGEMENT : **SAUL HOLIFF**
509 JARVIS STREET, LONDON, ONTARIO
TEL. 471-5519 (519)

Johnny Cash with daughter Kathy and her
husband Jimmy Tittle on their wedding day.
Cash performed the ceremony.

Rosanne Cash and family.
(Standing, from left: Chelsea, Caitlin,
Carrie, and Hannah. Husband John
Leventhal, and son Jake)

Johnny Cash with his first wife, Vivian
Liberto, and daughters (L to R) Rosanne,
Kathy, and Cindy in the early 1960s

Cash home in Dyess, Arkansas in 1968,
years after the family moved away

Tara Cash Schwoebel with her husband, Fred,
and sons Aran and Alex

Johnny Cash, John Carter Cash, Ezra Carter

Cash with daughter Tara

Johnny and June backstage after a show
in Trenton, New Jersey, 1963

Great-grandson Brennan Coggins
and grandson Joseph Cash

Rosanne and Johnny

John, June, and Kacy
Tittle (Kathy's daughter),
at Bon Aqua

Carlene Carter and June Carter Cash

Johnny Cash and John Carter Cash
on the set of Hee Haw

Johnny Cash performs on stage with Marshall Grant and Luther Perkins in February 1959

Johnny Cash and Elvis Presley, 1955

Johnny Cash backstage at the Odeon, London
May 15, 1966

June Carter Cash and Johnny Cash at their wedding, March 1, 1968

JOHNNY CASH

Johnny Cash outside Folsom Prison, January 1968. The recording was for Columbia Records, but the photo was picked up by Sun Records to promote their back catalog.

Johnny Cash and a young Marty Stuart

June Carter Cash and Robert Duvall

George Jones, Tammy Wynette, Cash, and June
at the Cash home in Hendersonville, Tennessee

Cash dining at his home with U2 members
Bono (right) and Adam Clayton, and friends
Doug Caldwell and Jack Clement in 1990

Luther Perkins, Johnny Cash, and Marshall
Grant at Sun Studios in Memphis, 1956

Cash with Johnny Horton, December 1963

"Cowboy" Jack Clement and Johnny Cash

Roy Orbison, June Carter Cash, Johnny Cash,
Jerry Lee Lewis, and Carl Perkins

Roy Acuff, June Carter Cash, and Johnny Cash
backstage in 1987

Johnny Cash, June Carter Cash,
and Rosey Nix meet a young Prince Charles

Cash with the Muppets, August 1980

Cash and Waldo, the ostrich
that attacked him in September 1981

Johnny Cash and June Carter hug each other in this late 1960s photo

pounds were distributed over a six-foot-two-inch frame, making him look alarmingly thin. (He had been five pounds heavier at the age of eighteen.) He had developed a number of nervous habits often imitated by people on the country scene—scratching his neck, the nervous cough, the twisting of his head. Kris Kristofferson, then serving in the army, first met Cash at the Opry in 1965. "He looked like a panther pacing around backstage," he says. "He was so skinny and wired out."

Cash's condition began seriously affecting his career. "Many times we'd have to go ahead and do the show without him just to try and save whatever the box office had taken," says Don Reid of the Statler Brothers. "We just had to walk out on stage and say 'Ladies and gentlemen, Johnny Cash is not here this evening. Anybody who wants their money back can go to the box office now, but the rest of us are here and we'll put on a show. We hope that you'll stay and that you'll enjoy it.' Surprisingly a lot would stay."

At other times Cash would perform, but in such an agitated state that everyone would be on tenterhooks. At the Grand Ole Opry in 1965, he lost his temper onstage, either because he couldn't dislodge a microphone from its stand or because he found the stage lights too bright. His tantrum resulted in his banishment from the Opry. "What I remember is that he dragged his microphone stand right across the footlights so that he'd take them out," says Don Reid. "It was because of the pills. It was the pills talking. He would do really bizarre things. I've seen him stop in the middle of a concert and take a microphone apart with a screwdriver while the audience sat there waiting for him to carry on. All of a sudden, right in the middle of the show, that microphone became the most important thing in his life. We were all standing there waiting for him. These strange urges would come over him."

These distractions could sometimes cost him days. He would drive to the desert for an afternoon and not come back for a week. Once, on the way home to Los Angeles from Nashville, he found himself partying in Dallas with people he didn't even know. "In 1965 he lost my Cadillac," remembers Johnny Western. "He was on an amphetamine jag. He had flown to California to do a TV show with me and asked if he could borrow my car for a couple of hours. The next day at around 9:00 a.m. I had a call from a rather sheepish Johnny who said that, er, he'd been up all night on pills and couldn't remember where he'd left it." It was later found outside the Farmers Market with a dead battery and the keys in the ignition.

The show he'd flown in to do was *Shindig* produced by Jack Good, who had introduced him to British television in 1959 on *Boy Meets Girl*. Good recalls that Cash was on pills when he first met him in Manchester, England, but that by 1965 he was barely controllable. It took them two hours to tape one song because Cash couldn't remember the words. "We introduced him as being 'In his famous role as Harry the Hobo,' but I think that was put in to disguise his strange behavior," says Good. "We also had to bring some dancers on so that we had somewhere to go if he was really out of it."

When he was working in Nashville he'd stay with Gene Ferguson and his family, but there were times when Cash's behavior was so unacceptable that Ferguson would make him stay in his office downtown. "When he was staying with me he'd sometimes take a ballpoint pen and write phone numbers on my couch," he says. "He'd go out into the rain with no shoes or socks on and in the morning there would be mud right through the house. There were a couple of times when I went to wake him when he didn't respond and I couldn't feel a heartbeat. Once I called Luther to ask him what I should do and Luther said, 'Well, he'll either wake up or die.' That was the answer I got."

Today such escapades would be widely reported and there would be public concern about his state of mind, but in 1965, as far as his fans knew, Johnny Cash was a happily married Christian who sometimes suffered from laryngitis. For Saul Holiff, who had had no previous experience of dealing with addictive personalities, his client's erratic behavior gave him quite a headache. "I was brought up in a rational, nonreligious, openminded household of logic," he says. "Suddenly I found myself in this chaotic, unpredictable, terrible atmosphere. Nothing could be finalized. Nothing could be definite. The cancellations were awful and I had to handle them and make good on them. I had to fend off lawsuits. There was never a tranquil period that lasted for more than a week."

Cash's drug-impaired ability to react quickly started to threaten his safety. He crashed cars and rolled them down banks. He sank a boat. He overturned a tractor on his land in Casitas Springs. In June 1965, while fishing in the Los Padres National Forest, he stalled his camper in the sand on the edge of the creek, and, as he revved the engine, the heat from the exhaust pipe set the grass on fire. He attempted to put it out, but the fire spread rapidly and eventually razed five hundred and eight acres, which were a significant habitat of near-extinct California condors. It took four hundred and fifty firefighters to put out the blaze.

In an unprecedented case, the federal government sued Cash for $125,127. He contested the figure and two years later settled for $82,000.

Things finally came to a head. On October 2, 1965, Cash played a show in Dallas, but instead of staying overnight, as expected, he checked out of his hotel and flew to El Paso, Texas, from where he took a cab across the Rio Grande to Juarez, Mexico. There, he'd been told, was a thriving black market in pills. From a Mexican dealer he bought 475 Equanil and 668 Dexedrine tablets, which he then hid inside a guitar. He returned to El Paso International Airport and waited for a plane home to Los Angeles. However, the dealer in Juarez had been under surveillance because he was believed to be selling heroin. Federal customs agents promptly arrested Cash and locked him up overnight in the county jail.

The next day, dressed in a black suit and a white open-necked shirt, he appeared in court at a bond hearing where he faced U.S. Commissioner Colbert Coldwell. Cash was charged with "willfully smuggling and concealing drugs after importation," ordered not to leave the continental United States until further notice, and released on a fifteen-hundred-dollar bond. After the hearing, he left the court flanked by two plain-clothes policemen, his wrists cuffed together in front of him. A press photographer pointed his camera at him and Cash kicked out in anger, but not before the shutter clicked. The next day, a photograph of the handcuffed Cash in dark glasses appeared in newspapers across the country. "It was on the front page of our local newspaper in Casitas Springs," says Cindy Cash. "I remember being terrified that my friends would see it."

Two months later, accompanied by Vivian, and with moral support from Don Law and Floyd Gressett, Cash returned to El Paso to plead guilty to the possession of illegal drugs. The misdemeanor criminal offense carried a maximum one-thousand dollar fine, one year in prison, or both. The district judge deferred sentencing indefinitely, pending a report from his probation officer.

When Cash left the court that day, he was again photographed, this time without dark glasses, wearing a suit and tie, and holding hands with Vivian. The picture that ran in papers the next day made Vivian's full lips and Mediterranean complexion resemble those of a light-skinned African American. For some reason, the Ku Klux Klan picked up on it and published the photograph in their paper *Thunderbolt* as well as on flyers. They described Vivian as a "negress," Cash as "scum," and their four children as "mongrelized." The Klan also ran advertisements in newspapers across the South, saying, "FOR CASH, CALL THIS NUMBER." The listed number connected to a recorded message warning people not to attend Johnny Cash concerts because the singer was "married to a n– woman."

Johnny was unaware of the KKK campaign until Porter Wagoner called him about a flyer he saw while playing in Ponchatoula, Louisiana. Cash hired a top lawyer for the case, John Jay Hooker, and filed a twenty-five-million-dollar lawsuit against the Klan. Cash released an official statement:

> What I resent is the attempt at defamation of character and the attempt to make my children ashamed that they were born. If there's a mongrel in the crowd, it's me, because I'm Irish and one-quarter Cherokee Indian [sic]. I've had no interest in politics. My business is making music, and I've sung "John Henry" as well as "Remember the Alamo." If I win this, I'm going to give the money to the defense budget.

"It became very serious for all of us in the Cash camp," says Saul Holiff. "Not only serious, but threatening. Columbia's top brass finally came to help us and we threatened a major lawsuit when it became obvious that the Klan had made an egregious error in Vivian's background. So we had them cold. When they saw the mistake that they had made they backed away, apologized, and stopped everything. Eventually, after making another serious mistake, they were sued and went bankrupt."

In October 1965, three weeks after the El Paso arrest, Cash's friend Peter La Farge, only thirty-four years old, was found dead in his New York apartment. Though he officially died of a stroke, the drug paraphernalia found in the room suggested an overdose—either deliberate or accidental.

Initially, this succession of events sobered Johnny right up. He stopped taking pills, began to gain some weight, and started recording a lighthearted album that used several songs written by his old friend Jack Clement. *Everybody Loves a Nut* appeared to be a deliberate diversion from all the morbidity around him. In the first session after his court appearance, Cash recorded "The Frozen Logger," "The Bug That Tried to Crawl around the World," "Flushed from the Bathroom of Your Heart," "Dirty Old Egg-Sucking Dog" and "Take Me Home." "I'd always written novelty songs and he just decided he wanted to cut a novelty album," says Clement. "I was all for it because I happened to have a bunch of material in that direction."

Cash didn't stay clean for long. Soon after starting a new tour he was back on the pills. In May 1966, he arrived in London to tour England, Ireland, Scotland, and Wales. From there he planned to go on to play in Europe. Bob Dylan's tour coincided with Cash's—they had many of the same cities scheduled, though on different dates. Since their last meeting in the summer of 1964, Dylan had grown his hair into an Afro, hired a band (the Hawks) to play behind him, and forsaken his political protests for surreal explorations of different states of consciousness. While this broadened his fan base and put him on equal footing with the Beatles and the Rolling Stones, it alienated some of his early supporters who believed he'd betrayed the folk movement. They viewed Dylan's electrified music and mod shirts and boots as a capitulation to modern pop. At a concert in Manchester a member of the audience famously shouted out "Judas!" when the set changed from acoustic to electric.

Although Dylan had a naturally fertile imagination, some of the perceptions and allusions in the new songs obviously came from drug experiences. Dylan took pills to keep up the pace, smoked pot to relax, and possibly dropped LSD to explore. He never directly answered when asked exactly what he took, but he did say, "I wouldn't advise anybody to use drugs—certainly not the hard drugs. Drugs are medicine. But opium and hash and pot—now, those things aren't drugs. They just bend your mind a little. I think everybody's mind should be bent once in awhile."[1]

The two men met up at Dylan's hotel in Mayfair, a meeting captured by director D. A. Pennebaker and used in *The Document,* his unreleased film of the 1966 tour. The sequence shows Dylan playing "I Still Miss Someone" on an upright piano while Cash, dressed in a dark jacket and an open-necked shirt, stands beside him harmonizing. At the end, a smiling Cash tells Dylan, "You know, the tune's completely different." He then sings it to him as it should have been. On May 11, one of Cash's days off, he traveled to Cardiff to see Dylan.

Holiff managed to book Cash a show at the Olympia Theatre in Paris immediately following the British tour. The prestigious engagement had taken a lot of negotiating, but when the manager arrived at Heathrow Airport to fly on to Paris, Cash didn't turn up. He'd apparently partied so hard with Dylan that he just couldn't make it. "That's when I resigned," says Holiff. "I spent the next week just walking around Hyde Park contemplating my future before buying myself a first-class ticket back home." The break between Holiff and Cash lasted for six weeks.

When Cash returned to the States, he made a brief appearance at Casitas Springs but left almost immediately on June 2, 1966, to tour. He didn't even come back at the end of the tour. Instead, he stayed with Gene Ferguson in Brentwood, but no one else knew where he was. "Vivian would call me to see if John was there," says Ferguson. "Then June would call me to see if John was there. I hate to admit it, but I lied to both of them. He put me in a real precarious position."

This desertion was the final straw for Vivian. She hired an attorney, Lawrence Storch, and on June 30 filed for divorce on the grounds that, "Since the marriage of the parties, defendant has treated plaintiff with extreme cruelty and has wrongfully inflicted upon her grievous mental suffering and anguish." She was particularly concerned about her share of the estate because she was, "without sufficient funds or means with which to support herself and said minor children." She claimed she had reason to believe that, unless restrained by a court order, Cash would try to "sell, dispose of, or encumber said community property . . . for the purpose of defeating plaintiff's rights and claims."

To prevent him from selling the property or concealing his earnings, a court order was issued, and because she had no idea where Cash was living, she had it published in the *Nashville Banner* four times during August 1966. It ordered John R. Cash to "appear and show cause before the above titled court (the Superior Court of the State of California), in the courtroom of said court, at the courthouse, in the City of Ventura, County of Ventura, State of California, on the 22nd day of August, 1966, at the hour of 9.00 a.m. of said day, or as soon as counsel can be heard, who this court should not make the said orders. . . ." The orders included custody and control of the children, support and maintenance during the action, attorney's fees, and restraint on disposing his property during the action.

Cash failed to appear in court on August 22. On August 29, his attorney, Bruce Thompson, responded to the complaint for divorce. He assured the court that Cash was neither guilty of extreme cruelty nor of causing grievous mental suffering and anguish. He further denied that Cash intended to conceal his wealth or dispose of property and that Vivian was without sufficient funds. In October Cash agreed that she should have custody of the children, pending a trial, and promised not to sell any property. Vivian agreed to withdraw her claim for maintenance during the same period.

"I was eleven years old at the time," says Rosanne. "There was none of this,

'Hey. Let's sit down and talk about this.' I think my mother was freaked out and she was of an age where you just didn't talk about these things, particularly with the children. So we were left full of anxiety and wondering what was wrong. I remember seeing it in a newspaper. It said that my mother was suing my father on the grounds of mental cruelty. I was at my grandmother's house, and she saw me reading this and said to me, 'Your daddy is not cruel,' I was so grateful to her for saying that." When Kathy asked her mother what it would mean if there was a divorce, Vivian told her that she shouldn't worry too much, because the only difference would be that Daddy's clothes would no longer be hanging in the closet.

Cash moved out of Ferguson's home and rented a one-bedroom, first-floor apartment at the Fontaine Royale Apartments off Gallatin Road in Madison, Tennessee. Close to Mother Maybelle and Pop Carter's home on Cude Lane, his new place was also near June's home on Gibson Drive, although he made a point of not being seen there. In August, he ran into Waylon Jennings looking for a new place, and the two soon became roommates.

It was a cramped and disorderly bachelor pad. Two king-sized beds filled the bedroom, dirty plates littered the kitchen, and each man hid his drugs in different secret places, thinking that the other wasn't aware of his habit. The only thing that made the arrangement bearable was that, for the most part, their tour schedules kept them from sleeping in the apartment at the same time. And, once a week, June and Maybelle would come by to tidy and clean.

It made no sense for someone of his fame and wealth to live in such modest circumstances permanently. With his divorce all but signed, Cash wanted to a buy a home where he could relax and write, where he could entertain and showcase his expanding collection of books and records. He contacted Braxton Dixon, a local builder, and asked to see available lots. At the time, Dixon was building a unique house overlooking Old Hickory Lake in Hendersonville, about twenty miles north of Nashville. He decided to show Cash the property, almost as an afterthought, because he knew Cash wanted something similar that was close to water. Dixon didn't think of it as a spec house but as one he might live in himself.

The house was built from stone and wood Dixon had collected from old barns and houses—some of them more than two hundred years old. The rafters were made of skinned tree trunks, and three of the outside walls were of glass. It was unusual and impressive, and Cash fell in love with it on the spot. He loved the lake and the roughness of the stones and wood. It filled him with a sense of peace and space. He imagined it as a place where he could straighten himself out and get re-acquainted with the trees, flowers, grass, and earth that had inspired him as a boy. Dixon tried to tell him it wasn't for sale. "Everything's for sale," Cash answered, and he negotiated a deal.

Moving in even before it was completed, he became close friends with Dixon, who quickly learned about Cash's drug problem. He genuinely wanted the new house to signify a new start and desperately wanted to kick his habit, because June refused to marry him until he went straight. "He called us one day and said he wanted us to come over and see his new house," says Don Reid of the Statler Brothers. "So we did. There wasn't a stick of furniture in it and I don't think there was even any electricity. He had asked us to bring a guitar. So the four of us went out and he was there with June and he said, 'I want you to christen my house.' I remember it was dusk and there were no lights. We stood in the living room and we sang 'How Great Thou Art.' He wanted that to be the first song ever sung in his house."

On August 30, 1967, Cash capitulated to Vivian. He withdrew his denials, dropped the counterallegations, and agreed to divorce proceedings without any further defense. He finally realized that the negative publicity from a public court battle would cost him far more than any financial judgment. Specific "written findings of fact" and "evidence" resulted in the court's opinion that "a divorce ought to be granted to plaintiff from defendant on the grounds of the defendant's extreme cruelty." Vivian was awarded custody of the children as well as the guarantee of four hundred dollars per month (plus medical care and insurance) per child. Finally, Cash would pay her sixty-five-hundred-dollar attorney's fee.

Vivian also received a substantial financial settlement that involved one of Cash's lucrative publishing companies and his share in Purple Wagon Square, a shopping center in Ojai, California, that he'd bought with Sheb Wooley, the writer and performer of the 1958 hit song "The Purple People Eater."

Willpower alone wasn't enough to get Cash drug free—not even with the additional support of Braxton Dixon, who got rid of pills he found hidden around the house, and June, who tried to dissuade his Nashville suppliers from driving up to Hendersonville. Maybelle enlisted local psychiatrist Dr. Nat Winston, former state commissioner of mental health for Tennessee and a banjo-pickin' personal friend of Earl Scruggs. Winston tried to admit Cash to several private psychiatric hospitals, but at the last minute, Cash would always back out, and legally no one but he could make that decision. However, his relationship with Winston was a life-changing one, and later he even credited Winston with saving his life.

Looking back from the 1990s, Cash pinpointed a visit with a friend in Chattanooga as the ultimate crisis point in his life. Thirty miles west of the city lay Nickajack Cave—an underground warren that was home to one hundred thousand gray bats—where he'd previously searched for Indian arrowheads and inscriptions left by Confederate soldiers. This time, he planned not to hunt for treasures but to end his life. He believed that if he crawled in far enough, he'd be unable to find his way out. When he starved to death it would look like a tragic accident.

In 1995 he told the writer Nick Tosches:

> It just felt like I was at the end of the line. I was down there by myself and I got to feelin' that I'd taken so many pills that I'd done it, that I was gonna blow up or something. I hadn't eaten in days, I hadn't slept in days, and my mind wasn't workin' too good anyway. I couldn't stand myself anymore. I wanted to get away from me. And if that meant dyin',' then okay, I'm ready. I just had to get away from myself. I couldn't stand it anymore, and I didn't think there was any other way. I took a flashlight with me, and I said, I'm goin' to walk and crawl and climb into this cave until the light goes out, and then I'm gonna lie down. So I crawled in there with that flashlight until it burned out and I lay down to die. I was a mile in that cave. At least a mile. But I felt this great comfortin' presence sayin', "No, you're not dyin'." I got things for you to do. So I got up, found my way out. Cliffs, ledges, drop-offs. I don't know how I got out, 'cept God got me out.[2]

In his 1997 autobiography he added another detail. He recalled that when he crawled back into the daylight, June was there with his mother, and together they drove him back to Nashville. He omitted saying how they knew where to find him, why they thought he might need their attention, or even what happened to the vehicle he originally drove to the cave. During the ride back home, he told his mother that God had pulled him back from death, and he was now ready to recommit his life to God and come off drugs.

This graphic and pivotal event wasn't referred to in the Christopher Wren biography or in his first autobiography, *The Man in Black.* In both of these books he dates his epiphany as his November 2, 1967, arrest in Lafayette, Georgia, when he was picked up with a pocketful of pills. If, as he has written, the Nickajack Cave experience was in October, his determination to come clean couldn't have lasted long.

Former sheriff Ralph Jones remembers the night in Lafayette well. "He was looking for a house and knocked on the wrong door on Mission Bridge Road," he says. "The woman who lived there was on her own and was a bit worried, so she called my office and one of my deputies, Bob Jeffries, picked him up and brought him in. He was searched and that's when we found out that he was Johnny Cash and that he had pills on him."

He was jailed overnight and Richard McGibony, a musician friend who lived nearby, was called in to make bond for him. According to McGibony, Cash had come to Lafayette to visit Albert Fullam, an old man who had once worked on the railroad with the singer Jimmie Rodgers. He parked his Jeep outside Fullam's property but later lost his way back, so he ended up looking like a vagrant checking out front yards and knocking on doors.

He could have charged Cash with disorderly conduct, but Sheriff Smith decided to show mercy. "I told him that I would like to know, for my own personal satisfaction, why he would want to throw everything away," he says. "I asked him why he would waste his career, his family, and all the money he had earned for the sake of getting stoned on these pills. I just felt led to say that to him and later he said that he didn't know whether God had sent him to me or whether God had sent me to him."

After bailing him out, McGibony drove Cash back to Nashville. Two days later, on November 5, 1967, June persuaded him to attend a service at First Baptist Church, Hendersonville. She felt that the only way to save Cash was to reawaken his faith. He constantly switched his trust from drugs to his own inner strength, but instead needed reminding to trust in God's strength working through him. He needed to be empowered.

Both incidents brought home to Cash his inability to control his behavior and yet revealed the forgiving nature of God. They were moments of grace. He was reminded of the words of the apostle Paul: "For I am convinced that neither death nor life, neither angels nor demons, neither the present nor the future, nor any powers, neither height nor depth, nor anything else in all creation, will be able to separate us from the love of God that is in Christ Jesus our Lord" (Romans 8:38–39).

Rev. Courtney Wilson, pastor at First Baptist since 1955, preached that morning on the gospel story of the woman at the well. While resting at Jacob's well in Sychar, Jesus meets a Samaritan woman there to draw water. Jesus engages her in a conversation, during which he offers her instead what he refers to as "living water." The woman is naturally confused about where to find this water of his. Jesus tells her, "Everyone who drinks this water [the water in the well] will be thirsty again, but whoever drinks the water I give him will never thirst."

"What Jesus was saying was that faith in him was for eternity," says Wilson. "I spoke about this in my sermon, and Johnny later said that it made him determined that he was going to try that living water, that faith in Christ, instead of going the way that he'd been going. He made his rededication that Sunday. There was something special to him about the experience. From that time on his relationship with God, with Jesus Christ, was very real. He kept it current in his life."

> For his water flows eternal from the well that never dries—
> It flows right out of heaven where the soul will never die.
> If you're hot, tired and thirsty; if you crave a tall cool drink;
> He will pour it right out for you a whole lot quicker than you think.
> He already knows you're thirsty, so let him just come on in,
> And he will give you living water, and you'll never thirst again.
>
> ("Have a Drink of Water," 1977)

8

The Voice of America

CASH HAD PLAYED PRISONS SINCE 1957, and since 1962 he had wanted to record one of these concerts. He believed that no applause equaled the applause of incarcerated men who had suddenly been treated to some entertainment. "The first time I played a prison I said that this was the only place to record an album live because I'd never heard a reaction to the songs like the one that prisoners gave," he said. "They weren't ashamed to show their appreciation." Despite his enthusiasm for such a project, Columbia wasn't interested.

Cash's opportunity came when Don Law, his producer since 1958, retired and was replaced by thirty-five-year-old Bob Johnston, who had come to Nashville from New York where he'd been a staff producer since 1965. Thirty years younger than Law, Johnston was on the cutting edge of contemporary music, having produced Simon & Garfunkel's *Sounds of Silence* and *Parsley, Sage, Rosemary and Thyme* and Bob Dylan's *Highway 61 Revisited, Blonde on Blonde,* and *John Wesley Harding*—all popular albums with the newly radicalized college-age generation. A no-nonsense Texan with a loud voice, who thought that record companies frequently failed their artists because executives played safe in order to keep their jobs, Bob Johnston was an ideal partner for Cash at this point in his life.

Johnston felt that the executives at Columbia had neglected Cash's career because they didn't know how to present or promote him. They also considered him well past his peak and, therefore, not worthy of too much attention. "They were producing garbage because nobody had any idea," says Johnston. "They thought of him as a bag of bones who crashed into telephone poles and tore up hotel rooms. They couldn't see that all he needed was his music. The second he got his music back, he got off all that stuff."

Johnston planned to revive Cash's recording career by first identifying his artistic vision and then enabling him to realize it. If Cash wanted to record in a prison, then he'd make sure that it was the best album that could be produced in a prison. He wouldn't take orders from New York–based accountants and marketing consultants. He'd trust the singer's instinct. "I signed on to do what the artist wanted to do because I believe in that," he says. "It has always worked for me."

They chose Folsom State Prison in Repressa, California, as the venue. Not only had it been the subject of one of Cash's best-known songs, but he'd also played there before at the suggestion of Floyd Gressett, his minister friend from Ventura, who regularly worked with prisoners on the West Coast. Situated twenty-five miles east of Sacramento, it was California's second-oldest prison and had a reputation for housing some of the state's worst offenders. Five massive cellblocks held over thirty-five hundred inmates.

After two days of rehearsals in the banquet room of the El Rancho Motel in Sacramento, Cash, the Tennessee Three, Carl Perkins, the Carter Family, and the Statler Brothers arrived at the prison on the morning of January 13, 1968. The dining hall, a cavernous room with a pitched roof, was thronged with two thousand men sitting at small white tables. Armed guards patrolled the overhead walkways, and because the men couldn't be left in darkness, rows of neon lights blazed down throughout the show.

Because the prisoners rarely had a chance to express themselves as a group, the room overflowed with tension. "Those prisoners were all power," says Johnston. "There was nothing but power. If he [Cash] had gone in there as a wimp, I don't think it would have worked. We would have had a pretty good album, but I don't think he would have done all those songs, and I don't think he would have done them the same way. That's why I made him say, 'Hello. I'm Johnny Cash as soon as he got onstage. He needed to assert control right from the start."

Cash had played enough prisons to know the songs that most touched the hearts of those forced to live there. Almost half of his set was either about prison or crime. Another quarter addressed loneliness, separation, and despair. The difference with the prison audience—and this is obviously what Cash knew would translate well onto the album—was that their applause didn't just come at the end of the songs, but whenever a line hit home. These men took his words seriously. They weren't there to appreciate or evaluate but to respond.

Although Johnston knew that the applause would be something special, Folsom State Prison wasn't an ideal setup for live recording. The dining hall's high, pitched roof and thick stone walls were an acoustical nightmare. They had to use five separate machines—running simultaneously in a truck parked in the prison yard—just to record the music. "When I got back to Nashville I spent about three weeks mixing it. I had to take the echo off. I was bringing it back and forth from these five tapes so that the end result was what it was supposed to be."

Johnny Cash at Folsom Prison kick-started his first major comeback. The album was as important to him in the 1960s as the single "I Walk the Line" had been in the 1950s. It sold six million copies, reached number thirteen in the pop charts, and led to *Johnny Cash at San Quentin,* which in turn led to his network television series. At the end of 1969, Columbia Records president Clive Davis would announce that Johnny Cash had sold more records in the U.S. that year than the Beatles.

The album cemented Cash's image as an outlaw. It didn't matter that he'd never served real time. What mattered was that he not only looked the part— rugged and weathered—but he identified with a huge audience of hardened criminals in a way that implied he was on their side—not that of the law. Many of the songs, written from the perspective of the imprisoned, addressed the guards with a mocking sneer. In "Cocaine Blues" the lines "Early one morning while making the rounds / I took a shot of cocaine and I shot my woman down," were met by a wave of applause, presumably coming from men who'd either done the same or wished they could. Cash did nothing to quell their enthusiasm.

Questioned closely, Cash would attribute his concern for prisoners to a belief that they needed to know that they were not forgotten. They may have earned society's punishment, but they also deserved their dignity, especially if they were ever to be rehabilitated. How could we expect prisoners to emerge more loving and caring citizens if they were deprived of love and care? "The conditions are the reasons for the crimes," says Johnston. "You can't lock people up and treat them like animals and then punish them even more when they act like animals. At Folsom I stood by the doors as they filed in and I stood there as they filed out and there wasn't one person who looked me in the eye."

Cash was also aware of the biblical edict to care for those in prison. In Matthew 25, Jesus distinguishes between those who are religious in name and those whose faith results in action. He says that the faithful who care for the sick and lonely are indirectly caring for Jesus himself. "For I was hungry and you gave me something to eat, I was thirsty and you gave me something to drink, I was a stranger and you invited me in, I needed clothes and you clothed me, I was sick and you looked after me, I was in prison and you came to visit me" (Matthew 25:35–36).

"There's three different kinds of Christian," said Cash. "There's preaching Christians, church-playing Christians, and there's practicing Christians. I'm trying very hard to be a practicing Christian. If you take the words of Jesus literally and apply them to your everyday life, you discover that the greatest fulfillment you'll ever find really does lie in giving. And that's why I do things like prison concerts."

Ten days before the Folsom concert, on January 3, 1968, Cash's divorce became final. Two days before the concert, Vivian married Dick Distin, a Ventura policeman. She met her new husband when Cash did a benefit he'd helped organize for the Ventura Boy's Club. To remarry as a Catholic, she had needed special dispensation from the ecclesiastical hierarchy or risk excommunication. Distin took special instruction during 1967 and converted to Catholicism by the time of the wedding. There was now no obstacle, and Cash could finally marry June. While performing in London, Ontario, on February 22, 1968, he proposed to her onstage. Just more than a week later, they wed at the Methodist Church in Franklin, Kentucky. Merle Kilgore stood up as best man and the reception was alcohol free.

Cash and June didn't honeymoon immediately but waited until after a tour of Britain in May to travel to Israel. They visited Nazareth, the town where Jesus grew up, the area around the Sea of Galilee where his early ministry took place, and sites of Jerusalem, including the disputed site of the Crucifixion and the Via Dolorosa. Cash, who had only been to Israel once before, was gripped by the sights, sounds and smells of this land and spoke his thoughts at each site into a tape recorder. At a jewelry shop they each bought the other a ring engraved with "Me to my love and my love to me" in Hebrew.

Just as *Johnny Cash at Folsom Prison* began to climb the charts in 1968, a thirty-year-old director, Robert Elfstrom, began shooting a documentary on the singer. His film opens with Cash out hunting in the woods with his rifle. He downs a crow but when he realizes he has only wounded it, he playfully caresses it. "Be still, be still," he urges it as it tries to peck his finger. "I already like you for some reason. I'm gonna charm you yet." With the bird firmly gripped in one hand and his rifle in the other, he strolls on through the long grass, composing a song as he goes:

> If I could fly like Mister Crow
> I know where I would go
> I would leave you
> I would leave you

He eventually completed and even copyrighted the song "Mr. Crow" in 1970, but never recorded it.

It was an unusual and arresting opening to a film about the life of a popular singer. Elfstrom used it because he thought that it encapsulated Cash's contradictions. Here was a man, though capable of destruction, who became overwhelmed with the desire to repair what he had destroyed; a nonviolent man who had a love affair with guns; an artist who could cause suffering and then turn that suffering into art. "John is all of those people," says Elfstrom. "He would sit around his house and get bored and so he'd say, 'Let's go outside and get a crow.' He wounded the crow and then he spent the next day or two trying to mend it. He was driving around to doctors and vets and buying gaffer tape to fix the bird's leg. There was a whole Doctor Doolittle thing going on."

The idea of making a documentary had originated with Harry Wiland, a twenty-two-year-old graduate film student at Columbia University, who with the help of a tutor secured one hundred and seventy-five thousand dollars from the Public Broadcast Library. They pitched the idea to Saul Holiff in a letter and secured Cash's participation. Elfstrom, active in the cinéma vérité school of filmmaking in New York, had filmed documentaries in Vietnam and Central America, was hired to direct even though he knew little about Johnny Cash. With no planned outline, he hung around Cash intermittently for eight months, filming him relaxing at home, traveling to concerts in his Dodge RV, recording, performing, returning to Dyess, and listening to his father sing.

"He was just in a great place in his life and so was June," says Elfstrom. "I just hit it off with both of them. John is the kind of guy who looks you in the eye when he makes a decision. He's very earthy. He makes decisions with his stomach and his heart, and I guess that he figured that I was good enough. Once he had made that decision he just opened and opened as the film went on. He became more and more revealing and trusting. I've been making documentaries for over forty years now and that was one of the highlights of my life."

Elfstrom captured Cash in July 1968 with Bob Johnston recording "Land of Israel" for the *Holy Land* album, based on the tape-recorded impressions Cash had made in Israel. Seven months later, in the same studio, Elfstrom filmed him cutting his first Kris Kristofferson song, "The Devil to Pay," with Carl Perkins on guitar and harmonies. Kristofferson, who'd been in Nashville for three years working at menial jobs to support his family while he wrote, pitched songs to Cash on a regular basis. Most celebrated is the time Kristofferson once flew a National Guard helicopter up to Hendersonville, landed on the Cash property, and hand-delivered a cassette demo. Legend has it that the track was "Sunday Morning Coming Down," but Kristofferson says it was "It No Longer Matters," a song that neither of them ever recorded. "I figured it would get his attention," he says of the stunt. "So many times Luther would say, 'John loves that song of yours,' but he wouldn't record them. You never knew what he was going to do."

Kristofferson was part of a new generation of songwriters who wanted to shake up Nashville by broadening the parameters of what was acceptable in country music. His songs were more sexually frank, drug aware, urban, and socially concerned than the traditional Opry fare. Kristofferson was also more consciously literary, having studied English literature at Oxford University for a year on a Rhodes scholarship. He enjoyed the poet William Blake as much as he enjoyed Hank Williams and wasn't afraid to use allusion, alliteration, and other rhetorical devices in his lyrics. As with his friends Mickey Newbury, Chris Gantry, and Vince Matthews, he had more in common with Bob Dylan, John Lennon, and the culture of the Monterey Pop Festival than he did with George Jones, Porter Wagoner, and the Grand Ole Opry.

For them, Johnny Cash remained one of the archetypal Nashville rebels, a man who defied the country ethos of his day by recording songs that drew attention to Native American rights, who'd been banned from the Opry, and whose credentials had been questioned by the country elite. "The rest of us wanted to be like him," says Kristofferson. "He had integrity. He went his own way boldly. He was an outlaw and that appealed to us. He went in his own direction and nobody told him what to do."

Later that year Cash would record another Kristofferson song, "To Beat the Devil," and he introduced Kris to the audience at the Newport Folk Festival. Kristofferson had gone to the festival—as a fan—with Vince Matthews. When Cash heard that he was sleeping in an old church that offered space to hippies, he invited him to perform two songs during his show. Time was tight and it was an extraordinarily prestigious spot to be given, especially to someone with no previous experience in performing for audiences.

"I got to sing 'Sunday Morning Coming Down' and 'Me and Bobby McGhee,'" says Kristofferson. "They went over so well that John told me on one of the last occasions that I spoke to him that the *New York Times* had said that I stole the show. I don't remember that. I do know that it went over well enough that they put me on at some of the afternoon workshops with people like Van Morrison, Joni Mitchell, and James Taylor and that it started my performing career. It took me from being a guy who sat on a chair at John's house to getting an invitation to appear at the Berkeley Folk Festival. I never looked back."

The third recording session that Cash permitted Elfstrom to film was one with Bob Dylan, who was in town to record *Nashville Skyline* with Bob Johnston. Since *John Wesley Harding,* also recorded by Johnston in Nashville, Dylan had turned away from the wild drug-warped electric blues of his *Blonde on Blonde* period and toward the simple melodies and sentiments of country music. He'd cut his instantly recognizable shock of unruly hair, had grown a beard, and now lived on a mountainside in Upstate New York. *Nashville Skyline,* for which Cash wrote the liner notes in the form of a poem, captured Dylan's exploration of the country sound.

The two men crossed paths at Columbia Studios on February 18, and Bob Johnston thought he should take advantage of the situation. "There was no purpose to the session other than my selfishness," he says. "I've always tried to put people together and I thought it would be wonderful if Dylan and Cash got together. They went out to eat and while they were gone I set up microphones, chairs, and stools and put the lights on in a special way so that when they got back and saw what I had done they just chuckled, got their guitars, and began playing. I started requesting stuff and four hours later Dylan said, 'We've finished.' Columbia never wanted it done."

Gone was the nervousness that had been obvious two years before when they'd sung in a hotel room in front of Pennebaker's camera. They were more confident in each other's presence. Not much more than an improvised jam, the session included all the false starts, faltering vocals, and forgotten words expected from such a spontaneous get-together. Though most of the eighteen tracks were too unpolished to ever be considered for release, one, "Girl from the North Country," became the opening track on Dylan's *Nashville Skyline* album.

Elfstrom's film illustrated the variety of live shows Cash was performing. Dressed formally at the Ryman Auditorium, he accepted the CMA Album of the Year award for *Johnny Cash at Folsom Prison.* With a voice filled with emotion, he accepted it on behalf of Luther Perkins, who had died two months previously of burns and smoke inhalation after falling asleep on a couch with a lighted cigarette. Cash played an unnamed county fair, a concert hall, Nashville's Tennessee State Prison, and the St. Francis Reservation in South Dakota. The day after the St. Francis concert, Elfstrom filmed Cash's visit to the site of the Battle of Wounded Knee, where, in December 1890, 146 members of the Miniconjou Lakota tribe were killed by the Seventh United States Cavalry.

This trip had been set up by John L. Smith, a fan who was not only an authority on Cash's recording career (and later his discographer) but was a student of Native American history. They first met after a concert in Des Moines in April 1967 and had since corresponded to exchange information about Native Americans. Cash promised to give Smith one of his guitars if he could supply him with detailed information about and photographs of Wounded Knee.

The St. Francis concert gave Cash an excuse to finally see Wounded Knee. He listened attentively as Jesse White Lance, Robert Holy Dance, and William Horn Cloud, descendants of those killed, took him around the site and showed him the grave markers. He was particularly taken with the story of the Indian leader known as Big Foot. "I took John and June back in my car after the visit," says Smith. "As we drove through the Badlands June fell asleep. When we got to the airport she woke up and John said, 'I think I've got something you ought to hear,' and he just sang this song called 'Big Foot' to both of us, keeping track of the melody by slap-ping his leg."

Some of the most revealing footage Elfstrom shot on tour was of Cash backstage before and after concerts. At thirty-six Cash looked like a man in his prime. The gaunt and skinny look of his amphetamine days had been replaced by a full, solid face, powerful shoulders, and a slow, swaggering walk. It was as though this was the look he had always been meant to grow into, and he seemed far more hand-some in his early middle age than he had as a teenager or a young man. He still twitched and scratched his neck but now with the natural energy of a man getting ready to meet his audience rather than the edginess of an addict. "Before he went onstage he was rolling everything through his head," says Elfstrom. "He was clear-ing his voice and psyching himself up. He was intense."

He also displayed a commendable courteousness to those who found their way backstage either to share their songs with him or to ask him to sing for them. In one clip, a singer called Buzz Martin comes by with a tape of his songs, and Cash gives him his guitar and asks him to play "the best song you've got that you think I might record." Martin responds by playing a song about his wife who he has nicknamed Biscuit, and Cash, after laughing throughout, commends him on his ability with words. Another young man comes by and asks him to play "Great Speckled Bird" for his girlfriend and Cash obliges.

In a longer sequence, an eighteen-year-old Canadian songwriter, Don Freed, plays him two Dylanesque folk songs that he had written, one of which was called "The Banks of Mariposa." Freed traveled from Saskatoon for this opportunity and came equipped with guitar, harmonica, and brace. Cash listens intently and prom-ises to get him an audition with Columbia. Freed looks disbelieving but Cash assures him that he wouldn't tell him he liked a song if he didn't.

While Elfstrom shot this documentary, a film production team employed by the commercial company Granada Television, three thousand miles away in London, considered the idea of producing an arts program on Cash. Mostly in their late twenties, they were possibly the hippest group of creatives in British television, regarded equally with suspicion and envy for their links to the burgeoning under-ground scene of avante-garde films, radical politics, fashion, and rock music. Two of them, Jonathan Cott and David Dalton, contributed regularly to *Rolling Stone*. Geoffrey Cannon was the first rock critic for a British daily newspaper. As a team, they'd recently made a film about the Doors that spliced concert footage with news coverage of napalm falling on Vietnam and antiwar protesters being clubbed by police. They would go on to cover the Rolling Stones's momentous 1969 Hyde Park appearance following the death of guitarist Brian Jones. Their mission, they'd decided, was to show that rock music was both a commentary on and a cause of cultural change in the modern world.

"It was in this context that I had a bad idea," says Geoffrey Cannon. "In those days people like us thought of country as music for redneck hoedowns. But the journalist in me, that I tried to suppress, could smell a story. So I came into our office one November morning and asked Jo Durden-Smith, Jonathan Cott, and David Dalton to join me at the big round table and I said, 'I have a bad idea, but I know it will be a hit. How about getting Johnny Cash to do a second gig at Folsom Prison and filming it?'"

Cannon had half hoped his friends would nix the idea, but instead they showed mild interest and one found a number for Saul Holiff. Cannon phoned but was told quite firmly that Johnny Cash had no interest in revisiting Folsom Prison. "Having made the dud call, the idea began worming its way into my consciousness," says Cannon. "I began to see that actually this was a good idea. Nothing like a concert where a jailbird [sic] sang songs about desperation to no-hopers and lifers in prison had ever been transmitted on national network television and this was one of our touchstones. So a couple of days later I rang Holiff a second time. He was still polite and still not interested. Then just as I was going to say 'bye' he said, 'but Johnny is going to San Quentin. He'd be happy to make a film with you there.'"

San Quentin State Prison was bigger, older and even more notorious than Folsom. Perched on four hundred and thirty-two acres of land in Marin County and overlooking the San Francisco Bay near the San Rafael Bridge, it housed almost six thousand inmates and had a staff of more than fifteen hundred. As with Folsom, Cash was comfortable with it as a venue because he'd played there before, back on New Year's Day in 1959 when future country star Merle Haggard was one of the prisoners in the audience. This time Columbia was more than interested in capturing the concert for posterity. They asked Granada what sort of percentage they would like in the recording. The film's director, Michael Darlow, suggested to his boss, Cecil Bernstein, that they ask for 4 percent. "Bernstein said, 'I don't want that. Nobody's heard of Johnny Cash. Take £800,'" remembers Darlow. "That was the worst decision Granada ever made. When I told the guy from Columbia that we only wanted £800, he couldn't get off the phone fast enough."

Darlow and producer Jo Durden-Smith flew out to California and met up with Cash before a show in San Diego. "One of the first things I did was to ask him if he'd be willing to write a song about San Quentin in the way that he'd written one about Folsom," says Darlow. He told Darlow, in no uncertain terms, exactly what he could do with his idea. "I was crestfallen. June came over to me and whispered in my ear, 'That means he'll do it.' I fell in love with her at once!"

They went on to San Quentin ahead of the concert, which was scheduled for February 24, 1969, to film the prison and interview inmates. "It was full of chaos, the whole thing," says Darlow. "I went to see the prison governor and he wanted to know what was in it for them. I did a deal where he got a cabinet radiogram and the prison got a sound system. Then twelve hard guys came and told us that we needed protection, and the senior guard advised us to accept their offer. So these guys looked after us, and they became the twelve guys in the front row at the concert!"

Darlow and Durden-Smith wanted make a documentary that, like the Doors film, interspersed social realism with art to underline the connection. They interviewed men on death row and were impressed with the stories told by the prisoners. Durden-Smith became so engrossed in some of their situations that years later he returned to write a book about one of its inmates: *Who Killed George Jackson?*

"There was enormous tension in the prison between blacks and Chicanos, and it got quite difficult," says Durden-Smith. "In a sense the eventual film got transmuted and slightly bent off course. I think we had started off with a notion that San Quentin was somehow a place where 'tales of regret and love and death and murder come home to roost.' The truth is, it wasn't exactly a country-and-western prison, so the music and the prison don't mix exactly. It was a bit of a mismatch but, nevertheless, not a bad film."

Bob Johnston remembers that the tension at San Quentin surpassed that at Folsom. "All the guards were nervous," he says. "They thought that there was going to be a riot. He [Cash] said that when he was singing 'Folsom Prison Blues' and the men were up on the tables yelling when they were only supposed to clap sitting down, he realized that all he had to say was, 'Let's go!' and there would have been a full-scale riot. He told me after, 'I was tempted.' I mean, if there was ever a three-word sentence pregnant with meaning, it was that one. People got carried away." Ralph Gleason, who reviewed the concert for *Rolling Stone,* observed: "What he did was right on the edge. If he had screwed up one notch higher the joint would have exploded. He knew when to stop."

This is an opinion shared by Darlow. "He knew exactly what he was doing," he says. "He would take it up to a certain point and then he'd take it down because the guards were getting really jumpy. It was all an act. All that stuff on the record was kind of fixed because he made very sure that the camera was on him before he said anything. He was very skillful."

Other than repeating "Folsom Prison Blues" he presented a different set than the one recorded at Folsom, with the added spontaneity of playing recently written songs. "Starkville City Jail," about his arrest for picking flowers in Mississippi, he'd written the night before the show, and he played "San Quentin" since Darlow suggested it two days before. The words of "A Boy Named Sue" had been given to him by Shel Silverstein at a songwriters party at Old Hickory Lake just five days before, where Graham Nash had premiered "Marrakesh Express"; Bob Dylan "Lay, Lady, Lay;" Kris Kristofferson "Me and Bobby McGhee;" and Joni Mitchell "Both Sides Now." There was no tune; so he propped the lyric sheet on a music stand and asked the band (which now included guitarist Bob Wootton, who had replaced Luther) to improvise behind him as he sang it for the first time.

"I knew pretty much what he was going to do in the concert, but I didn't know about 'A Boy Named Sue,'" says Darlow. "He just told me that he had something new that he was going to try."

The shaved-headed but bearded Silverstein was a versatile writer and hard to categorize. To children he was the author of "Uncle Shelby's Story of Lafcadio," "The Lion Who Shot Back" (1963), and *The Giving Tree* (1964). Readers of *Playboy* knew him as a cartoonist. The folk crowds of New York and Chicago knew him as the composer of "The Unicorn" (recorded by the Irish Rovers) and "25 Minutes to Go" (recorded by Brothers Four as well as Johnny Cash). Uniting all his work was a quirky view of life and a love of long and strange titles.

"A Boy Named Sue" told the story of a father who named his son Sue, knowing that he'd be teased and ridiculed as he grew up and would therefore develop tenacity to survive. The prison crowd hung on every word and exploded at the punch line. Released as the first single on the *Johnny Cash at San Quentin* album, it rose to number two in the singles charts—his best position ever. Cash developed ambiguous feelings for the song. Though he naturally enjoyed its staggering success, he didn't relish the idea that his most commercially successful song was a novelty number written by someone else.

The Granada Television documentary was screened in Britain during April 1969, before the single or the album had been released, creating a sense of anticipation. The American networks didn't pick it up, probably because the combination of Cash's salty language and the sympathetic portrayal of death row inmates was considered unsuitable for a mainstream audience. "I think that the film was quite pivotal in the Johnny Cash revival," says Durden-Smith. "He was someone who had become quite forgotten. In all the fuss about the Beatles and the Rolling Stones he'd got left behind. The fact that he was on network TV may have been something of an indication that hip young things in Britain were shooting Johnny Cash and that he therefore might reach a much wider audience."

Holiff also thinks that the documentary was crucial. It not only helped to push the album (and the single) in Britain, but it showed what a charismatic and televisual performer Cash was. Soon after, he was approached by ABC to see if Cash would be interested in becoming a summer replacement for *Hollywood Palace,* a fifteen-show run transmitting from June through September. The accepted wisdom was that few people watched summer television, which made it the perfect time to try out new shows. Holiff accepted the offer with two provisos: first, that Cash would only do the shows if they could be filmed on his home turf at the Ryman Auditorium, and second, Canadian Stan Jacobson, who'd made a 1967 CBC special about him, would produce the shows. ABC agreed to both conditions.

Although Cash had done a lot to get his life back in order, it was still a battle to stay completely free of drugs. "When the TV series was scheduled he was as wild as a guinea," says Marshall Grant. "However, anytime he wanted to come back down he could do it. He'd do what he needed to do and then he'd get blown out again. He wasn't drug free during the TV show years but he had it totally under control. Six months before they started filming he looked like death warmed up, and he gained weight and he looked excellent."

Filming began in April 1969 and the schedule was tough. Rehearsals took place on Mondays, Tuesdays, and Wednesdays, and tapings (an average of two shows a week) were on Thursdays. Weekends were kept free for Cash's concert commitments. Cash planned to keep the show fresh and to use it to introduce acts that the average

American viewer may not have seen. He wanted to use his privileged position to shake up mainstream television entertainment, and in this he was initially successful. His opening show coup was having Bob Dylan and Joni Mitchell perform. On subsequent shows in the summer series he did duets with the likes of Merle Haggard, Buffy St. Marie, Ramblin' Jack Elliott, Mama Cass, Odetta, Gordon Lightfoot, and Linda Ronstadt, none of whom were then household names and who all came from the folk, blues, or country tradition. These choices won him new friends who saw him as a man willing to take risks.

Rick Rubin, his future producer, was then a six-year-old living on Long Island. "I was only a kid, but he definitely made an impression on me," he says. "He had an accent that was very unusual to hear on TV in those days. Also, he looked cool. He had a presence that was different from anyone else."

Bono, later to become part of U2, was a nine-year-old living in Ireland. "People will tell you that this was when Johnny Cash sold out," he says. "But that's not right. The *Johnny Cash Show* on TV was an amazingly generous act, a great gift to the world. Bob Dylan goes on and on about this. It saw him moving from the fringes to the center of the stage. I used to see those shows in America, and that's when I became a fan."

Nick Cave was a twelve-year-old living in Australia. "I used to watch it with my parents," he says. "Up until that point I had basically been listening to children's music. Then I started to watch the *Johnny Cash Show* and from somewhere way down I understood that this music was talking about something different. To my young mind, Johnny Cash appeared to be an outlaw. His voice had so much weight. The idea of this guy doing songs that were about God, murder, and love, and getting away with it, seemed like some kind of an achievement."

The summer series coincided with the release of *Johnny Cash at San Quentin,* which soared to the top of the album charts. "Normally a summer replacement show like this would have died a quiet death," says Holiff. "But the hit single and album meant that people started watching the show in summertime. The idea of being at the Ryman Auditorium clicked, and people from all walks of life seemed to find his charisma very appealing." Happy with the summer ratings, ABC picked the show for the next season starting in January 1970 and lasting for seventeen shows.

They kept the format of the show consistent. Cash sang a selection of his better known songs, performed duets with guests, and then one with June, and for the finale, he would join the Carter Family and the Statler Brothers for a gospel song. The caliber of guests remained high with appearances by Ray Charles, Judy Collins, Roy Orbison, Roger Miller, Waylon Jennings, Burl Ives, Roy Acuff, and others.

In the middle came "Ride This Train," a filmed section focusing on a particular aspect of Americana: the Wild West, trains, religion, prisons, hobos, cotton picking, rivers, or the land. Cash, usually dressed in period costume and, in a relevant location, would talk to directly to the camera from scripts prepared by, among others, Merle Travis. Two or three pertinent songs underscored the narration.

This segment became his favorite part of the show and, according to producer Stan Jacobson, was the most popular with viewers. It helped position Cash as a curator of American traditions and a preserver of stories. "The train in the title became a symbol," says Jacobson. "We were saying to people—ride with us along this trail and we'll take you anywhere. These segments were really like the first videos."

Although Cash had a lot of control over the content of the shows, television naturally demanded some compromises. The greasy-haired punk with the irreverent line of banter at Folsom and San Quentin had to be cleaned up a little for family viewing. Instead of the dark three-piece suits he usually wore onstage, he started to wear long gambling jackets that he'd designed himself, shirts with ruffles and even bow ties. Instead of greasing his hair back, he began having it blow-dried and lacquered. He learned to fix the camera lens with a loving look and deliver prescripted lines. Even his once spontaneous welcome of, "Hello, I'm Johnny Cash" became ritualized into a James Bond-like opening sequence as he whirled round each week and delivered his signature greeting. "He learned the craft of performing on television as he went," says Holiff. "He learned how to smile differently. It took a lot of courage to do what he did and to do it well. The fact is that he was able to withstand the garbage that came out of New York about how he should do it, who his guests should be and all that."

Although the *Johnny Cash Show* wasn't designed to rehabilitate Cash, it did. The bad guy who stomped out lights, used profanity, kicked photographers, and smuggled drugs slowly transformed into a good guy who loved his wife, praised the Lord, and upheld the values of decent Americans. "The Man in Black became an embodiment, like Gary Cooper, of the American male's most flattering picture of himself," wrote Jack McClintock in *Family Weekly*. "[He was] the strong but gentle man who came from nowhere, excelled through talent and effort, indulged a spiritual weakness and was nearly ruined by it, but kept the faith and triumphed through strength and the help of a good woman."[1]

Stan Jacobson describes what he believes was the unequivocal reason for the success of the show: "Johnny, at the time," he says, "became the voice of America. He became the voice of a nation. It was during the Vietnam War when there were huge divisions, often along generational lines, but the older country music people loved him and so did the youth of America. The young people believed him. They saw him as a bit of a rebel and they liked that."

Kris Kristofferson, whose career got a further boost after appearing on the show in April 1970, watched the change from close quarters. When he first wrote home in 1966, bragging to his mother that he'd met his hero, Johnny Cash, she wrote back saying she was shocked that her son still idolized a man who everybody else just thought of as a dope addict and a felon. "By the time he did his TV show he was such a figure of stability," says Kristofferson. "It was like he was the father of our country. He was Billy Graham's friend. Presidents had respect for him. It was wonderful to see my mother change. I got an honorary doctorate from Pomona College, where I had gone to school, and John and June attended the ceremony. John had written her a letter and she came up to him and gave him a big hug. She was quite proud."

Though patriotic and religious, Cash was hardly a conventional conservative. He opposed American involvement in Vietnam, for example, but at the same time, he supported the troops by playing concerts in Saigon in January 1969. Visiting wounded soldiers in the hospital and ducking incoming mortar fire only served to increase his desire for peace. His nephew Roy Cash Jr. joined the navy in 1963 and spent a thirty-year career flying fighter planes off aircraft carriers. He remembers that Cash was always more interested in asking him questions about military life than he was in recounting his show-business tales. "He wasn't particularly for the Vietnam War and I wasn't either. I just felt that it was my duty to serve my country, and he supported us. He gave me tapes and records to give to the folks in my outfit. He even came and did a free concert at the naval college up in Newport, Rhode Island."

At a time when many of his generation were dismissive of the spiritual quests and political protests of the campus rebels, Cash, perhaps mindful of his own excesses and stumbling pilgrimage, liked to listen and understand. He shared many of their concerns for peace, freedom, equality, and human dignity. In a song premiered on the March 18, 1970, show, he took the question asked by Pontius Pilate, "What is truth?" and made it the hook of a song that looked at the failure of his generation to understand the young.

> The old man turns off the radio
> Says, "Where did all the old songs go?
> Kids sure play funny music these days
> And they sure do play it in the strangest ways!
> It seems like the whole darned world's gone wild.
> It was peaceful back when I was a child."
> Well, man, could it be that the girls and boys
> Are trying to be heard above your noise?
> And the lonely voice of youth cries, "What is truth?"

Another song specifically written for one of the shows was "Man in Black." For years he'd been asked why he dressed predominantly in black jackets and trousers (although he actually frequently wore white jackets in the 1950s). He usually gave one of three answers: (a) black stayed the cleanest for the longest time; (b) black was good for wearing in church, and his first concert had been in a church; (c) black was easier to color coordinate. The new song offered the explanation that he wore black in remembrance of all the sadness and injustice in the world. "Are you becoming a political radical?" Cash was asked. "No, I sure don't," said Cash. "I look at it the other way. I'm just trying to be a good Christian."[2]

> Oh, I'd love to wear a rainbow every day,
> And tell the world that everything's OK,
> But I'll try to carry off a little darkness on my back,
> Till things are brighter, I'm the Man in Black.

A third television series was commissioned starting in September, this time lasting for twenty-six shows. While taping Cash always maintained his boundaries. He wasn't concerned about pleasing a particular constituency—liberal or conservative—but wanted to stay true to himself. When he performed Kris Kristofferson's "Sunday Morning Coming Down," the network wanted him to leave out the reference to being "stoned." Someone suggested that instead of singing the line "wishing, Lord, that I was stoned" he could sing "wishing, Lord, that I was home." "John didn't let me know what he was going to do with it," says Kristofferson. "When he sang it that night he looked right up at me in the balcony and sang 'wishing, Lord, that I was stoned' and, to me that saved the song. I don't think it ever would have been that big if it had not had that word in it. He fought to preserve the integrity of the song. And he won."

On another occasion Cash dared to offend the liberals by making an explicit declaration of his Christian faith. He had always included gospel songs on his shows but had not yet revealed the precise details of his religious commitment. The fact that he loved gospel made him little different than Little Richard, Jerry Lee Lewis, or Elvis—performers from the South who grew up loving gospel songs and hymns. He knew from the fan mail that came into the show that a lot of people wanted to know whether the gospel songs had a deeper meaning for him.

Cash prepared a statement that he wanted to include in the show that aired on November 18, 1970, but Jacobson warned him against using it on the grounds that it would alienate a section of the public who didn't share his views. It wasn't a simple statement of his faith, something that would fit comfortably into the show-business format, but a short polemic that seemed out of character with the easygoing mood they'd established over the past eighteen months. He said,

> All my life I have believed that there are two powerful forces: the force of good, and the force of evil; the force of right and the force of wrong; or, if you will, the force of God, and the force of the devil. Well now, the force of God is naturally the Number One most powerful force, although the Number Two most powerful force, the devil, takes over every once in a while. And he can make it pretty rough on you when he tries to take over. I know. In my time I fought him, I fought back, I clawed, I kicked him. When I didn't have the strength to kick him, I gnawed him. Well, here lately I think we've made the devil pretty mad because on our show we've been mentioning God's name. We've been talking about Jesus, Moses, Elijah the prophet, even Paul and Silas and John the Baptist. Well, this probably made the devil pretty mad alright, and he may be coming after me again, but I'll be ready for him. In the meantime, while he's coming, I'd like to get in one more lick for Number One.

He then sang "I Saw a Man," by Arthur Smith.

Jacobson approached him afterward and suggested cutting it, but Johnny told him, "If you cut that out I'll never talk to you again. That's how I feel." It aired, but Jacobson believes that it had a catastrophic effect on the third season. "It was a seminal moment," he says. "John said something that he shouldn't have said. I left it in and our ratings began to dip. When the ratings started to dip, the powers that be in L.A. began to panic. They were saying, 'We gotta do something!' They started putting the pressure on me and on John. I tried to deflect it as best as I could, but I think by then he'd had enough."

The program was now running out of steam. The "Ride This Train" sections merely reworked past ideas, studio executives determined the guests, and old staples like "Big River," "I Walk the Line," and "Folsom Prison Blues" took up more of the playlist. Then, in a last-ditch effort to spice up the format, they introduced theme programs: comedy, youth, the Wild West, country music, circuses. A gospel-themed show even featured Billy Graham in a "duet" with Cash in the specially written song "The Preacher Said," in which the evangelist recited passages of Scripture. Though the *Johnny Cash Show* rated seventeen in the 1969–70 Nielsen Ratings, it didn't break the top twenty for the 1970–71 season.

In May 1971, while the third season still aired in the States, Cash flew to Australia for a tour. On arrival he was greeted by reporters asking him why the *Johnny Cash Show* had been cancelled. Apparently, in his absence, a decision had been reached in L. A. to pull the plug after fifty-eight shows spread over almost two years. Although totally shocked because he had agreed to film another season, he was nevertheless relieved that the decision to quit had been made for him. Cash had felt increasingly restless and was eager to embark on projects that had "more meaning" for him.

"It was all right for the first year," he said. "But I soon came to realize that to the networks I was just another piece of merchandise, a cog in the wheel, and when the wheel starts squeaking and wobbling they'd replace me with another cog." He told Robert Elfstrom that he felt that every part of his personal and family life had been exploited. "Television steals your soul," he said.

In December 1969 Billy Graham contacted him, and Cash invited Graham and his wife, Ruth, to Hendersonville for a meal. It was the start of one of the deepest and most valuable relationships of his life. On the surface they seemed an unlikely couple—Graham, the untainted and conservatively styled evangelist, and Cash, the unpredictable and wild musician—but they shared backgrounds as Southern Baptist farm boys, high-profile lives, and a love of the Bible.

Cash admired Graham's resoluteness and quiet confidence in God. Graham had met and advised some of the most powerful people in the world, and yet the most striking thing about him was his humility and his integrity. Graham, in turn, was intrigued by Cash's ability to be candid about his faith and yet find acceptance with sections of society that were traditionally cynical about Christianity.

Graham encouraged Cash to write more songs addressing the questions posed by the Woodstock generation. He also invited Cash to make a guest appearance along with the Carter Family and the Statler Brothers at a youth revival on May 24, 1970, in Knoxville, Tennessee. Posters advertising the event used psychedelic graphics, and Graham preached on what he called "the Jesus revolution." Cash spoke of his drug abuse that in fact had only ended a mere two months beforehand when his first son, John Carter Cash, was born. "It ain't worth it," he told the stadium crowd. "I'd like the young people to take it from a man who's been there and knows what he's talking about." Later he referred to the appearance with Billy Graham as "the pinnacle of my career."

9

Personal Jesus

THE END OF THE *JOHNNY CASH SHOW* marked the beginning of the most intensely evangelical period of Cash's life. His previous acts of spiritual rededication often appeared more motivated by a need to survive than an unselfish desire to serve God. When his life was falling apart it seemed that, as a last resort, he would turn to the teachings of Christ in the hope that he could be restored. Yet, when his situation improved, he gradually forgot his commitments to Christ and would soon find himself back where he started.

In the spring of 1971 Cash was nowhere near the end of his tether. His ratings had dropped during the final season of his television show, but he was still a huge international star, gaining celebrity status akin to John Wayne or Muhammad Ali. The previous year his movie career had been revived when he'd starred with Kirk Douglas in *A Gunfight*, his first screen role in almost a decade. His marriage to June made him happy, and the birth of his longed-for son reinvigorated him. Earning a reputed three million a year, he lived in a custom-built, luxurious home surrounded by one hundred and forty-six acres of land and had purchased a home nearby for his parents.

Apparently now able to offer forgiveness, Cash treated his father with loving care, visiting him daily when he was off the road and always remembered to dedicate songs to him in concert. "I've heard it said that he mistreated his children, and have read what Dad said in his book, but I never heard my father say one negative word about my grandfather," says Tara. "I never saw him treat him with anything other than complete, devout respect. I think that he had a lot of struggles and showed a lot of anger before Jack died, but my father always said that after that he turned his life around and was a changed man."

—

CASH'S COMMITMENT TO CHURCH had always waxed and waned. Often when he was on the road, he would creep into the back of a church on a Sunday morning, and when he was home in Tennessee he'd visit different churches in Hendersonville and Madison hoping to find somewhere that he felt comfortable. As someone with such a recognizable profile, he faced an added challenge. If word got out that he attended a particular church, songwriters and unsigned singers would interrupt his worship to hand him demo tapes.

As an adult he had always felt slightly uncomfortable with collective worship. By nature he enjoyed solitary activities—shooting, fishing, walking, reading, writing, climbing, observing—and he preferred equally solitary methods of worship. He enjoyed praying and meditating alone or reading the Bible and works of theology at home in his book-lined study, off the master bedroom. His great theological sparring partner was June's dad, Ezra "Eck" Carter, who similarly enjoyed studying the Bible alone and rarely went to church. As Cash once said, "I find my church in my heart, 'cause sometimes I just can't drag my body into one."

Cash had known Jimmy Snow since the mid-1950s when he was a performer on the same circuit as Elvis. The son of Hank Snow, Jimmy ended up with a recording deal with RCA, but his career derailed when his addiction to alcohol and amphetamines dropped his weight from 150 pounds to 117 pounds. In 1958, at the age of twenty-two, he underwent a Christian conversion, abandoned his show-business career, and became a full-time preacher for the Assembly of God. CBS filmed him preaching a fire-and-brimstone sermon against the evils of rock-'n'-roll and the clip is still used in documentaries to illustrate the Christian reaction to what many at the time considered to be "the devil's music."

Cash and Snow became reacquainted in 1969 when their paths crossed at

Saigon airport, and later, during the taping of the *Johnny Cash Show* at the Ryman Auditorium in Nashville, where Snow became a familiar figure backstage. By then he was the pastor of his own church, Evangel Temple, on Dickerson Road in Madison, and had a vision for making a Christian impact on the country music industry. One of his earliest musical recruits was Larry Lee, a songwriter signed to House of Cash. He later persuaded Cash's sister Joanne to join the choir. Because of Joanne, June's twelve-year-old daughter, Rosey, started to attend services at the church, and ultimately, so did June and then Cash.

The unimposing church impressed Cash with its unconditional love, joy, and unselfconscious worship. As a Pentecostal denomination, the Assembly of God emphasized the more demonstrative "spiritual gifts," such as physical healing, prophecy, visions, and speaking in tongues. It also stressed the importance of "holy living," discouraging too much close contact with "the world." A comparatively recent denomination, it was founded in Hot Springs, Arkansas, in 1914, and at one time counted Elvis Presley and Jerry Lee Lewis among its members.

Initially Cash felt uneasy about the differences between the Assembly of God and the Southern Baptists. June, raised in a Methodist church, had similar reservations. In the end, they realized they agreed more than they disagreed with the Assembly of God tenets. Snow came over to Cash's log cabin and prayed with him. "We knelt right there and prayed together," the preacher later said. "When we did, God's spirit met with us and confirmed the experience we had there. I could really feel God."

Snow convinced Cash he would benefit from making his commitment public. He did, at Evangel Temple on May 9, 1971, when Snow made an altar call after preaching a sermon on the responsibility of a father as the spiritual leader of a family. The text was Acts 16:31: "Believe on the Lord Jesus Christ and thou shalt be saved and thy house." As he had at age twelve, and more recently at First Baptist Church at age thirty-five, Cash knelt at the altar, declared that he was sorry for his sins, and promised to endeavor to live a life of obedience to the will of God. June knelt beside him. Later Snow said, "It is one thing for a public figure to join a church. It is another thing for him to humble himself enough to get down on his knees and crawl and cry in front of a congregation."

Cash became noticeably more diligent about his faith. Influenced by Assembly of God teachings that tend to divide activities into either "secular" or "sacred," he began to prioritize gospel promotion over art or entertainment. For a while, it seemed to him that his wealth and fame had been built on the "stubble" that would be burnt away on the Day of Judgment. What was the value of singing to people about trains and prisons, cotton fields and love gone wrong if they were perched on the edge of hell? Wasn't it an abuse of his power if he neglected to tell his audience about the way of salvation? "I don't have a career anymore," Cash announced. "What I have now is a ministry. Everything I have and everything I do is given completely to Jesus Christ now. I've lived all my life for the devil up until now, and from here on I'm going to live it for the Lord."

The most obvious manifestation of this new attitude was the film *Gospel Road,* a presentation of Christ's life through narration, song, and drama made for the big screen. He wanted to make it, Cash said, "because I think Jesus was the most misquoted, misread, and misunderstood man in history. People have twisted his words to suit their needs. People also died for him. They died for his words." It was an ambitious and not obviously commercial project, yet when Cash approached Robert Elfstrom (who had filmed *Johnny Cash: The Man, His World, His Music)* to direct it, he had no storyboard. Besides a working title *(In the Footsteps of Jesus),* all he had was the idea that he would visit locations in Israel connected with Christ's life and deliver lines to the camera in almost the same way that he had composed the *Holy Land* album. Relevant songs could later be interspersed. He also wanted to dramatize some of the more crucial biblical scenes. Perhaps most importantly, Cash planned to finance it himself—to the tune of seven hundred and fifty thousand dollars—in order that he could maintain complete artistic control.

"He felt it was payback time," says Elfstrom. "He had made a lot of money doing the TV series, and he wanted to use that money to make a film about something he really believed in. I don't think that the TV series made him that happy. It wasn't his cup of tea. What he liked was to do things the way that we made this film. It was his money and he liked to do things the way he wanted. He liked to do things impulsively. He wanted to roll the dice."

After two intense years working with shooting scripts, rehearsal schedules, and words written for him by other people, Cash wanted to take things as they came, believing that some creative good would emerge. Elfstrom, who went to Israel ahead of Cash with writer Larry Murray (who had worked on the *Johnny Cash Show),* says that the script they began shooting with had no more than eight pages. The actors they'd hired for the dramatic pieces were all untrained, and most of them had been recruited from the backpacking community in Tiberius. "We were winging it," says Elfstrom. "When we started he told me that we should just do a lot of shots of the feet of Jesus walking here and there. That was all he had. He thought you could take repeated shots of a pair of feet and put music on top."

A team of forty or so worked on the film in Israel throughout November 1971. They based themselves in Tiberius on the Sea of Galilee and shot many of the scenes in an abandoned Palestinian village close to Jericho. They also filmed in Nazareth, Samaria, near the Dead Sea, and in the Negev Desert. One sequence they filmed but never used captured Cash being baptized in the Jordan River by Jimmy Snow, who'd been invited to join the trip as the film's religious consultant.

Key roles were cast in a way more befitting a home movie than a feature film. June became Mary Magdalene, Johnny's sister Reba became Mary the mother of Christ, Jimmy Snow had a brief appearance as Pontius Pilate, and Larry Lee appeared as John the Baptist. They spent days looking at European and American backpackers who could pass for Jesus Christ but couldn't find a suitable candidate. "Then one day they just looked at me and said, Bob, why don't you do it?" says Elfstrom. "I had blond hair, I was a hippie, and that was it. All of a sudden I was directing the film, shooting it, and playing the role of Jesus!"

Cash had started recording the songs for the film with producer Larry Butler before he left the U.S. They continued to work on the songs and incidental music throughout the first half of 1972. Christopher Wren, a senior editor from *Look* magazine was researching Cash's biography *Winners Got Scars Too* at this time and, being an ex-folkie from New York, wrote the song "Jesus Was a Carpenter" while hanging out at the Cash house. "I was in the living room and there were guitars all over the place. I was fiddling with some chords and he asked me what I was doing. I told him I was writing a song and he said, 'Well, I'm going upstairs for a nap. If you've finished when I come down and I like what you've written, I'll record it.' He liked it and recorded it. I was surprised!" Another song Wren had already written, "Gospel Road," provided the title for the film. Cash rerecorded "He Turned the Water into Wine" and wrote "I See Men as Trees Walking" and "Praise the Lord" specifically for the project.

In the meantime, at the invitation of country star Connie Smith, Kris Kristofferson had paid a visit to Evangel Temple in 1971. During the service Snow asked a member of the congregation, aspiring singer Larry Gatlin (who was then working as a janitor for a local TV station), to perform a song he'd written about his dependence on God. The song was called "Help Me":

> I never thought I needed help before,
> I thought that I could get by, by myself,
> Now I know I just can't make it any more,
> With a humble heart, on bended knees,
> I'm begging you please, help me.[1]

For reasons he finds inexplicable even today, Kristofferson was so moved by the song that, against all rational judgment, he walked down the aisle in response to Jimmy Snow's altar call. "It was what I guess you would call a religious experience," he says. "I've never had one before or since. To this day I don't know why I did it. I think Jimmy sensed that I didn't know what I was doing because he asked me if I was ready to be saved and I told him that I didn't know. He put his hand on my shoulder and told me to get down on my knees. There were a number of us kneeling and I don't remember what he was saying. It was something about freedom from guilt. All I can remember is that I broke into tears. I was weeping and when it was over I felt like I'd been purged. I was carrying a lot of guilt at that time. I felt that I had disappointed my family, my friends, my ancestors, and everybody that knew me. So I wrote that song." The song he wrote later that day in the back of Connie Smith's car was "Why Me."

Early in 1972, Gatlin repeated his performance of "Help Me" at Evangel Temple when June was in the congregation. She loved the song so much that she scribbled Gatlin's name down on the back of a blank check and went home to tell Cash about this exciting new singer, Larry Gatlin. A few months later, in April, Cash attended a Sunday morning service, and Snow, presumably having noticed Cash's presence, again asked Gatlin to perform. "As I was putting up my guitar afterward in the pastor's study John walked in behind me," says Gatlin. "John Cash could walk in a room behind you and you'd know he was there. You could feel his presence. I turned around and he said, 'Er, son. I like that song, son. You know, we're making this movie about Jesus and tomorrow we're in the studio and I'd love for you to come over and help us. Can you do that?' I said, 'Mr. Cash. I just got fired from my job on Friday. I'll be there first thing Monday morning.'"

At CBS studios Cash viewed the partially edited film on a monitor and pointed out sequences that he felt needed music. He told Gatlin that he needed something to go over a scene of the Last Supper, so Gatlin went home and wrote "The Last Supper":

> Have a little bread Simon
> Give a little wine to James my brother
> Go ahead and eat boys
> And love one another.[2]

A week later they moved to the recently completed House of Cash Recording Studios in Hendersonville and cut "Help Me" and another Gatlin song, "Steps." "That was the start of one of the most meaningful and cherished relationships of my life," says Gatlin. "He put me on my first national TV show in New York. He took me to concerts. He wrote the sleeve notes for my first album. He launched my career."

The symbiosis between Cash, Kristofferson, and Gatlin went even further. Kristofferson recorded "Why Me" and the last track on side two of his new album, *Jesus Was a Capricorn*. As the last track on side one he sang "Help Me" with Gatlin. "I did it because I loved the song and was so grateful for the effect that it had on me," says Kristofferson. "To further demonstrate my gratitude, I put it on the B side of my single 'Why Me' instead of one of my own, giving Larry mechanical royalties on the biggest single I ever had. Payback!" Cash used Kristofferson's "Burden of Freedom," a song about personal responsibility that alluded to Christ's suffering, on the *Gospel Road* soundtrack and later recorded both "Why Me" and Gatlin's "Help Me."

Radical Christian groups who mixed countercultural style (long hair, rock festivals, communal living) with traditional biblical content emerged in the 1970s as a belated response to the cultural changes of the 1960s. They worshiped with rock music, adapted "hip" terminology, and often met in abandoned buildings rather than in churches. Like Johnny Cash, an influential number of what the media dubbed "Jesus Freaks" had experimented with drugs, sex, and alternative spiritual beliefs, and, significantly, they came to prominence just as the idealism of the 1960s was fading. The murders carried out by members of the Manson

Family showed what a dangerous cocktail hallucinogenic drugs, occultism, and half-digested Eastern mysticism could make. The death of an African American music fan at the hands of Hell's Angels guards at the Rolling Stones' Altamont concert illustrated the limits of freedom. The breakup of the Beatles proved that more than love was needed to stop people warring.

Though not directly inspired by what *TIME* magazine, in its cover story of June 21, 1971, called "The Jesus Revolution," *Gospel Road* did exemplify the new mood of openness in popular culture to the name and image of Jesus. Recent songs by John Lennon, James Taylor, Simon & Garfunkel, the Rolling Stones, and Eric Clapton had all referenced Jesus. Even a new genre of music known as Jesus Rock, with proponents like Larry Norman, Randy Matthews, and Love Song, emerged, harnessing the rhythm and beat of rock music to often explicitly Christian statements. And two rock musicals about the life of Jesus premiered that year on the American stage. *Godspell,* written by Stephen Schwarz and John Michael Tebelak, opened off-Broadway on May 17 and *Jesus Christ Superstar,* with words by Tim Rice and music by Andrew Lloyd-Webber, had its Broadway premiere on October 12.

Buoyed by this new fascination for Jesus, Campus Crusade for Christ, a conservative evangelical organization working with students, organized a week of teaching evangelism for eighty thousand young people in June 1972. Held in Dallas, Texas, Explo '72 attempted to make Christianity relevant to a generation that had grown up with rock music, student protests, ecological concerns, spiritual quests, and alternative states of consciousness. The week's culminating event was a massive outdoor concert for more than one hundred fifty thousand on an abandoned racetrack just outside the city. Billy Graham, a cosponsor of the week and the keynote speaker at the nine-hour show, referred to it as a "religious Woodstock," which was exactly how Campus Crusade wanted it to be perceived. They wanted the opportunity to prove that non-Christians didn't have the monopoly on "love, peace, and music."

Cash was by far the best-known performer on a bill made up of Jesus Rock artists whose records sold through churches and Christian bookstores and who were predominately unknown to readers of *Rolling Stone* or *Creem.* He in turn invited Kris Kristofferson and Rita Coolidge, thinking that it would be good for them to see the Christian crowd and for the Christian crowd to hear songs like "Why Me" and "Burden of Freedom." Dressed in black and overwhelmed by a stage set full of brightly colored Peter Max–style clouds, rainbows, and flowers,

Cash sang "I've Seen Men Like Trees Walking," "A Thing Called Love," and "Supper Time." Between songs he told the crowd, "I have tried drugs and a little of everything else, and there is nothing more soul satisfying than having the kingdom of God building inside you and growing." Kristofferson, who still couldn't make sense of his experience at Evangel Temple, felt decidedly uncomfortable performing his slim gospel repertoire in front of thousands of fresh-faced young people, knowing that his appearance would be interpreted as a public declaration of faith. "I was singing songs that I thought were spiritual, but people wanted to hear more songs specifically about Jesus," he says. "Eventually I had to tell John that I couldn't do these type of shows anymore. I felt like a hypocrite."

Cash however, continued to play at similar events. He went to London with Carl Perkins and the Tennessee Three to perform at Wembley Stadium for the closing concert of SPRE-E '73, a British version of Explo '72. He performed songs from *Gospel Road* ("the best album I've ever made"), and he told the thirty-thousand-strong crowd that in the past he'd given his "flesh to the devil and left only the bones to God." Billy Graham warned people that he feared Russia was about to attack China and that this would launch Armageddon. "I see no glimmer of hope in the scientific world," he said. "There is no place to hide. The whole world is a problem . . . Jesus Christ is the answer. There is no other."

Jimmy Snow started a gospel music version of the *Grand Ole Opry*. It took place late on a Friday night at the Ryman Auditorium after the regular Opry show and was called the *Grand Ole Gospel Hour.* There Kristofferson premiered "Why Me" and Larry Gatlin first performed "Help Me" outside of a church. Cash played there and at the All-Lutheran Youth Gathering in Houston. He played at the Youth for Christ Super Rally in Kansas City and at the Johnny Cash Country and Gospel Festival at Mount Pocono, Pennsylvania. He showed no reservations about being associated with mainstream American evangelicalism and was unconcerned that it might damage his career.

Besides appearing with Billy Graham, Cash performed for other evangelists like Oral Roberts, Tommy Barnett, and James Robison. A preacher's theological stripe didn't bother him at the time, as long as somewhere in their message they preached the gospel of salvation through Jesus Christ. He didn't appear to mind whether that gospel came wrapped in a prayer cloth, a charm, or a warning about the imminent end of the world. Cash would either brush aside the criticisms of those who thought that some high-profile evangelists were manipulative, insincere, dishonest, and greedy, or even suggest that their suspicions were demonically inspired. In a song titled "Billy and Rex and Oral and Bob" he celebrated the ministries not only of Billy Graham, Rex Humbard, Oral Roberts, and Bob Harrington, but the late Billy Sunday, James Robison, Kathryn Kuhlman, Garner Ted Armstrong, Tommy Barnett, Jimmy Snow, and Reverend Ike.

> Ordained for proclaiming the gospel of Jesus
> The great super preachers go crusading on
> And the people all gather in great congregations
> To hear of a Savior who came to atone.
> And they kneel at the altar and walk away happy
> Then the Devil starts gossip 'bout money and sex
> And making it hard on the good men of God
> Like Billy and Bob and Oral and Rex.

Cash's lack of discrimination later affected him when some of the individuals he supported were found guilty of the very sins their enemies had accused them of. Through his relatively newly opened eyes, all evangelists and all teachings bearing the Christian name had seemed equally valid. He had an almost childlike trust in preachers. "I really don't know too much about doctrine," he once confessed. "I just simply believe in God and Jesus." In *The Man in Black* he asked himself why televangelists were criticized and abused by so many and concluded that it was because they had "been to the top of the mountain. They had seen heaven a little clearer than I had. Maybe things had been revealed to them that don't get passed around freely to the rest of us. The wind of the spirit had blown through their minds."[3]

During a seven-night run in Las Vegas during 1972, a report surfaced that Cash was using his commercial concerts to evangelize. A religious news service quoted an Episcopal clergyman as saying that fifteen hundred people had responded to altar calls at the Hilton shows and that Cash had received a "wave of the Holy Spirit" during these times. Cash was forced to issue a disclaimer in which he said that he had undergone no spiritual experience and that there had been no altar calls, though he often closed the evenings with a gospel song during which members of the audience tended to rush to the stage.

His statement only made matters worse. Once published, he realized that it could have been interpreted as a denial of the presence of the Holy Spirit in his life. He wrote to his local newspaper, the *Tennessean,* in order to correct this impression:

> The headline stating "Johnny Cash Denies Baptism" is pretty strong language." You asked me if I had received the baptism of the Holy Spirit on stage in Las Vegas and if I gave an altar call. The answer was no—but I didn't mean that the Holy Spirit wasn't alive in me and guiding me.
>
> Months before that in Jimmy Snow's church I had received the baptism of the Holy Spirit, and that was the most beautiful feeling in my life—to feel that the Spirit of God had come to live in me. Several months following that I felt a strong indwelling of the Holy Spirit, like the time last November when I was baptized in the Jordan River. For a Christian to say that the Holy Spirit does not dwell in him is to deny he is a child of God, and I do not deny that I am a child of God. I am very eager to tell it.
>
> I feel the Holy Spirit dwells in me at all times. Sometimes it's like a grain of mustard seed, but it's there and at times, like when we sing those gospel songs, I think it does shine through me. That's what happened at Las Vegas and at most of our concerts recently. The people feel that special something, and they come down to the front to shake my hand. That's what happened in Las Vegas.[4]

Cash's marriage, the birth of John Carter Cash, the success of the TV series, and Cash's reignited Christian faith combined to make him a calmer, more respectable person. He was turning into that classical mythological figure, the hero who, through his own weakness, is dragged to the depths but who is rescued and comes back wiser and more powerful bearing a message for the world. Even though he was only in his early forties, Cash had the rugged features and the *gravitas* of a much older man, and his slow, swaggering walk had the imprint of the gunslinger arriving to sort out the troublemakers. His past brushes with the law and his battle with addiction only added to his authority. They gave him a slightly dangerous edge.

He now found himself invited into the most prestigious circles in American society. President Nixon asked him to perform at the White House in front of an audience of two hundred and fifty congressmen and other dignitaries. An aide asked him to include "Welfare Cadillac" in his set, not realizing that it wasn't a Cash song. When he introduced Cash, Nixon said, "I don't know how to describe Johnny Cash's music. I'm no expert on music. I found that out when I told him to sing 'Welfare Cadillac.' He owns a Cadillac, but I understand that Johnny isn't on welfare."

Cash played for an hour at the White House. At the end of his show he made some personal comments about the war in Vietnam. He didn't believe in war, he said, but he didn't think that anyone was going to get America out of Vietnam quicker than President Nixon. "We elected our man as president, and if you don't stand behind him, get . . . out of the way so that I can stand behind him. We pray that he can end this war in Vietnam sooner than he hopes, and all our boys will come back home, and there will be peace in the mountains and all of the valleys." Then, joined by the Carter Family and the Statler Brothers, he sang "Peace in the Valley." After a standing ovation, he came back and performed "Coming Home." According to reporters in attendance, he reduced some in the audience to tears.

The invitation to one of only four such events organized so far by the Nixon White House illustrated Cash's growing stature, and his comments on the war displayed a newly acquired gift for diplomacy. He simultaneously presented himself as thoroughly American, an outspoken supporter of the president, and a campaigner for peace. His refusal to sing "Welfare Cadillac"—not just because he hadn't written it, but because the song appeared to mock the poor—was widely reported and drew attention to his integrity. Here was a man who wouldn't compromise his art even for the holder of the highest office in the land.

Cash's friendship with Billy and Ruth Graham grew stronger, and this too helped to establish him in the pantheon of great living Americans in the eyes of the watching public. Graham, after all, had been meeting major world dignitaries since the 1950s, and though living a life of modesty and humility, had enjoyed unparalleled access to those in power. When Ruth, Billy, and their son Ned spent Christmas with the Cashes in 1974 in the aftermath of the Watergate crisis, Graham put a call through to the then-disgraced former president. After wishing him the best for Christmas, he handed the phone to Cash and forced him into a conversation.

Cash and Graham became close friends over the years, primarily maintaining their relationship through written correspondence. Their families would visit one another at the Cashes' home in Hendersonville, the Grahams' home in Montreat, or at the Cashes' vacation home in Jamaica. These times were important to both families in keeping their personal and spiritual lives refreshed.

Montreat, NC 28757
January 7, 1975

My dear Johnny and June,

Words are inadequate to express our appreciation for one of the most marvelous weeks of our lives. When we left, Ruth and I had tears in our eyes—not only of appreciation, but affection for the two fo you and your wonderful family. We have come to love you all as few people we have ever known. The fun we had, the delicious food we ate, the stimulating conversations, lying in the moonlight at night, the prayer meetings, the music we heard, etc. There has been running over and over in my mind "Matthew 24 is knocking at the door." I have a feeling this could be a big hit.

Please give our love to the staff and all those who made our stay so memorable, especially John Carter—who is one of the most remarkable little boys we have ever known.

With warmest affection,
Billy

GARDNER-WEBB COLLEGE, a small Baptist college in North Carolina, awarded Johnny an honorary doctorate in humanities. The citation, read by the chairman of the college's board of trustees, referred to him as "one of the princes of American country music" and conferred the doctorate for "his humanitarian activities on behalf of the humble and the poor, those who are the victims of drugs and alcohol, and the thousands locked behind prison walls." Accepting the award Cash said, "Anything legislative bodies of the world may do, with all their speeches, is not worth two cents unless you care for people."

Although he had performed for prisoners since 1957, the concept of Johnny Cash "the humanitarian" didn't develop until the 1970s when, in addition to his vocal concern for the welfare of prisoners, he committed random acts of generosity for the deserving poor and willingly spoke out about the dangers of addiction. Stories of his big-hearted gestures toward ordinary people found their way into the press, like the time he gave ten thousand dollars to a Nashville man in desperate need of a kidney machine, or the phone call he made to a twelve-year-old boy in Texas who had lost both his arms in a farming accident, or the five-thousand-dollar check he sent to the correction commissioner of Arkansas to "do something special for the prisoners."

With just a few steps, "Cash the humanitarian" became "Cash the great American." As early as 1972, committees set up to organize various celebrations for the bicentennial in 1976 recruited Cash. His statesmanlike qualities represented the best qualities of American life—not only was he a family man, a patriot, and a military veteran, but he'd overcome physical and spiritual hardship, rooted for the underdog, supported the president, and was a practicing Christian. The Spirit of America Festival gave him the Audie Murphy Patriotism award. In a 1969 review of a Madison Square Garden concert, the *New York Post* pop critic Al Aronowitz, made the prescient observation that Cash "was bringing the country to the city with an authority that nobody else possesses in this fragmented nation. Johnny Cash knew how to talk to prisoners and to presidents. He knew, as a matter of fact, how to talk to all America."

A naturally self-analytical man, Cash had long been interested in his identity as an American. His albums *True West, Bitter Tears* and *Blood, Sweat and Tears* examined the nature of America and her people. As a traveling musician he'd seen more of the American landscape than most and he loved it all: the woodlands of Tennessee, the mountains of Virginia, the arid desert of California and Nevada, the cotton fields of Mississippi. He pored over books of American history, collected presidential autographs, and loved to dig up the spent bullets of Civil War soldiers and the arrowheads of Indian hunters. "This is my country," he once said, "and I'm proud of every inch of its soil."

In 1974 he'd made the TV Special "Ridin' The Rails," which writer-producer Dyann Rivkin describes as being, "the story of the building of America as seen through the building of the railroad from 1880 up to the 1970s." The filming involved recreating many of the seminal moments in railroad history, allowing Cash to imaginatively enter his country's past.

Johnny Cash made a great American icon, especially since, as Stan Jacobson observed when producing the *Johnny Cash Show,* he had the ability to unite the generations. Older people appreciated his military service, his gospel songs, and the success story of the boy from the cotton fields of Depression-era Arkansas who rose to sing to the president. Young people identified with the way he challenged authority, his protest songs, his inner questing, and his plea for peace at the White House.

Cash never unconditionally approved of his country. When asked what made him the most proud of America, he said,

> Our freedoms were won at a very high cost and I think there's a lot to be said for a little flag waving in my country. You know, "God bless America." I think God has blessed America and I don't know how much longer he's gonna go on blessing it the way we're screwing it up by getting involved in everybody's little battle. But the family unit, the home, our freedoms, that's what's precious. Then the pioneer spirit of America that still prevails in a lot of the country is precious to me. The spaciousness of the country, I love the West, the American West.

In December 1970 he started work on a collection of songs about the most important events in American history. Originally, he planned to send a tape of them to the moon with astronaut Stu Roosa on the *Apollo 14* mission. He thought the songs would keep the astronauts' thoughts "down to earth" while they were in space. The tape never made it on the mission, and Cash didn't pick up the project until June 1972 when, after recording three additional songs, he released *America: A 200-Year Salute in Story and Song.*

The conventional and uncontroversial approach to American history highlighted Paul Revere, the Battle of New Orleans, the Alamo, the Gettysburg Address, the assassination of President Garfield, World War I, the advent of flight, and the Moon landing. Cash's narration filled in the historical gaps. The one note of rebellion was the inclusion of "Big Foot," the song that he'd written about Wounded Knee.

Shortly after its release, Saul Holiff retired as Cash's manager and Lou Robin replaced him. "Nobody could believe that anyone would voluntarily leave Johnny," says Holiff, "but I have the documentation to prove it. He had just come through being a superstar and he was still a star. He was in good shape. He'd quit smoking and had straightened himself up. He had a good marriage and he adored his son. However, I truly believed that it was going to be anticlimactic from then onward, and it was. For the next ten or twelve years he went into a tailspin until Columbia even reached the point where it dropped him."

There was another side to Holiff's departure. He'd made no secret of the fact that his ambition in life was to travel the world at someone else's expense, make a clear million dollars, and then retire at a relatively young age to raise a family and pursue his own interests. He was able to do all these things by 1973, and naturally his appetite for business waned. After leaving Cash, he returned to Canada and earned a degree in English literature.

However, Lou Robin, an economics graduate from Chicago, still had the hunger for deal-making and a vision for Cash's career. Robin worked for an aerospace company before becoming a concert promoter. He'd started with jazz concerts as a student, and during the 1960s went on to work with the biggest acts in the business, including the Beatles and the Rolling Stones. He first became involved with Cash in 1969 when, as part of the Agency for Performing Artists with Marty Klein, he organized some of the California shows, including the concert at San Quentin State Prison. And although he never signed a formal contract, Robin would remain Cash's manager to the end.

In some ways it was a difficult time for Robin to take the reins. As Holiff indicated, 1969 through 1972 were Cash's superstar years—where could his career go but down? The nature of Cash's new projects only compounded the sentiment. Though a worthy film, *Gospel Road* was unlikely to boost him into the Hollywood stratosphere. Now drug free, he was far easier to deal with and he was as diligent as ever on the road, but his music lacked its experimental edge. His songs all started to sound the same and sales were slumping. Not one single or album released between August 1972 and April 1976 made the pop charts.

Distressed with the sales slump, Columbia decided that he needed a firmer hand. Cash wanted to do another gospel album, but the company refused, unless he accepted their choice of material ("Amazing Grace," "Rock of Ages," "The Old Rugged Cross"). In return for permission to record a gospel album *(Johnny Cash Sings Precious Memories)*, Cash had to record a commercial album with Columbia's choice of producer, Gary Klein. Cash went along with the deal, although he later admitted that he had no feeling at all for the project (the album

John R. Cash). To add to the indignity, both albums bombed.

The Bicentennial couldn't have come at a better time for Cash. In 1976 he was ubiquitous. He started the year off by hosting an NBC special celebrating two hundred years of the American circus, receiving a coveted star on Hollywood Boulevard, being honored with a Homecoming Day in his birthplace of Kingsland, Arkansas, and performing a benefit for the Bicentennial Freedom Train. Finally, on July 4, as grand marshall in the Washington, D.C. parade, he held a concert in front of the Washington Monument, after which he rang a replica of the Liberty Bell two hundred times to the enthusiastic cheers of the crowd and was taken through the streets in a horse-drawn carriage.

Cash's single, "Sold out of Flagpoles" playfully celebrated the Bicentennial, but kept an eye on the forthcoming presidential election. The Vietnam War, followed by the Watergate scandal, had left people feeling cynical about politicians, and Cash caught the mood:

> "What this country needs," I said
> "Is someone everyone can trust,
> Someone everybody knows
> Will always keep his word or bust."
> "How about me and you," said Loney
> "Or the Lone Ranger, or Tonto, or Mickey Mouse, huh?
> And I'm sold out of flagpoles."

The album that produced this single, *One Piece at a Time*, produced by Charlie Bragg and Don Davis, was heralded as a return to form, and the title track was Cash's biggest hit in years. Written by Wayne Kemp, the comedic song describes an auto factory worker who systematically steals parts until he is finally able to create a new car. The downside is that the parts are all from different cars. One fan was so enamored of the song that he built a car based on the description in the lyrics and had it delivered to Cash in Hendersonville.

Despite languishing record sales, 1976 found Cash, in every other respect, a satisfied man. His marriage, family, and faith had provided a tranquil center to his life. He started spending more time in Montego Bay, Jamaica, where he'd come across an eighteenth-century plantation house. The mansion, 280 feet above sea level, captivated his imagination in the same way the house on Old Hickory Lake had just a few years before. Built in 1747 for Richard Barrett, great-grandfather of the British poet Elizabeth Barrett Browning, it had fallen into disrepair; but the owner, American businessman John Rollins, planned to refurbish it for his retirement. Cash eventually persuaded Rollins to part with it, and the Cinnamon Hill Great House became his second home.

"Johnny and June met my husband in Jamaica on their first trip, which was around 1972," says Michele Rollins. "When they came back they stayed in our guest house and then Johnny was thinking what he could do for John, who was going through one of his down cycles, and he concluded that the best thing he could do would be to buy something from him. They asked him if he would be willing to part with the house and John said, 'Absolutely.' They said, 'Are you sure? It's so old and so historic.' And my husband, who had been brought up as poor as Johnny on a farm in Georgia, said, 'I've been in old houses all my life. I'll never live in one again. I'm happy for you to buy it.' That was how Johnny and June came to have Cinnamon Hill Great House."

Nestled against the hills, surrounded by cinnamon and allspice trees and with a view over the ocean, the house became the Cash family's favored winter retreat and John and Michele Rollins two of their most trusted friends.

In September 1975, Cash and June had enrolled in an intensive Bible-study course with the Christian International School of Theology, earning sixty-eight semester hours of college credit. Sixteen units covered a survey of the Bible, the Gospels, the tabernacle, and the life and teachings of the apostle Paul. The college president, Dr. Bill Hamon, remembers Cash as a straight-A student who read well beyond the requirements. "I personally graded several of his courses," says Hamon. "I was amazed at his grasp of spiritual truth. I couldn't tell the difference between his work and that of some of the outstanding ministers we had. He had a good biblical knowledge."

In May 1977, Hamon flew to Nashville and presented Cash with his associate of theology degree in a ceremony at the House of Cash. Cash gave a brief account of his conversion and performed a gospel song. Shortly afterward he approached Hamon to ask whether he could be ordained as a minister. "Johnny was going to Israel," Hamon says. "He wanted to baptize some people in the Jordan, and so we ordained him so that he would feel free to do it. A lot of people don't realize that he was really spiritual and that his spirituality and his life in Jesus Christ meant so much to him. People don't bring out that part of his life." Cash also used his new status as an ordained minister to conduct the weddings of a few close friends.

Some people who'd known bad-boy Cash in his carousing days found the new religious, family-man version hard to take, preferring the irreverent, dangerous, and unpredictable man to the level-headed, abstemious one. "They'd rather I be in prison than in church," he admitted. They didn't like the fact that Cash no longer kept alcohol in his home, voiced disapproval of sex outside of marriage, and was on intimate terms with the political and religious establishment. These people felt slightly awkward because they no longer knew how to behave around him. Waylon Jennings commented to writer Peter Guralnick that Cash had "sold out to religion." The politically motivated folk singer Phil Ochs, who'd met Cash during his days hanging out in Greenwich Village, said, "He used to write a lot of good songs before he started hanging out with the wrong company there at the White House. . . . He was once one of the greatest living Americans. He now stands as proof that television can kill."

By being a Christian in show business, Cash was performing a difficult balancing act, and there were few good examples for him to follow. He would be attacked by agnostics and atheists if he appeared too pious. He would be denounced by the religious community if he appeared too worldly. "There are times that I want to go off into the woods and cry, because what I feel is too big a load for me to carry," he once admitted. "We're only called to be Christians, and I don't feel any special calling, but I seem to have been given much by God. And much seems to be required of me."

10

The Beast in Me

T HE FIRST SIGNS OF A DISTURBANCE in Cash's otherwise placid new life came when he stopped attending Evangel Temple in 1977. The reasons he left are unclear, but he continued to grow uneasy with the way his celebrity status affected the church. Tourists came by to catch a glimpse of him and the church had to post signs forbidding photography inside the building. "We even had one guy who went to the altar to become a Christian," says Jimmy Snow. "John came up and knelt down and was actually praying with the man when the guy turned round and started to pitch him some songs. I couldn't believe it! John handled it very well."

Now that he was ordained, Cash thought that the solution was to start his own church meeting at the House of Cash, but after a few months he faced similar problems there. "People came in flashing cameras," says Dr. Bill Hamon. "He felt so grieved because he thought it was dishonoring to God. He had a hard time going to any church without people taking advantage of him, so he closed the services down."

After that he attended Hendersonville Church of God, pastored by John Cobaugh, who baptized John Carter Cash in the Jordan River when he was nine. Cobaugh also baptized Cash in the river that day, which was his third baptism. But

163

his attendance there came to an end after about a year and a half, and he found himself again without a spiritual home.

Although he struggled to remain involved in church, the discipline had helped stabilize his spiritual life. Belonging to a group and being accountable to a minister kept a check on his excesses, whereas solitary meditation in the woods involved no such responsibility. Organized Bible study at church was thorough and systematic rather than cursory and random. He acknowledged this when he was at Evangel Temple, saying, "My policy of aloneness and severed fellowship from other committed Christians would weaken me spiritually. . . . Jesus never meant for us to try and make it on our own. Missing it would leave me vulnerable and easy prey for all the temptations and destructive vices that the backstage of the entertainment world has to offer."

In his second autobiography Cash remembered the early 1980s as the start of his drug relapse, but Marshall Grant says it began earlier, coinciding with the cooling of this intense evangelical period. Besides slowing record sales, there didn't appear to be any obvious triggers. He just started to scrounge pills from musicians he met on the road and was soon just as addicted as he had been in the mid-1960s. "If anything, it was twice as bad after he got back on in the late 1970s," says Marshall. "He would have been dead on more than one occasion if I hadn't have found him."

Oddly enough, as this new decline set in, Cash developed a passion to write about the apostle Paul. His final course at Christian International School of Theology on the life of Paul had captured his imagination. Undoubtedly he saw himself in the story of this passionate Jew who persecuted Christians before undergoing a profound spiritual transformation while traveling the road to Damascus.

Initially Cash envisioned a film, *The Reborn Man,* and then that idea changed into an idea for a novel, *The Gospel Ship.* Describing the apostle to *Country Music People,* he said Paul was "a man who suffered and hurt, but who was also highly spiritual. A man who had the strength of body and the power of will to overcome every obstacle in his path in order to accomplish his desired mission. He was always looking for new ground to cover and new places to go."[1] It sounded uncannily like a description of Johnny Cash.

Ironically, just as he began to explore the life of the man who recorded New Testament theology, Cash was almost always too stoned to put his own ideas on paper in a cohesive way. He read books, studied the Bible, and he even sought the wisdom of Bible scholars and the knowledge of historians, but he couldn't focus his mind long enough to create a narrative flow. Embarrassingly for Cash, Billy Graham would sometimes announce from the podium in front of mass audiences that his good friend Johnny Cash was writing a book about the apostle Paul and that he expected it to be one of the best books on the apostle.

On August 16, 1977, Elvis Presley died of a heart attack at his home in Memphis. At forty-two, he was only three years younger than Cash. His bloodstream contained a cocktail of eleven drugs. Hearing of the death, Cash issued a formal statement:

> June and I loved and admired Elvis Presley. We join his family, friends, and loved ones in mourning his death. He was the King of us all in country, rock, folk, and rhythm and blues. I never knew an entertainer who had his personal magnetism and charisma. The women loved him and the men couldn't help watching him. His presence filled every room he walked in. He, of course, will never be forgotten, and his influence will always be felt and reflected in the music world.

For someone whose career had started alongside that of Elvis's and who had shared a manager, producer, friends, dressing rooms, and stages with him, Cash seemed oddly detached. According to Marshall Grant, this was partly due to the fact that Cash was back on the pills himself and incapable of deep emotional feelings.

It was also partly due to the fact that the two men had never had a close friendship. They last met in Hollywood in May 1960 when Elvis was filming *GI Blues* on the Paramount lot and Cash was living in Encino. Richard McGibony (the songwriter friend who put up Cash's bond when he was arrested in Lafayette, Georgia), recalls Elvis being in Nashville in the 1970s and wanting to see the house on Old Hickory Lake, but Cash deliberately avoided him. "He just took off with me," he says. "He told me that Elvis and his goons were coming over but that he didn't want a whole lot of people hanging around."

The rivalry that had started in 1954, when Elvis cut his first record with Sun, had continued through the years. Freddie Bienstock managed the music publishing company Hill and Range. Not only did the company have a British publishing deal with Cash, but Beinstock also collected songs for Elvis Presley, whose companies Elvis Presley Music and Gladys Music were held by Hill and Range. The one thing that Bienstock recalls about his many meetings with Cash is his curiosity about Elvis and his success. "I think that to some extent he resented my relationship with Elvis," he says. "Even though Johnny wrote most of his own songs, he always thought I was giving the best songs to Elvis."

Drugs dulled Cash's conscience—he engaged in his most excessive behavior only when drunk or high. When asked to explain his fall from grace in the 1970s after telling the world that he'd cleaned up, he said, "I never lost my faith during that time but I lost my contact with God because anyone on drugs or alcohol chronically [sic] becomes very selfish. You don't think about anyone else. You think about yourself and where your next stash is coming from or your next drink. I wasted a lot of time and energy. I mean, we're not talking just days but months and years."

In the summer of 1978 Mother Maybelle's health deteriorated sharply. She had problems with her thyroid, circulation, and bladder, and the doctors predicted that she wouldn't outlive the year. They were right. She went to bed on the night of October 22, after playing a game of bingo and watching a rerun of Bonanza on TV, and didn't wake up. Cash had lost not only his mother-in-law and musical colleague, but his fishing buddy and one of his most dear friends. Three months later she was followed in death by Sara Carter, the last living member of the original Carter Family, thus closing a great chapter in the history of American music.

In December 1978 he and June took part in the "Billy Graham Christmas Special" and in March and June of 1979 he appeared at Billy Graham crusades in Tampa and Nashville. In December 1979, he released the gospel double-album *A Believer Sings the Truth*, which contained the last recordings he'd done with Jan Howard.

Columbia chose to celebrate Cash's silver show-business anniversary in 1979, although it had actually been only twenty-four years since his first release on Sun. His recording career was clearly flagging, and his music had become formulaic and uninspiring. He'd made his name with the boom-chicka-boom sound and seemed afraid to move too far from it lest he lose his distinction. Columbia decided to put him in the studio with Brian Ahern, a Canadian producer who had built his reputation working with Emmylou Harris and who had a sharp ear for delicate sounds.

The resulting album, *Silver*, turned out to be one of Cash's better recordings. His voice had a fresh clarity, and there was a vibrant quality to Ahern's instrumentation. In addition to the familiar guitars, bass, and drums, there were flourishes of fiddle, banjo, trumpet, and even flugelhorn.

Silver was the last Cash album that featured Marshall Grant. By early 1980 he'd been fired from the band that he'd helped form in 1954 as a twenty-six-year-old mechanic. Though Cash fired off the bitter letter that formally terminated the partnership, Marshall shared the feeling that things were at an inevitable end.

Cash had his reasons for releasing Marshall. Wanting to grow musically, he thought that Marshall's style of playing was restrictive. He also decided that Marshall had become too controlling. He became suspicious that Marshall was not acting solely in Cash's best interests, and had become alarmed by the power Marshall wielded, taking on the responsibilities of a tour manager.

As he slipped back into his drug habit, Cash probably also resented Marshall's attempts to restrict his pill-popping. Marshall had absolute disdain for drug abuse and little sympathy for those who partook. For him it was a simple question of restraint. "There was no excuse for it," he says. "I'm seventy-five years old and I've never tasted a drop of alcohol. I've been in the business fifty years and that's the proof that you can do it if you have the fortitude. If you want to make something of yourself and come back to your family then that's what you've got to do. It's a matter of self-control. That's all it is. That applies to everybody."

Earl Poole Ball recalls the incident that he believes finally severed the relationship between Cash and Marshall. "They were all on the tour bus and Johnny was studying a map to find the place that we were going," he says. "Marshall then grabbed the map and said, 'Here. Let me show you where it is,' and I think that was just the topper on whatever else was going on. I think Johnny felt that he was losing control of his organization. Sometimes people have known each other for so long that they just can't sit down together and talk things out."

From Marshall's point of view, Cash needed controlling. Marshall believed that he and June were the only people totally committed to saving Cash from himself, and that because they frequently had to step between Cash and the object of his selfish desires, they took the brunt of his venom. In many ways the men were diametric opposites—Cash being ruled by instinct and Marshall by reason. "He was at his worst at that time, even though they tell me that after I left the show he got even wilder," says Marshall. "June couldn't do anything with him and no one else cared."

The formal end for Marshall came by letter via Cash's sister Reba. Ironically, it arrived at Marshall's home in Mississippi just as Marshall and his wife returned from buying Cash his silver anniversary gift. The cold dismissal angered Marshall and triggered an exchange of letters. "I got a rude letter from him," he says. "In fact, I got a lot of 'em. But I sent him a couple too. It was an unfortunate situation."

In June 1981, Marshall filed a $2.6 million lawsuit in federal court, charging Cash with breach of contract and slander. The pivotal breach of contract allegation centered on a claim that Cash had promised Marshall one hundred thousand dollars per year for the rest of his working life. The slander charges emerged from statements supposedly contained within the letters. Near the same time, in a separate suit, three relatives of Luther Perkins asserted that his estate had not received its full share of royalties.

Cash's lawyer at that time, James Neal, the famed Watergate prosecutor, responded to Marshall's suit by arguing that a partnership never existed and that Marshall had been fired because he wasn't willing to learn songs or attend rehearsals. All that Grant will say of the matter now is that some of the news reports were inaccurate and that toward the end of Cash's life the two of them were reconciled. The case was settled out of court.

Marshall also sought to have Cash barred from using the names "Johnny Cash and the Tennessee Two" or "Johnny Cash and the Tennessee Three" because he considered himself an essential part of both bands. Whether in response to Marshall's action or not, Cash reformed his band, adding guitarist Marty Stuart, bassist Joe Allen, and trumpeters Jack Hale Jr. and Bob Lewin. He named it Johnny Cash and the Great Eighties Eight. He was ready to expand the basic sound identified with his music.

In the midst of all these troubles, Cash was elected into the Country Music Hall of Fame, receiving his award from Kenny Rogers on October 13, 1980. In his acceptance speech, he thanked his mother for her faith in him and encouraged younger artists not to "get caught in a bag" but to do things their own way. He added a warning that he hoped that he would provide them with competition for some years to come. At the age of forty-eight he was the youngest person ever to be elected to the Country Music Hall of Fame.

Throughout the early 1980s, Cash flailed around in search of a new musical direction, seemingly unsure of where to land. He tried a back-to-basics approach with Earl Poole Ball as producer on *Rockabilly Blues,* but although the album received critical acclaim, it flopped commercially. "We had a lot of good songs," says Ball. "I thought that it was one of his better albums, but Columbia didn't get behind any of the three singles."

Cash then tried his other traditional approach—an album of Christmas carols embellished with an orchestra and chorus—before trying his luck with veteran Nashville producer Billy Sherrill, who'd had great success sweetening up country music for the pop market with hits like Tammy Wynette's "Stand By Your Man" and Charlie Rich's "The Most Beautiful Girl." The resulting album, *The Baron*, was disappointing, and Cash regretted being pushed into recording such unsuitable material. He didn't have a hand in writing any of the songs, although Sherrill cowrote the title track and one other. "Sometimes you go in a direction that your producer convinces you that you need at the time," said Cash. "I listened to too many of those people. I know what I want when I get in the studio and I let too many people tell me otherwise."

Even while recording with Sherrill, Cash continued to cut tracks with Jack Clement, his long-trusted friend who'd supported him at so many other difficult junctures in his career. Cash remained virtually absent as a songwriter, coauthoring only one song. In retrospect, Clement believes that he overproduced *The Adventures of Johnny Cash*. "I put way too much echo on," he says. "I just love putting echo on Johnny Cash sessions, because it didn't matter how many instruments you put in there, his voice would still boom out. We used to call him Captain Decibel."

Although he'd always studiously avoided hijacking the latest musical trend, Cash had always been open to new ideas, never forgetting that in 1954 as the new boy on the block, his style had been discarded as too simplistic by traditionalists of the time. His daughter Rosanne, who'd moved to Nashville after graduating from high school in 1973 and joined the *Johnny Cash Show*, was by 1981 an accomplished recording artist. Her album *Seven Year Ache* produced by her husband at the time, Rodney Crowell, had gone gold. June's daughter Carlene, who'd also been part of the show, moved to London and married British musician Nick Lowe, who later produced her albums *Musical Shapes* and *Blue Nun*.

Through Rosanne and Carlene, Cash met a generation of musicians in the vanguard of the postpunk era, musicians who'd taken advantage of the spring-cleaning effect punk had to experiment with less obviously commercial forms of music. Nick Lowe played a crucial role in what, for convenience, became known as New Wave music. He cofounded Stiff Records, produced Elvis Costello's first five albums, wrote "What's So Funny 'Bout (Peace, Love and Understanding)" and with Dave Edmunds formed the band Rockpile. On one of his visits to Carlene in London, Cash cut a version of George Jones's "We Oughta Be Ashamed" with Costello (discovered in Cash's tape vault after his death and due to be released by Costello in 2004) and Nick Lowe's song "Without Love."

"I think he was always interested in what was happening at the younger end of the market," says Rosanne. "He always loved being around young people. He said he learned more from nineteen-year-olds than people his own age. I'm sure that when I started having success that was a catalyst for him."

Toward the end of 1981, Cash faced two setbacks. In September, while walking through the animal park he'd created across the street from his lakeside home, he was attacked by an ostrich he'd named Waldo. Apparently the ostrich had recently lost his mate in the cold weather, and when the bird became aggressive, Cash attempted to ward him off with a long stick. Thinking he was being attacked, Waldo struck out with one of his feet and caught Cash on the right side of his stomach, cutting the skin open above his leather belt and breaking two ribs. As he fell, Cash landed on a rock and broke three more ribs.

He went to the hospital but kept the incident quiet, mostly to avoid the embarrassment of having been floored by a big bird. Though the idea of the broad-shouldered Man in Black being kicked into submission by an irate ostrich could have been the theme of a novelty song that Jack Clement might have written for *Everybody Loves a Nut,* the accident had serious and long-lasting consequences. Cash began taking painkillers and gradually, over the months, upped his dose until he was hooked. As he once explained it, "The label says one tablet every four hours but you eventually find you're taking four tablets every one hour."

Then Cash went to Cinnamon Hill for the Christmas holidays. On December 21, just as he and June sat down to dinner with their guests (his sister Reba and her husband Chuck, friend Ray Fremmer, John Carter, and his friend Doug Caldwell), three men with stockings over their heads burst through the open doors and demanded all their money and valuables. One carried a machete, one a knife, and the third a gun. They initially demanded one million dollars and said, if they didn't get it, they'd kill one of the family members. For four terrifying hours the thieves held them hostage, forcing them to lie on the floor. While two men guarded the group, the third escorted each of them, in turn, around the estate, demanding an inventory of the property most worth stealing. Finally the thieves bundled them into a basement storage area and escaped in June's Land Rover with an estimated fifty thousand dollars in haul.

They freed themselves from the room by battering down the two-inch-thick mahogany door with a coat tree and summoned the police. Almost immediately, the authorities caught two of the men trying to board a plane to Miami at Donald Sangster International Airport. They apprehended the third suspect in Jamaica on January 5, but he was killed while resisting arrest. The two men who were jailed later died trying to escape. A rumor circulated that authorities allowed the escape to facilitate a speedy but legal solution to the potentially embarrassing situation for the Jamaican government. Prime Minister Edward Seaga apologized personally to Cash for the ordeal.

The experience shook Cash, especially because the gunman had selected eleven-year-old John Carter as his intended murder victim. He'd remained extraordinarily calm though, and his lack of panic probably ensured their safety. Their homecoming must have been particularly joyous when they returned to Nashville on January 9 for a ceremony renaming a five-mile stretch of Gallatin Road (between Drake's Creek Lane and Shute's Lane) Johnny Cash Parkway.

In 1983 Cash returned to producer Brian Ahern, who tried to revitalize his sound by bringing him out to Hollywood to record with some of the city's top session musicians, including drummer Hal Blaine, guitarist James Burton, bass player Jerry Scheff, and fiddle player David Mansfield. The title track, "Johnny 99," and the opening track, "Highway Patrolman," both came from Bruce Springsteen's recently released, stripped-down recording *Nebraska*, which, ironically enough, had been written by Springsteen after repeated listens to Cash's early Sun recordings.

Springsteen, a longtime Cash fan, also wrote about blue-collar life, social entrapment, and the need for redemption. "I think Springsteen says it better than any of us did," Cash said.

> He's the master of these kinds of songs. He's such a prolific writer. I guess youth has got a lot to do with it. When I was in my twenties and thirties I was writing more. It's not that I don't have the inspiration, it's just that when I write something I'm more thorough than I ever was. They take me

longer to finish. In the fifties I would leave them exactly as they came to me, but now I'm aware of the competition of writers like Bruce and so I work on every line until they're to my total satisfaction. I want my songs to be as good as theirs.

There was something ironic about Cash, the great innovator, trying to emulate the work of artists who'd originally been inspired by him. Cash's own writing barely came through on his recordings. Of the five albums from *Silver* to *Johnny 99,* he'd contributed only seven songs and increasingly relied on the work of younger songwriters like Tom T. Hall, Rodney Crowell, and Billy Joe Shaver.

He still hadn't abandoned his acting ambitions. In 1981 he'd received a lot of critical acclaim for his role in the CBS-TV movie *The Pride of Jessi Hallam,* which focused on the problem of adult illiteracy. In 1988 he appeared in *Murder in Coweta County,* a made-for-TV movie based on a true story about a sheriff who attempts to bring a corrupt Georgia land baron to justice. Cash had spent seven years trying to get a network interested in filming this story.

On November 10, 1983, while in Nottingham for the tenth stop on a twelve-show European tour, Cash began hallucinating from the combination of drugs and alcohol. Back in his hotel room with June, he became convinced that the wooden wall panels concealed a pull-down bed. June told him not to be ridiculous, but Cash was so sure of what he saw that he began repeatedly punching the wall, because the "bed" wouldn't budge.

He hit the wall with such force that he cut his hand. It became so swollen and infected that, by the time he returned to Nashville three days later, he required surgery. Checking into Baptist Hospital for the operation, he learned that he had a much more serious condition—he was suffering from internal bleeding and needed his duodenum and part of his spleen, stomach, and intestines removed.

Although he'd packed his own stash of Valium and Percodan, these pills became unnecessary once doctors prescribed morphine. Besides relieving his pain, the drug gave him intense hallucinations. He began imagining the hospital as a gigantic plane taking off, circling through the air, and landing. At times he'd react so violently to his imagined flight that he'd flail his arms and knock down the poles holding the IV drips.

Meanwhile, those closest to Cash used the opportunity to make plans to admit him to the Betty Ford Center. A doctor from the center flew to Nashville to facilitate an intervention. In his private hospital room, his inner circle attempted to show him, in the clearest terms possible, the effect his selfish behavior was having on those he loved and who loved him. His wife, mother, and children all participated, each having written out a specific example of how his drugs had affected them.

"We had to tell him how he was hurting us," says Rosanne. "We told him that it was making him seem distant from us. We told him that we couldn't connect with him when he was in a state like that, that we didn't like the way his personality had changed, and that we all worried about his health and were afraid that he was going to die." John Carter told him how humiliated he had felt when he brought a friend home and his dad was stoned.

The challenging session concluded with a simple statement from the doctor: "We all want you to go to the Betty Ford Center." Cash was humbled. He knew that the statements they'd read to him weren't written out of vengeance but out of love and concern. He agreed to go. "It was pretty heavy," says Rosanne, "but he just sat there and nodded."

Treatment at the Betty Ford Center in Rancho Mirage, California, close to Palm Springs, is based on a Twelve Step philosophy. After a complete medical and psychosocial assessment, doctors and patient devise an individualized plan. Patients live in a dormitory and receive no privileges, regardless of their status in society. Celebrity or not, Cash had to make his own bed and vacuum his own room. When he and fellow guest Elizabeth Taylor planned a New Year's Day party complete with ordered-in delicacies, the head of the center stepped in and banned it. "Neither of them was used to having anyone tell them what they could or couldn't do," says Lou Robin's wife, Karen, who visited Cash during his stay. "But they got through it. June was surprised that Johnny acquiesced so quickly."

The Twelve Step philosophy requires that addicts acknowledge that they cannot control their own lives without recognizing "the Power greater than ourselves." The Betty Ford Center distinguishes this "spiritual" approach from a "religious" cure. The center's literature emphasizes, "Particular religions, while honored, are separate from the treatment experience, and no specific religion is promoted." When it refers to "God" the philosophy is quick to add "as we understand him."

For Cash, who naturally interpreted the Twelve Steps within a Judeo-Christian framework, nothing clashed with his convictions. The first step forced him to admit his powerlessness over his addiction. The second step, accepting that the "Power" could restore him, led naturally to the third step, in which he had to commit to turning his life over to the "Power." The program sounded as familiar as the voice of Hal Gallop back in Dyess or Jimmy Snow in Madison. He thought he'd learned this lesson in Nickajack Cave the day he'd wanted to end it all.

The fourth step required him to take a moral inventory before he could, as the fifth step, admit to himself and one other person the nature of his wrongs. By the sixth step he had to be ready to have these defects (or sins, as he would have seen them) removed, and by the seventh, he had to ask the "Power" to do so. So far it was almost like an altar call.

The eighth step involved listing everyone he'd harmed and being willing to make amends. Actually making those amends completed the ninth step. For the tenth step he had to take another personal inventory and admit any further wrongs and for the eleventh step he had to solidify his bond with the "Power" for guidance and strength. Finally, he had to apply these principles to every area of his life and seek to carry the message to others in the same situation.

He stayed at the Betty Ford Center for forty-three days. After three weeks, he found himself coming alive and enjoying the journey of self-discovery. During Family Week he was joined by June, John Carter, manager Lou Robin, and agent Marty Klein, who sat in on sessions in order to monitor progress. "We had to go through all the procedures that they were doing over five days," says Robin. "In some of those sessions people laid their souls so bare it was embarrassing. The idea was that they would get up in front of the public and talk about themselves. It was a big step."

Lou Robin picked up Cash from the center upon his release and took him straight to a hotel restaurant in Palm Springs, where they were joined by Gene Autry. Cash had lost weight, looked more fit than he had in years, and had all the zealousness of a convert to a new way of life. After reuniting with June in L.A., he played a concert that night with Waylon Jennings at the Universal Amphitheater and afterward tried to persuade Jennings to give up his cocaine habit. "I just want you to see my bright, brown eyes to show you what can happen," he told him. "If you ever want help, I know what to tell you to do."

John Carter Cash and Johnny Cash at the House of Cash Studio in 1974

Cash on Old Hickory Lake, Hendersonville, Tennessee

Johnny and June at London Airport, May 1968

Performing at the premiere of The Johnny Cash Show, taped May 1, 1969

Johnny and June in New York recording studio, 1975

Johnny Cash with his kids at Bon Aqua, July 4, 1975. Left to right: John Carter, godson Tony Bisceglea, friend Chris Brock, Cindy, Rosanne, Johnny, grandson Thomas Coggins, Tara, and Kathy.

Johnny Cash cheers up a young child at the Hadassah Medical Center in Jerusalem, 1977

John Carter, Johnny, and June Carter Cash at the dedication of a star honoring him
in the Hollywood Walk of Fame on March 10, 1976

Johnny Cash adored mother-in-law, "Mother Maybelle" Carter. This photo captures a moment of tenderness at the 50th Anniversary celebration of Carter Family recordings at the Carter Fold, August 4, 1977.

Pastor John Cobaugh baptizes Cash in the Jordan River in 1979

Ray and Carrie Cash, parents of Johnny Cash

Johnny Cash on a tour bus in Europe, 1981

Copyright © Laura Cash
Anna Maybelle and Joseph Cash

Copyright © Laura Cash
The Cash Cabin Studio

Courtesy of House of Cash
Cash and June talk backstage

Copyright © Laura Cash
Dustin Tittle

Copyright © Anne Goetze
June Carter Cash and Laura Cash

Courtesy of John Carter Cash
The Carter family at Mexican border radio station XERA. Clockwise: AP, Janette, Announcer "Brother Bill," Sara, Maybelle, June, Anita, and Helen Carter

Courtesy of House of Cash
Jack Cash

Copyright © Laura Cash
John Carter Cash with his dad in the studio

Courtesy of Cindy Panetta
Eddie Panetta and Cindy Cash Panetta

Courtesy of Cindy Panetta
Cindy Cash Panetta and daughter
Jessica Brock

Courtesy of John Carter Cash
John Carter, Laura, and
Anna Maybelle Cash at
Cinnamon Hill in Jamaica

Copyright © Martyn Atkins
June Carter Cash
in the studio during
The Man Comes Around
recording session

Copyright © Tara Schwoebel
Carlene Carter's daughter
Tiffany Lowe and grand-
daughter Luna Kai Darling

Copyright © Laura Cash
Johnny Cash with granddaughter
Anna Maybelle Cash, in Maces
Springs, VA on June 23, 2003

Courtesy of Lou Robin
Manager Lou Robin, Cash, and
Karen Robin, at Johnny's sobriety
anniversary party—with a '50s
theme

Courtesy of John Carter Cash
Ray and Carrie Cash's 50th Anniversary
—August 20, 1970. (From left: Louise, Roy,
Carrie, Ray, Tommy, Johnny, Joanne and Reba)

Copyright © Laura Cash
Carlene Carter's son Jackson Routh
with wife Emily and daughter Anni

Kris Kristofferson, Johnny Cash, Willie Nelson, Hank Williams Jr., and Waylon Jennings
at a six-month sobriety celebration for Cash at Jennings' home, July 1984

Cash talks on the phone from his truck
in the early 1980s

The sign outside of the House of Cash,
early 1980s

Johnny and June Carter Cash, Billy and Ruth Bell Graham

Johnny Cash and Billy Graham
at a Billy Graham Crusade in Denver, Colorado, in 1988

June Carter Cash
New York City, 1988

Cinnamon Hill, Jamaica, January 1999

Tom Petty, Cash, Rick Rubin, and Marty Stuart
in the studio for the American Recordings

Copyright © Laura Cash

Johnny & June's last portrait together, taken at his private office at home, March 2003

I'll be Satisfied

When I am dead, If men can say,
"He Helped the world upon its way,"
If they can say, If they but can,
"He did his best. He played the man,
His way was straight, His soul was clean
His life was not unkind or mean
He always did his best, and tried,
To help men," I'll be satisfied

unknown
Author

Courtesy of House of Cash

Handwritten by J.R. Cash in the late 1940s

According to Karen Robin, the new Johnny Cash took some getting used to. "Johnny and June had to work on their marriage after he came back from Betty Ford," she says. "He wanted her to be totally accepting of him right away, and she had to tell him to hold back because she wasn't used to him being like this—so sober and lucid all the time and so excited by what he had learned. I think at first she didn't trust him to have changed so totally, but then she realized that he really had turned a corner. It was quite wonderful."

11

Riding the Highway

EVERY YEAR SINCE 1976, Cash hosted a Christmas special for TV. The first one, "Johnny Cash at Home," featured various sites around Hendersonville, including the House of Cash and his farm, Bon Aqua. Guests included Roy Clark, Tony Orlando, Merle Travis, Barbara Mandrell, and Billy Graham. Subsequent specials were filmed either at studios or partly on location: Israel (1977), Scotland (1981), and Memphis (1982).

In 1984 the special aired from Switzerland, where Cash ended a ten-date tour in Europe. His special guests, Waylon Jennings, Willie Nelson, Kris Kristofferson, Toni Wine, Connie Nelson, and Jessi Colter, flew in and stayed at the Montreux Palace Hotel on Lake Geneva. At the press conference, the inevitable question was asked: why a Christmas special from Montreux? What was the significance? "Because this is where the baby Jesus was born," deadpanned Waylon.

The special in Montreux laid the groundwork for a country music supergroup made up of Cash, Kris Kristofferson, Willie Nelson, and Waylon Jennings later known as the Highwaymen. The music producer for the TV show, Chips Moman, had, in October, begun recording an album with Cash in Nashville. "We were passing the guitar around, and John asked Willie why he'd made duet records with everyone in the business but him and suggested that they should do one," says Kristofferson. "Willie said that, if that happened, I should be there to pitch songs because, although Willie wasn't wild about my voice, he loved my songs."

The idea of the country supergroup may have come and gone had Cash not recorded Willie's song "They're All the Same" three weeks after returning to the States. The next day he cut Kristofferson's "Here Comes That Rainbow Again." While still at Moman's Nashville studio, Willie and Kristofferson, on the spur of the moment, called in Waylon to cut some tracks with them. Backing them were some of Nashville's most experienced session musicians, including keyboard player Bobby Emmons and guitarist Reggie Young. Before Christmas the quartet had recorded ten songs, including "Highwayman," a 1977 song by singer-songwriter Jimmy Webb that they'd played together informally in Switzerland.

"One thing led to another and the next thing we knew, we had an album," says Willie Nelson. "Then we found ourselves playing together onstage and having a . . . lot of fun. We are all fans of each other's work and that's why I loved it. I could stand onstage with three guys I really admired and respected and listen to them perform." The resulting album, *Highwayman,* and the title single both topped the country charts in 1985.

Work on Cash's album *Rainbow* was temporarily suspended, first for *Highwayman* and then for *Heroes,* an album of duets with Waylon, which Moman also produced. They didn't pick back up on *Rainbow* until after their debut concert at Willie's Picnic, an annual concert and cookout, in Austin, Texas. Almost immediately after the final session, Cash returned to Sun Recording Studio for the first time in twenty-seven years to record *The Class of '55,* a nostalgic album with Carl Perkins, Roy Orbison, and Jerry Lee Lewis that was released by Polygram.

Another reason *Rainbow* took so long to produce was that Columbia had lost faith in Cash as a solo artist. By playing with the Highwaymen, he received some much-needed attention and even sold some other albums. Released without any promotion, *Rainbow* consequently died a quiet death. When interviewed years later, Chips Moman was convinced that it had never been released. Kris Kristofferson, who had two songs covered on it, has still never heard it. He was particularly puzzled when he read that Cash called "Here Comes That Rainbow Again" (the song that gave the album its title) his favorite song, when as far as Kristofferson knew, he had never recorded it.

"The album was released but Columbia buried it," says Lou Robin. "Rick Blackburn, who was running the company in Nashville, was not interested in the stuff that John was doing and he was acting like 'judge, jury, and executioner.' When I sent him the final mixes he probably put out twenty thousand records, which is like one in every record store. It certainly wasn't going to be promoted."

—

BY THIS TIME RAY CASH had become seriously ill. Confined to his home in Hendersonville, he had almost completely lost his sight. Cash did a few scattered shows but managed to stay nearby much of the time, making the film *The Last Days of Frank and Jesse James* with Kristofferson and Waylon in and around Nashville.

Ray Cash had mellowed over the years, and the tough drinker who'd done so much to belittle his son was gone. He, now, without pretense, summoned his children and grandchildren to pray and sing gospel songs to him on his deathbed. "He was very sincere," says his daughter Joanne. "He asked us with tears. I feel assured in my heart that he made things right with God."

On December 23, at the age of eighty-eight, Ray Cash died. Courtney Wilson officiated at the funeral, which took place at First Baptist Church in Hendersonville. His gravestone held the same question engraved over his son Jack's final resting place: "Will You Meet Me in Heaven?" Cash had ambiguous feelings about his father's passing. On one hand, he had lost the man from whom he had inherited so much of his temperament, but on other hand, he was now finally free of the man responsible for so much of his self-doubt.

While he was alive, Cash showed his father nothing but the greatest respect— almost as if "honor thy father and mother" was the one commandment he was determined not to break. He never spoke publicly about his father's violence, verbal abuse, or drunkenness. Instead, he always appeared to go out of his way to shower his father with praise for his hard work, sacrifice, exemplary military service, and love of country. Whenever Cash introduced the song "These Hands" onstage, he always dedicated it to his father.

A decade later, when he wrote his autobiography, *Cash,* he made the startling confession that he rarely thought about his father anymore, and even though he passed the cemetery where his father was buried almost every day, he didn't visit his father's grave any longer. He told how his father never praised him until he became a star, and even then he never brought himself to tell Cash that he loved him. Cash revealed some of his violent behavior but made a point of remarking, "He never laid a hand on Jack or me either."

His father ruled supremely in the home. Questioning his behavior constituted insubordination. "The father was a pretty strong personality," says Saul Holiff. "I would say that Johnny was always intimidated by him."

The abuse was a source of the pain that Cash was always trying to heal, but he learned things from his father—like respect for elders and love of his country—that he desired to emulate. However, Cash was determined to be different with his own children. He avoided violent punishments, praised them endlessly, and often professed his love. He preferred to correct their behavior by talking with them or writing them letters, even when they lived in the same house. Asked in 1979 how he'd like to be remembered in one hundred years, he said simply, "I'd like to be remembered as a good daddy."

Cash felt guilty that he hadn't been around as his girls grew up and worried that his behavior had negatively affected them. (By 1986, three of his daughters had already been married and divorced.) For a short time, he regularly sent questionnaires that required them to search through the Bible for answers. "I think it always bothered him that he had made some mistakes," says Tara. "Looking back I think that sending us these questions was a really sweet way of trying to get us to pay attention to what he was trying to show us."

John Carter was the main beneficiary of his improved parental skills, not only because he was taken on the road from earliest childhood and so enjoyed the company of both his parents, but also because Cash was able to do everything with him—from playing with toys on the living room floor to hiking in the woods and taking fishing trips in Alaska.

—

SINCE LEAVING THE BETTY FORD CENTER, Cash had been clearheaded enough to return to his manuscript about the apostle Paul, and in March 1986, he completed it during a writing stint at the farm in Bon Aqua, Tennessee—his two-story country retreat outside of Nashville. For someone used to telling stories in three verses and a chorus, a ninety-thousand-word novel had been an ambitious task. His favorite novelists were James Michener *(The Source),* Colleen McCullough *(The Thorn Birds),* Jack Higgins, and Stephen King. He was a great lover of historical fiction, and even in his last days was reading *Aztec,* by Gary Jennings, on a magnified image projector. He modeled his novel of the apostle Paul, *The Man in White,* on the biblical novels he'd first read when he and June married: *The Robe* by Lloyd C. Douglas, *The Silver Chalice* by Thomas B. Costain, and *Ben Hur* by Lew Wallace.

The publication of *The Man in White* coincided with news that Columbia would not renew its contract with Cash. After thirty-one years as a recording artist (twenty-eight of them with Columbia), Cash was suddenly a man without a label. Columbia's Nashville head, Rick Blackburn, cleaned house and Cash was one of the casualties. The reason was basic. Cash was no longer selling records in large volumes, and radio stations pursuing the coveted eighteen-to-twenty-four-year-old market share, didn't think a fifty-four-year-old (whose first hits appeared on the charts in the 50s), should top their playlists.

"They didn't care for what he was putting out," says Lou Robin. "When John's contract expired, Rick Blackburn called me and told me he wasn't going to renew it. I was a little surprised. I'm sure that Rick had been given orders from higher up."

It was 1986, and Cash's statistics as a solo artist didn't help his case. He hadn't had an album in the (pop) Top 200 since *One Piece at a Time* a decade before. Columbia argued that shifting demographics left little hope of a career revival, especially since his songs were plowing the same old furrows. He argued back that because Columbia lost faith in him, they stopped promoting him—so *they* were to blame for the poor sales figures.

Cash hadn't made it easy for himself. He'd clearly lost his enthusiasm for recording and often skipped the mixing sessions. Even his staunchest fans considered one of his last singles for Columbia, "The Chicken in Black," rock bottom (he actually dressed up in a superhero blue cape, yellow jersey, and tights for the video, which was shot at Citizen's Bank in Nashville). In 1988 he admitted to Bill Flanagan of *Musician* magazine that the song was indeed awful, but he blamed it on producer Billy Sherrill. "I hated it from the first day and I refuse to admit that I even know the words to it anymore. It was an embarrassment. Every once in a while I'll do something that embarrasses me, like anybody. It's good to let the people know you have a sense of humor."[1]

There may be some truth to the amended story since the B side of that release,

"The Battle of Nashville," was an undisguised attack on the record company:

> Many times I've regrouped my emotions
> And smiled through the struggle and pain
> And made believe I'm all together
> Just like I'm doing again
> But my little defeats keep on coming
> Cause you keep on holding the line
> I'm losing ground with you daily
> And it's just a matter of time.
>
> And the Battle of Nashville is raging
> There's a troubling deep in my soul
> Here's my swan song for Music City
> Cause my forces are out of control
> I have hoped against hope that you'll love me
> And my heart won't give up the fight
> So the Battle of Nashville continues
> And pray you'll surrender tonight.

("The Battle of Nashville," 1984)

Despite the layoff from Columbia, Robin remained upbeat with the press. He said that they already had a lot of interest from other labels and reminded them that Cash was far more than just a recording artist—he was a touring performer, a TV host, an author, and a movie actor. On August 21, Cash signed a new deal with Polygram Records in Nashville, to release his records on the Mercury label.

Polygram Nashville's president, Dick Asher, and vice president of marketing, Steve Popovich, both got to know Cash while working for Columbia. Their view was that Cash was a prestige artist and that the association with him would be good for their Mercury label. They also thought Cash could sell some records if handled well. "We knew that Columbia was about to drop him," says Popovich. "There was a change about to happen. As Rick Blackburn put it, the torch was about to be handed to another generation. I was always totally against this idea of getting rid of these older artists. They were the people who had built country music and they had millions of fans."

For his first Mercury album, *Johnny Cash Is Coming to Town,* he worked again with Jack Clement, whom he regarded as something of a talisman in his career but others thought had steered him away from his vision by going for the lightweight and the obviously commercial. Clement had produced "Ballad of a Teenage Queen" and "I Guess Things Happen That Way" when Sam Phillips lost interest in Cash at Sun, helped restore Cash's reputation at Columbia with his work on "Ring of Fire," and was around to supply songs for *Everybody Loves a Nut* after Cash was arrested. He produced *The Adventures of Johnny Cash.* He was almost family.

David "Fergie" Ferguson, an engineer who played an important role in the last ten years of Cash's recording life, came along as Clement's assistant. "He wanted attention," says Ferguson. "Columbia had slammed the door on him. He was happy to have a new buddy engineer and to be working with Jack Clement again. He recorded the songs he wanted to record and was happy to be sparing no expense on recording and to be able to use any instrumentation he wanted to. He loved all that. He was having a good time but he was disappointed because every time we recorded something nobody would do anything with it. He made great records but nobody would push them. That's the pity of it." Interviewed in 2000, Cash confirmed that working with Jack Clement in the 1980s was "the happiest period of my recording career."

Johnny Cash Is Coming to Town was promoted as Cash's comeback album, but in 1988 he commented, "That's what they said, but that album didn't make it very big. If I'm going to make a comeback recordwise, I've still got that comeback to make. But meanwhile I'm doing what I enjoy; so what's the difference? I've always done what I wanted to do. I've never looked at the charts and grieved because my name wasn't in there."

Cash's next recording was an album of duets, *Water from the Wells of Home,* which started with a song he recorded with June, "Where Did We Go Right?" followed by the title track, co-written with John Carter. Also on the record were songs with Roy Acuff and Glenn Campbell. "Then I was in the studio and Waylon came in, so Waylon and I did a duet," he said. "We got talking about other people I'd like to sing with; so I got Emmylou Harris and Hank Williams Jr. I have a track cut for my daughter Rosanne and the Everly Brothers."

When last at Cinnamon Hill he'd been visited by Tom T. Hall and Paul McCartney, and the three of them had written a song, which was also included on the album. When Cash was next in England he recorded it with the former Beatle at his studio in the West Sussex countryside. "It sounds terrific," Cash said the next day. "We were at my house right after New Year having one of our all-night singin's and guitar pulls on the front porch. We'd been singing for about six hours and the moon started setting and Tom T. Hall had this idea for a song called 'New Moon over Jamaica.' We wrote the song together."

—

The late 1980s also, unfortunately, marked the start of Cash's serious health problems. On May 16, 1987, while playing a concert in Council Bluffs, Iowa, he stopped in the middle of his second song. He started to talk to the audience but found his speech slurred and indecipherable. Realizing something was horribly wrong, June stepped forward from the wings and escorted him backstage, where he remained for ten minutes. When he reached the coronary unit of Mercy Hospital, doctors there diagnosed an irregular heartbeat. The concert was cancelled. Photos of him coming offstage show him staring wildly, looking confused and afraid.

Cash's publicity team attributed the incident to exhaustion from his heavy schedule of recording, touring, and signings for *A Man in White*. Lou Robin confirmed that, though he had no history of heart problems, he did suffer from high blood pressure. He spent two nights in the hospital and then flew back to Nashville. He didn't play again until June 13.

In March 1988 he checked into the Eisenhower Medical Center in Palm Springs, California, to be treated for laryngitis and bronchitis. Then, on December 13, he went to Baptist Hospital in Nashville for a routine checkup and learned the following day that he had a 90 percent blockage at the junction of two coronary arteries supplying blood to his left ventricle. He needed immediate bypass surgery.

His operation started at 8:00 a.m. on December 19 and lasted for two hours. According to Cash, he smoked a cigarette thirty minutes before being given the anesthetic. Surgeons used blood vessels from his chest and leg to bypass the blockage. Waylon Jennings, who'd undergone the same operation exactly a week before, was resting in a private room after coming out of intensive care on December 17. Roy Orbison had died of a heart attack on December 6 at his Hendersonville home. Cardiologist Dr. Charles E. Mayes noted that the age and lifestyle of the singers probably contributed to their heart problems. Jennings was fifty-one, Orbison fifty-two, and Cash fifty-six.

Cash entered intensive care listed as "stable but critical" but then developed pulmonary problems over the weekend. Journalists were called and asked to prepare Johnny Cash obituaries, while June asked Lou Robin to fly in from L.A. on Christmas Day. Though apparently alert and able to watch television, he'd nevertheless suffered a setback. He wasn't discharged from the hospital until January 3, when he vowed to waiting journalists that he was going to change his lifestyle by exercising and giving up fatty foods and cigarettes. "It has been a great soul-searching experience for me," he said. "I never want to go through it again."

Cash didn't return to work until March 6, 1989, when he began recording a second album with Kris Kristofferson, Willie Nelson, and Waylon Jennings. His first concert since the heart operation came four days later at the Embassy Theater in Fort Wayne, Indiana, and he continued touring for the rest of the year. In Paris in May he was admitted to the American Hospital with what was described at the time as "a torn ligament," but which was in fact a life-threatening chest condition. "He was booked at the Zenith Theater and the doctors told him that whatever it was could have started a chain reaction and that he shouldn't perform," says Lou Robin. "They said it could kill him, but he played it anyway, and in fact he played for longer than he usually did. That's the way he was when someone told him not to do something. Then, after the show, I took him back to the hospital and he was kept in for three days."

In August, Cash was forced to cancel three dates in Washington and Oregon because of bronchitis and respiratory infections. On November 19, he entered Cumberland Heights Alcohol and Drug Treatment Center for a two-week course of "relapse prevention therapy." Thankfully, he recognized the warning signs of a potential relapse after the heavy doses of painkillers he'd taken following surgery, and took precautionary measures.

The words "Johnny Cash" and "hospital" were popping up together in headlines with worrying frequency. Many of his friends date his serious decline in health not to his heart surgery but to what initially appeared to be a minor problem. In January 1990 he had an abscessed tooth removed in New York, and instead of healing smoothly he developed a cyst between his gum and his jaw. Later in the month he required oral surgery to scrape the cyst from his jawbone. On February 7, while at the Grand Ole Opry hosting a TNN tribute to country music broadcaster Ralph Emery, he had to stop two-thirds of the way through the taping because of the extreme pain in his jaw. Concert appearances from February 15 to 24 had to be cancelled.

Despite the lingering pain, Cash appeared at the Country Radio Seminar at the Opryland Hotel on March 1 to take part in the first Highwaymen press conference. The group performed new songs, announced its new album *Highwayman 2,* and promoted its first tour—which would begin March 3 in Houston, Texas, and end March 17 in East Lansing, Michigan. Discussing the four personalities in the group, Kristofferson said, "Willie's the outlaw coyote, Waylon's the riverboat gambler, and John's the father of our country. I'm still trying to get over the image of being their janitor."

The Highwaymen, bound together by mutual respect and shared history, also maintained a sharp sense of rivalry expected of four men at the top of their profession sharing the same stage. "I think they enjoyed being with each other," says guitarist Reggie Young, who was the musical director for the tour, "but one of them would always be trying to outdo the other. There were some big egos involved. When the four of them sang parts of the same song they'd do joke things to throw the others off. For example, Willie would deliberately sing behind the beat so that it would throw Waylon off, and when Waylon came in he'd come in wrong."

Kristofferson, though not that much younger than the others, didn't get into the business until a decade later and always had the most jitters. He never quite got over the fact that the other three were already well established in their careers when he was still cleaning their cigarette stubs out of the studio ashtrays. Willie had written "Crazy" for Patsy Cline, Waylon had given up his seat on Buddy Holly's fatal last flight to the Big Bopper, and Cash had toured with Elvis. "For me, it was like being up on Mount Rushmore," he says. "It was like these legendary people were up there along with the janitor."

Cash played the tour in terrible pain, but he didn't discover until its end that the surgery had weakened his jaw so much that he'd accidentally broken it while eating a steak. He cancelled his European tour scheduled to start on March 22. The surgery to mend Cash's jaw proved unsuccessful, and he was forced to cancel the rescheduled European tour altogether.

The repeated operations and original damage to Cash's jaw, altered his appearance. The lower left side of his face seemed permanently swollen, and he developed a habit of leaning it into his collar when being photographed. The nerves in his jaw had also been permanently damaged, and he said it left him feeling like a blowtorch was being held to his chin.

—

ON MARCH 11, 1991, Cash's mother, Carrie, died at the age of eighty-six, six weeks after coming out of a hospital where she was being treated for cancer. It was a bitter blow for Cash, who cried publicly for the first time that anyone could remember. His mother had been the biggest single influence on his life. She had not only encouraged his music and taught him about Christian faith—both through her Bible reading and the example of her life—but she had convinced Cash that his voice was a gift from God.

By all accounts, she led an unwaveringly dedicated Christian life and no one has a bad word for her. Rosanne remembers her as incredibly longsuffering. "As far as I know she was a saint," she says. "She was very much like my dad in that she suffered silently. She never said anything. She avoided confrontation at all costs." Marshall Grant recalls that "Carrie Cash was a wonderful lady who really knew no wrong and loved her family beyond anything. She was a gracious lady."

Carrie remained cheerful and optimistic despite the hardships of her life in Kingsland and Dyess, her husband's alcoholism, and Jack's unexpected, early death. She stood by Cash throughout his battles with drugs and yet didn't hesitate to wag her finger at him, reminding him of marital vows when he began his affair with June in the 1960s. Fortunately, she lived to see her son survive all the calamities and emerge as one of the best-known Christian laymen in America.

Cash, for his part, never forgot the debt he owed his mother. He knew that the best part of himself came from fulfilling the vision she'd had back in postwar Dyess, when she told him that God's hand was on him and that he had a special task to carry out. So convinced was he of her vision that it kept him going during the darkest days of his life. From the bowels of Nickajack Caves where he considered suicide, to the bed in intensive care after his double-bypass operation, the same thought stayed with him: "I can't die yet because God has more things for me to do."

Carrie was a constant presence in Cash's career. When he sang gospel songs and hymns, he was singing the songs she'd taught him to love. She twice played piano on the *Johnny Cash Show* and added vocals in the studio. Johnny even wrote the sleeve notes for *Silver* as a letter to her, remembering the day she told him,

"God has his hand on you, son." The letter ended: "There hasn't been a day passed in the last thirty years that I haven't recalled that scene in the kitchen with you, Mama, and the things you said and how you said it as if you *knew*. I remember that afterward, I nodded my head and almost said, 'I know it, Mama,' but I didn't. I just started singing. Now, after twenty-five years in the profession, I think maybe my voice is still suitable at times to be played on the radio. You still like it, don't you Mama? That's what matters to me."

The years 1992 and 1993 marked the beginning of what Cash would later call his third career, or his second comeback. His first career started with "Hey! Porter" in 1955, and *Johnny Cash at Folsom Prison* signified his first comeback in 1968. Comfortable and enjoying himself in the 1980s, his "best of" album *The Mercury Years*, boasts some terrific tracks recorded between 1987 and 1991, including "Cat's in the Cradle," "Sixteen Tons," and "I'd Rather Have You." But he wasn't jumping any artistic hurdles. Neither was he winning over a new generation of listeners as Roy Orbison did with his 1988 album *Mystery Girl*. Cash had yet to make his comeback album.

He'd reached the point where people admired him more for his past achievements than for his present output. He received a Living Legends Award at the Grammy Awards ceremony (1991) and was inducted into the Rock and Roll Hall of Fame (1992) at a time when he was playing small venues like Roadie's Roadhouse in Mississauga, Ontario, and Toad's Place at Yale University in New Haven, Connecticut. Only with the Highwaymen did he now play the large arenas and have an impact on the charts. "Highwayman" had topped the country singles charts, and both *Highwayman* albums had made it into the Top 100 of the *Billboard* charts. After a second U.S. tour in 1990, the group toured Australia and New Zealand in 1991 and then Europe in 1992.

Cash's dwindling status coupled with the frustrations of touring with a variety of health problems, may have clouded his judgment when it came time to commit to Cash Country, a planned thirty-five-million-dollar entertainment complex in Branson, Missouri. The music theme park, spread over one hundred acres, would include three theaters, a horse arena, a go-cart track, an amusement park, a water park, an auction house, a Cash museum, a thirty-five-unit hotel, three motels, and a twenty-thousand-square-foot shopping mall.

The guaranteed seventy-five nights a year in one of the twenty-five-hundred-seat theaters appealed to Cash, and Branson was only four hundred miles from Nashville. Veterans Roy Clark and Mel Tillis already had long seasons in Branson. "It's not running away from Nashville," said Lou Robin. "It's just part of the road activity he does one hundred days a year. There comes a time after thirty-six years that you look for an easier way to do it. In Branson we'll work five days at a time, essentially every other week. The rest of the time we'll be doing other things."

Cash never put any money into the project being designed and built by California property developer David Green, but he did allow his name to be used and was promised that he and June would be given some creative input. Cash wanted one of the theaters to be devoted to gospel music, and June had ideas about developing shows for children. The museum would be modeled on the existing Cash Museum at House of Cash (which opened in March 1979 at a cost of ten million dollars) and would include separate sections devoted to different aspects of Cash's life, from music and history, to patriotism and Americana, to causes like prisons, guns, and Native Americans. With the opening date scheduled for May 1992, it looked like the ideal way for Cash to celebrate his sixtieth birthday.

But Cash Country didn't open on May 1, 1992, with a headline show by Johnny Cash as announced. By the spring, cash-flow problems forced the builders to stop work. November found David Green in a Springfield, Missouri, bankruptcy court where the judge approved a $4.1 million sale of the half-completed theater.

The failure of Cash Country drastically altered the shape of the final decade of Cash's career. Had it taken off, he may well not have embarked on the European tour in January 1993 that took him to Dublin on February 8. If he hadn't gone to Dublin, he wouldn't have sung on a track for U2's album *Zooropa,* which, as time would tell, became a turning point in his career.

Although a monumental figure assured his place in the history of twentieth-century popular music, it had been years since Cash had been considered hip. Not since 1968 to 1970, when he was cutting the prison albums and introducing people like Bob Dylan, James Taylor, and Joni Mitchell to the television viewing public, had his influence really mattered.

Then, starting in 1988, a reevaluation began to take place. The first indication was a Johnny Cash tribute album made in Britain to raise money for an AIDS charity. *'Til Things Are Brighter,* produced by Mark Riley and Jon Langford for Red Rhino Records, featured members of some of Britain's more avant-garde post-punk bands—That Petrol Emotion, Cabaret Voltaire, the Mekons, the Triffids, and Soft Cell. It was a fascinating link between Cash and the world of alternative rock. Mark Riley explained: "Generally speaking, for the young audience in Britain, the country and western singers are pretty much figures of fun. But Johnny Cash comes across as this cool dude who plays in prisons and wears black. Everybody was instantly keen to do it."

That same year Cash met Bono, who came to Hendersonville during a driving trip across America with U2 bass player Adam Clayton. When they sat down for a meal, Cash intoned a long and elaborate grace, thanking God for his wonderful provisions and asking him to bless the food to their bodies. Then he opened his eyes, winked at Bono, and said, "Sure do miss the drugs though." The demonstration of piety coupled with the admission of weakness endeared Cash to the young Irish musicians. In May 1989 Cash recalled the meeting: "We sat around and played some songs afterwards and then we started writing a song together ["Ellis Island," which was never completed]. We were going to finish it off by fax, but that didn't work out. I hope to go and see him when I get to Dublin."

The early period of Sun Records fascinated Bono. He was interested in knowing the origins of rock-'n'-roll and was also intrigued by the theological struggles of people like Elvis and Jerry Lee Lewis as they fought to reconcile this deeply sensual music with their Pentecostal understanding of Christianity. Rock-'n'-roll encouraged rebellion, abandon, pride, and self-indulgence. Jesus Christ preached obedience, self-control, humility, and sacrifice. Was reconciliation possible?

Of all the Sun Records artists, Cash was the one closest in spirit to U2. Cash was the one who'd developed a social conscience, placing his music at the service of the downtrodden and marginalized. He was the one unafraid to explore the darkness within himself. He was the one to incorporate spiritual material into his non-gospel albums. He was also the one to explore folk, blues, gospel, and country roots. For a contemporary band attracted to rock-'n'-roll, the teachings of Jesus, and political justice, Cash was a unique example.

"Johnny Cash was a saint who preferred the company of sinners," says Bono. "It's an amazing thing. I've seen the Bible he read from. I've seen his life from various different quarters, and what I was left with was the feeling that I'd met someone with the dignity of an age we don't know. I feel it's as though I'm reading about Jacob or Moses. He was so not twentieth century. He was a mythical figure. I don't know how that happens. Elvis, Johnny Cash—they were mythical figures and they lived mythical lives."

In February 1993, when Cash was in Dublin to play a concert with Kris Kristofferson, Bono invited him to Windmill Studios, where the band was recording with producer Brian Eno. As Cash later remembered it, they told him they were recording a track that was part of an experimental music project. The day before, Bono had written the words to a song he was calling "The Preacher" (it later became "Wanderlust" and finally "The Wanderer"). It was inspired by the Old Testament book of Ecclesiastes, in which the unnamed narrator systematically explores all avenues of fulfillment before concluding that everything is worthless unless people remember their Creator.

"Ecclesiastes is one of my favorite books," says Bono. "It's a book about a character who wants to find out why he's alive, why he was created. He tries knowledge. He tries wealth. He tries experience. He tries everything. You hurry to the end of the book to find out why, and it says, 'It's good to work,' 'Remember your Creator.' In a way, it's such a letdown. Yet it isn't. There's something of Johnny Cash in that."

Cash added the necessary gravity to the "The Wanderer." When he intoned the lines "I went out there / In search of experience / To taste and to touch / And to feel as much / As a man can / Before he repents" he seemed to sum up a large part of his own life. "It's like a post-apocalyptic search," said Cash. "It's the search for three important things: God, that woman, and myself." Bono instinctively spotted one of Johnny Cash's unique talents. "He's got this great voice which loves certain words," he said. "I just wrote those words for him."

Cash returned home assuming the track would never be used, but Bono called to tell him that it would be the final track on *Zooropa*. A Johnny Cash track on a U2 album would expose him to a totally new audience—U2 was the biggest band in the world at the time. The following year, *Zooropa* became a number-one album in both Britain and the U.S., selling more than seven million copies worldwide. Johnny Cash was, once again, hip.

12

American Recordings

O N FEBRUARY 27, 1993, two weeks after flying home from Dublin, Cash played the Rhythm Café, a small dinner theater in Santa Ana, California. After the show he met with a thirty-year-old man with long dark hair and a thick beard down to his chest who said that he was interested in producing him. The man was Rick Rubin, owner of Def American Records.

It's unlikely that Cash would have known any of the artists Rubin had produced up to that point. He wouldn't have heard rap acts like LL Cool J, the Beastie Boys, or Run DMC, heavy-metal acts like Slayer or Wolfsbane, or even the politically incorrect comedian Andrew Dice Clay. The Red Hot Chili Peppers might have rung a bell, but not for long. Nevertheless, Cash was intrigued to know what this guy, whom he thought looked like a wino, imagined he could do for his career.

Although he now based in Los Angeles, Rubin was from Long Island, and his musical roots were as far removed from Cash's as it was possible to imagine. He liked hard, aggressive metal—AC/DC and Led Zeppelin had been his favorite boyhood bands. He formed his first record label, Def Jam, with rap impresario

Russell Simmons, and they specialized in synthesizing elements of heavy metal with elements of rap, the most commercially successful result being the single "Walk This Way" that paired Aerosmith with Run DMC.

Rubin had produced the multiplatinum albums *Licensed to Ill* for the Beastie Boys, *Raisin' Hell* for Run DMC, *Mack Daddy* by Sir Mixalot, and *BloodSugarSexMagik* for the Red Hot Chili Peppers, as well as the platinum albums *Reign in Blood* for Slayer and *Electric* for the Cult. Wealthy and celebrated, he was looking for a fresh challenge. He'd even specifically entertained the idea of finding a great artist, without a recent smash album, to revitalize.

Whenever he thought about great artists, Rubin kept coming back to Johnny Cash, whom he considered a primal force with a currently uninspired career. Although Cash's style of music differed from anything he'd produced so far, it had common elements. Rap and heavy metal, like country, had been born on the other side of the tracks and dealt with the life experiences of the crushed and frustrated. Both genres were rife with songs about drugs and alcohol, guns and knives, light and darkness, lost love and jail.

"I have always been drawn to things that are edgy and extreme," says Rubin. "Johnny Cash was always an outlaw figure who didn't fit in anywhere. He was looked upon as a country artist, but I don't think that country people ever totally embraced him. He was an outsider, and I think that's what drew me to him more than anything else."

In October 1992 Rubin and his label manager, Mark Geiger, had seen Cash make an appearance on Bob Dylan's 30th Anniversary Celebration at New York's Madison Square Garden. Both of them were highly impressed with the way in which Cash grabbed the crowd and particularly noticed his ability to capture the younger members of the audience. They talked about the possibility of doing something with him, and a couple of weeks later Geiger was talking to Cash's agent, Jim Gosnell.

"It just so happened that a couple of weeks earlier I had been talking to Lou Robin, who had told me that John wasn't happy at Mercury," says Gosnell. "He felt that country radio had just abandoned him. When Mark mentioned this idea about Def American I was over the moon about it. I called Lou, and Lou had never heard of Rick Rubin but he had an open ear. He responded to my enthusiasm and agreed to set up a meeting between Rick and John."

Cash was reticent at first. "It was just another record company as far as he knew," says Robin. "I took Rick into the dressing room before the show in Santa Ana, and they sat there and stared at each other for two minutes. They didn't say a word. They were sizing each other up. Then they started chatting and found that they had a lot in common. There was Rick with this big scruffy beard, and suddenly Johnny found that here was someone who thought about handling his music the same way that he did. That's how it all started."

Cash was slightly bemused that someone from the alternative side of the rock market thought he could do something with a sixty-two-year-old Baptist from Arkansas. What did Rubin imagine he could do that hadn't been done before? Rubin explained that the first thing he wanted to do was to get Cash to sit down with an acoustic guitar and play through all the songs he loved, and, perhaps more importantly, perform them exactly the way he heard them. That way, he could get a sense of what Cash really wanted to record, and they'd take it from there.

This happened to fit with an idea Cash had been nurturing. In a just-published interview with *Country Music* magazine, he mentioned that he'd been collecting a cache of songs, explaining, "When I get in the right situation I'm going to record the best album I've ever had. There are a lot of albums I want to do. I want to do an album of real 'heart' folk songs, or country songs, or love songs, mainly with just me and my guitar and I want to call it *Johnny Cash Alone and Late.*"

Cash already had a busy schedule touring the country with the Highwaymen as well as playing the Wayne Newton Theater in Branson (in lieu of dates that should have been at Cash Country), but he found time to meet with Rubin in California while he was filming the TV series *Dr. Quinn, Medicine Woman* with Jane Seymour. Between May 17 and 20 he recorded thirty-three songs, almost all of them with his acoustic guitar as the only backing. These were songs in his own back catalogue that he felt hadn't been properly recorded ("Drive On," "Flesh and Blood"), traditional songs ("Bury Me Not on the Lone Prairie," "Banks of the Ohio"), country classics ("Long Black Veil," "Waiting for a Train"), songs by friends (Dolly Parton, Willie Nelson, Kris Kristofferson), and songs recommended by Rubin (Glenn Danzig's "Thirteen").

The purity of the results was striking. The absence of record-company pressure lifted a burden from his shoulders, and for the first time in years Cash openly explored his own tastes. Rubin's purpose at this point was not to cut an acoustic album, but to find out what Cash had inside him and to suggest some songs that might challenge beyond the boom-chicka-boom sound. Above all, he wanted to create an environment that would reignite Johnny's passion for the recording process.

Being picked up by someone who believed in him and who wanted him to explore his music beyond the constraints of demographics was truly a godsend for Cash. It made him feel wanted. Cash and Rubin shared common interests in spiritual matters, poetry, and issues of justice and would spend hours talking to each other on the phone. "Rick became not just his producer but his muse," says Rosanne. "He was like this angel that swooped down into his life. He gave Dad this wonderful focus, inspiration, and passion."

Over the next six months they continued to record in the living room of Rubin's home, just off Sunset Strip. They also went to Ocean Way Studios in Santa Monica to experiment with other musicians who had previously worked with Rubin: the Red Devils, Tom Petty's guitarist Mike Campbell, Chad Smith, and Flea from the Red Hot Chili Peppers. For Rubin, any combination was worth trying—time and money were irrelevant. The overriding goal was for Cash to rediscover his authentic voice. Back in Hendersonville, Cash continued the process, recording gospel songs alone in his cabin studio and finding fresh approaches to some of the songs he'd worked on in Hollywood.

"I was always trying to find songs that fit the mythical image of Johnny Cash," explains Rubin. "What would the Man in Black sing? Well, the Man in Black would sing serious songs. He would sing weighty songs. He might sing spiritual songs. They would be songs with gravity."

By December 7, he'd recorded ninety-four songs, the most reworked being Tom Waits's "Down There by the Train," Glenn Danzig's "Thirteen," and Nick Lowe's "The Beast in Me." As one last experiment, Rubin suggested a first-ever solo performance in public—a full-length show using only his acoustic guitar. As a venue, he picked what was then one of the hippest clubs in Hollywood, the Viper Room on Sunset Boulevard, and booked Cash for three days, beginning on a Thursday evening. It was only a few minutes from Rubin's house.

The object of the experiment was twofold. The show would be taped and therefore would yield different performances of the songs than those given in the living room. It would also test Cash with a totally unfamiliar audience. The Viper Room, owned by Johnny Depp, was the favored hangout of young musicians, actors, models, and filmmakers. Few of them would be likely to have an extensive knowledge of Cash's back catalogue. If he could make an impression on this crowd with his simple, timeless songs, then the word would quickly spread. As Rubin says, "Word travels fast from shows like this."

Cash agreed to play but was initially very nervous about being alone in front of an audience. "There's one thing about doing a solo," he said to Jim Gosnell before walking onto the stage. "You can't blame the drummer for screwing up." Only when he got in front of the microphone and halfway through his opening number, "Delia's Gone," did his fears evaporate. The 150-strong Hollywood crowd, well known for its coolness, voiced its appreciation early and continued to do so for the full ninety minutes. Songs that made no concession to contemporary trends, that used no hip language, cut through the superficial surface fashion to the universal heart. When he'd finished playing his newly recorded material, he gave them a selection of his greatest hits.

"My first reaction was to run," Cash later said. "But then I got to thinking, why not? Young people especially see so much video and film that they know what's real when they see it. They appreciate the honest and open baring of emotions. And you can't have any more honesty than just taking a guitar up there and singing your songs."

His success that night helped spread the word that Johnny Cash was hot again. The gossip columns noted that members of the Red Hot Chili Peppers, Henry Rollins, Gibby Haynes (of the Butthole Surfers), as well as actors Sean Penn, Juliette Lewis, Pierce Brosnan, Randy Quaid, and Patricia Arquette had attended. Johnny Depp had introduced him. "I think Rick's real talent with Johnny Cash was in being able to know what to do in order to make young people connect with him again," says engineer David Ferguson. "That was his big contribution, plus making Johnny feel good. Rick created a big buzz about Johnny and that really helped."

After listening to all two hundred and eighteen takes and the tape of the Viper Room concert, Rubin concluded that nothing had bettered the early performances in Rubin's living room. He then boldly gambled by using what they'd originally considered the "research" sessions as the basis for the album. "I've recently gone through all those tapes and I've heard every word and every note on them, and basically the tape machine was turned on and left rolling and Johnny just sang one song after another for several hours," says Ferguson. "The whole of the first *American Recordings* album came from that except for one cut I did at the cabin on

'Drive On' and the live recording of 'Tennessee Stud' and 'The Man Who Couldn't Cry' that were recorded at the Viper Room."

Released in April 1994, *American Recordings* was not only a testament to a great musical talent and a fine collection of songs but the first time Cash success-fully integrated his faith into an album rather than added it as an appendage. Although not conceived as a concept album, the theme that emerged through the thirteen songs was that of bondage and freedom, fall and redemption. In this context, murder songs like "Delia's Gone" and "Tennessee Stud" ceased to be celebrations of male violence and revealed themselves as tales of men caught in cycles of jealousy, revenge, and guilt.

Nick Lowe's song "The Beast in Me" deftly painted a portrait of human sinfulness. It's not difficult to see why Cash identified so closely with it. The beast, or penchant for evil, is always present, and when it's not overtly display-ing itself, it shouldn't be assumed it's dead. Lowe had started writing the song in 1981 with Cash in mind, but he didn't complete it for ten years. "Something clicked and I suddenly finished it in an evening," Lowe says. "It was as if some-one else had come along and shown me how it went."

No song has ever come so close to identifying Cash's central dilemma. "The first time I heard Dad singing 'The Beast in Me' it just killed me," says Tara. "Even though it was written by Nick, that song to me is the essence of Dad. He had a way of being able to speak his darkness and that's what made him a great artist. His darkness was essentially everybody's darkness, the demons we all have and wrestle with."

Seen in this way, the rest of the songs divide into those that deal with an aspect of being enslaved—to the restless search, to the instincts, to the beast—and those that deal with an aspect of salvation ("Why Me," "Redemption," "Down There by the Train"). "Like a Soldier" was his personal testimony:

> But the wild road I was rambling
> Was always out there calling
> And they said a hundred times I should have died
> But now my present miracle
> Is that you're here beside me
> So, I believe they were roads that I was meant to ride.
> Like a soldier getting over the war

Like a young man getting over his crazy ways
Like a bandit getting over his lawless ways
Every day is better than before
I'm like a soldier getting over the war.

Cash's strength as a Christian writer was his compassion born from experience. He wrote of sin, not as it affected other people, but as something with which he'd become intimately acquainted. Yet the older he became, the less he enjoyed wallowing in the details of his wrongdoing. Cash was fond of saying that the only reason he didn't carry a burden of guilt for his errors was because he figured that, if God had forgiven him, the least he could do was to forgive himself.

There were nights I don't remember
And there's pain that I've forgotten
Other things I choose not to recall.
There are faces that come to me
In my darkest secret memory
Faces that I wish would not come back at all.

In my dreams' parade of lovers
From the other times and places
There's not one that matters now, no matter who
I'm just thankful for the journey
And that I survived the battles
And that my spoils of victory are you.

Bono understood Cash as a Moses figure. "When the children of Israel start worshiping the golden calf after being delivered from Egypt, God gets really angry with them," he says. " 'I've just delivered you,' says God. 'All you've asked of me, I've given you. This is no way to say thanks. You're returning to these barbaric ways, and I'm angry.' He tells Moses to leave them because he's going to destroy them, but the Bible then says, Moses, knowing the heart of God, went down among the people and says, 'If you're going to take them, take me.' In that moment of empathy and grace you hear everything that Johnny Cash sang about. That was his whole thing."

The packaging of the album underscored this Old Testament feeling. On the cover was a photograph of Cash dressed in a long black cloak, standing in a wheat field looking as though he was about to deliver a word from the Lord God. Directly behind him were banks of puffy clouds, suggesting an imminent deluge or at least a roll of thunder. Sitting to his right was a black dog with white markings and to his left, a white dog with black markings. Their participation wasn't planned. Photographer Andy Earl flew out to Melbourne, Australia, in February 1994 to shoot the cover in nearby Geelong while Cash was on tour with Kris Kristofferson. There wasn't enough available time to do the shoot in America.

The original plan was to shoot Cash walking along a deserted railroad that would look as though it was somewhere in America, but, as photographer Andy Earl explains, "It just didn't have the kind of presence that I thought the photographs needed. Then I noticed these storm clouds brewing and a field of wheat, and because he was all dressed up like a religious figure, I stood him in front. The two dogs belonged to the station master, and they were just running around, but when Johnny stood for the picture one sat on one side of him and one on the other. I just went 'boom!' and captured the moment, and it was just one of those wonderful things. None of it was planned. The whole thing just came together."

Once the shot had been selected for the album cover, the dogs took on metaphysical significance for Cash. "Their names are Sin and Redemption," he told Lisa Robinson of the *New York Post*. "I've got to remember that the black stripe is always there. Nobody's all good. Nobody's all bad. I guess I'm personally afraid of my dark side."[1] To *Rolling Stone* he explained, "That's kind of the theme of the album, and I think it says it for me too. When I was really bad, I wasn't all bad. When I was really trying to be good, I could never be all good. There would be that black streak going through."[2]

Reviewers were ecstatic about *American Recordings*, thoroughly vindicating Rubin's faith in Cash and his decision to go with the home recordings. *Rolling Stone* called it "unquestionably one of his best albums." *Billboard* gushed "never has the man in black produced a work of such brilliance." To the *Los Angeles Times* it was "a milestone work for this legendary singer." *Newsweek* noted that "the alternative-rock community has been buzzing about it for months."

Cash's hip quotient increased even further. He was being chased for interviews by alternative magazines, and invitations to perform poured in from rock clubs and campuses. "He's the original rebel," said James Lien, the editor of the *College Music Journal.* "He has all the mystique of being the outsider and the loner." He played an invitation-only concert at the Fez Club in New York, attended by model Kate Moss and Johnny Depp. A week later he filmed a video for the first single from *American Recordings,* "Delia's Gone," in which Moss played the violently murdered Delia. In Los Angeles he played the Pantagers Theater near Hollywood and Vine with Beck as his support act.

In June, Cash went to England to play the main stage of the prestigious Glastonbury Festival, a huge outdoor event held on Somerset farmland, attended by fifty thousand, mostly young, fans. He was given an afternoon spot traditionally reserved for established performers climbing the charts. Previous performers included Tom Jones (post-*Prince)* and Tony Bennett (post-*Unplugged).* The announcer for the slot was Andy Kershaw, a British D. J. with a special interest in roots music who had revered Cash since childhood. When they met backstage, Kershaw detected Cash's anxiety about the performance. Cash wanted to know how many people were out there and whether they were all young. He was sweating profusely.

Kershaw was equally nervous about introducing him. He knew that Glastonbury fans could be spirited in their rejection of an act, showing their distaste with showers of empty bottles. The omens hadn't been good that afternoon—honky-tonk records played between acts had been loudly booed. Also, he wasn't sure how to word his introduction and Cash hadn't helped by telling him that he had no preferred way of being announced. In the end, he went up to the microphone and said simply, "Please welcome a giant of American music and a giant of a man—Johnny Cash."

"Fifty thousand throats roared back," Kershaw later said. "I turned slightly to my right, and the great man was already standing at my shoulder, guitar in place. . . . The applause went on and on. It came in waves, crashing over that huge stage. Again and again. Glastonbury was going daft. I stepped aside to let Johnny move to the mic. For a moment, he just stood there and looked out either in relief or disbelief. Tears were falling down those Mount Rushmore features. Tears were rolling down my face too." Cash went on to do a fourteen-song set that many thought was the highlight of a festival that featured, among others, Rage Against the Machine, Elvis Costello, Peter Gabriel, the Beastie Boys, Oasis, and Radiohead.

Cash would compare these and similar experiences with the way things had been when he started out: the huge standing audiences, the simple style of recording, the excitement of choosing material, the media buzz, the young people. There was no one else from the Class of '55 who not only had an unbroken recording and performing career, but who was still breaking new ground. In February 1995, *American Recordings* won the Grammy for Best Contemporary Folk Album.

The challenge facing Rubin for the next album was to create something that built on the momentum of *American Recordings* but that was different. He didn't want to repeat himself by doing another acoustic album. He introduced Cash to contemporary songwriters both as a way of tuning him in to the music of a new generation and of stretching him as a singer. The lyrics were always of paramount importance, because given a song he identified with, regardless of who'd written it, Cash had the extraordinary ability to make it his own. Hearing him sing "The Beast in Me," for example, it's hard to imagine that he didn't write it—he takes such command of every word. When Glenn Danzig heard Cash's version of "Thirteen" he commented, "It's his song now. I wrote it, but it's his now."

"There are a couple of different ways to look at Johnny Cash as a recording artist," says David Ferguson. "You can make Johnny's voice and the instruments sound as one instrument, or you can take Johnny's voice and just complement it. You make the music about the voice. You color around the voice. That's basically the way Rick looks at it."

Ferguson recalls, "Rick got him to do songs that weren't easy for him. Sometimes he gave him songs where he was singing on a different beat than he was used to singing on. It was a little more difficult for him singing on the rock-'n'-roll feeling songs because when you sing on the beat it's different. His whole thing all of his life was singing with that syncopation. On the first record Johnny was basically singing Johnny songs. Then on the second album it started to get away from that a little bit. You can tell the songs that Rick chose and the songs that Johnny chose."

Cash obviously chose his own songs: "Country Boy," first recorded in 1957, "Mean Eyed Cat," and "Meet Me in Heaven," a beautiful song based on the words of his brother Jack's headstone. He probably picked "Memories Are Made of This," a hit for Dean Martin in 1956; "I Never Picked Cotton," a hit for Roy Clark in 1970; "Sea of Heartbreak" recorded by Don Gibson in 1961; "The One Rose" recorded by Jimmie Rodgers; Geoff Mack's "I've Been Everywhere," a hit for

Hank Snow in 1962; and "Unchained" by Jude Johnstone, a friend of his daughter Kathy's husband, Jimmy Tittle. Rubin definitely chose "Rowboat" by the then up-and-coming singer Beck (featured on his 1994 album *Stereopathetic Soulmanure*), "Rusty Cage" (from Soundgarden's 1991 album *Badmotorfinger*), and "Spiritual" by Josh Haden.

Some of Rubin's choices were inspired. Most people could never take originals and imagine them as possibilities for Cash. Even Cash couldn't imagine himself doing "Rusty Cage" when he first heard the track by Soundgarden. He was also acutely sensitive to Cash's Christian world-view and picked contemporary songs that expressed aspects of the human struggle. In order to help Cash in the selection process, Rubin would record demos to show him how specific songs might sound with his interpretations.

"The way I picked songs for him would always be about what they said, not about the music," says Rubin. "I would ask myself whether it was something I could imagine him singing and it feeling right. If he sang, 'I'm gonna break this rusty cage and run,' would I believe that? Yes. All the songs we ended up with resonated with who he was. They sounded like they could have been his words. With some of the less-well-known songs, people still often assume that he wrote them."

Although the second album didn't have a conscious concept, many of the songs focused on the same themes of bondage and release, sin and redemption that pervaded *American Recordings*. Songs such as "Unchained," "Rusty Cage," and "Spiritual" were pledges or prayers emphasizing the need to be set free, whereas "Meet Me in Heaven" was a song of hope about the world to come.

Backing Cash were Tom Petty and the Heartbreakers, a band that Rubin had produced in 1994 on *Wildflowers* and was now producing for the soundtrack of the movie *She's the One*. Petty played a Byrds-inspired music, which acknowledged the blue-collar rock of Bob Seger and Bruce Springsteen. He'd toured extensively with Bob Dylan and had been part of the Traveling Wilburys with Jeff Lynne, George Harrison, Dylan, and Roy Orbison.

The speed of recording was hampered by Cash's recurring medical problems. His broken jaw required repeated operations—over thirty he once said—and when he arrived in Britain in May 1995 he was only able to play one show before hurrying back home in pain. Additionally, he was suffering from an undiagnosed nervous disease that saw him stumbling, shaking, and sometimes unable to sing.

Despite the illness, Cash continued to tour and record, and *Unchained* was released in November 1996. *Entertainment Weekly* called it "a travelogue of Cash's sticky psyche—the repentant sinner wrestling with dark desires." *Musician* said that *"Unchained* seems such classic Cash it almost doesn't matter who's playing with him." *Alternative Press* reported, "Cash slips on [these] tunes as comfortably as a black mourning coat." *Rolling Stone* voted it number five in its list of the Ten Best Albums of 1996.

Cash started 1997 optimistically, playing dates in the U.S. and then touring in Czechoslovakia, Germany, Norway, Sweden, Denmark, France, Austria, Switzerland, and England. In September he began another tour of the country, but by this time he knew that his health was deteriorating and that he just didn't have the stamina to continue. Before a show at the Ford Theater in Washington, D.C., on September 16, he and June called a meeting with the musicians. "Everybody on the show was there," says Earl Poole Ball. "He wanted to let us know that he wouldn't be able to go on forever." The idea was to reduce the number of concerts each year and retire by 2000.

The end though came abruptly. At a concert in Flint, Michigan, on October 25, he stumbled and almost fell as he bent down to pick up a guitar pick. He then told the audience that he was suffering from Parkinson's disease. Many of them thought he was joking, but he wasn't. It proved to be the last concert Johnny Cash ever gave. He would continue to make an occasional guest appearance, but never again would he mount a full-length concert.

He had been scheduled to make a seven-city tour to promote his book *Cash: The Autobiography,* which he'd written with country music journalist Patrick Carr, but it had to be cancelled at the last minute. He thought at the time that he had Parkinson's Disease and that as soon as the condition was stabilized with medication he would resume the promotional tour. However, on October 29 all the remaining concerts of the year were cancelled when he was admitted to the hospital with a combination of pneumonia, diabetes, and nerve damage.

It turned out to be his most dangerous battle yet. Cash lapsed into a coma for twelve days. His family became so anxious that June arranged for a special prayer request to be put on fan Web sites. What they didn't know was that for much of the time Cash was aware of what was going on in the hospital room. He could hear people discussing his fate. "I remember things they were saying," he later said. "I couldn't respond. [I couldn't] wake up and tell them, 'I heard what you said . . . I'm not dying.'"

June believed that prayer had brought Cash back from the brink of death. "There seemed to be no way to reach him," she said. "I couldn't think of anything but to pray. So we prayed and within a matter of hours he just started squeezing my hand." The joy was short-lived. Doctors informed Cash that he didn't have Parkinson's disease but a rare condition known as Shy-Drager's syndrome. His life expectancy was no more than eighteen months.

13

The Man Comes Around

THE ENFORCED SECLUSION at Old Hickory Lake was not to Cash's liking. He wasn't officially housebound, but travel presented fresh difficulties, and he had more and more doctor appointments to keep. He'd spent most of his adult life on the road—with his musicians as a surrogate family and his tour bus as a home away from home. Moving from city to city suited his restless nature. Basking in the applause of the crowd was a safe and controllable form of intoxication. "It gives me a high like none you can get," he said in 1988.

As Cash the man slowed, so did Cash the business. The Johnny Cash Museum shut its doors in 1995 and now, with Cash off the tour, talk of selling the House of Cash began. The payroll that once listed over forty people now ran in single figures. In January 1998, Carl Perkins died after suffering a series of strokes. In June, Helen Carter died at the age of seventy. Just over a year later, Anita Carter died at the age of sixty-six.

"It depresses him," Rosanne said at the time. "He's not used to sitting around. He's a very powerful person and not to feel well—that's really hard for him. He spent over forty years on the road, and suddenly he's not there. When that energy comes to a screeching halt, there's a lot to deal with just inside yourself."

Perhaps he could have managed a single illness, but almost every part of his body decided to rebel at the same time. His asthma only compounded the chronic obstructive pulmonary disorder in his lungs, his jaw remained a constant source of pain, and his stomach regurgitated food. Partially deaf in his left ear and partially blind from glaucoma, he suffered also from damaged nerve endings and abscessed feet.

It's difficult to say whether Cash's years of drug abuse contributed to his ailments. Anecdotal evidence suggests that there may be a connection between heavy amphetamine use and diabetes in later life. Some family members thought he'd been overmedicated for years, and others thought that he had been operated on more than necessary. Neither of his parents had suffered ill health at his age (now sixty-six) and both had lived well into their eighties. He insisted that years of hard work on the road, not the drugs, wore out his body. "Maybe I did [wear myself out]. But it was to a good purpose. They [the pundits] should be thankful that I wore it out . . . writing and recording and touring and doing concerts."

As Cash's faculties declined, public and professional acclaim for his work increased. People seemed to realize that they may not have many more chances to tell him face to face just what an exceptional contribution he had made to music. In December 1996, Cash received a Kennedy Center Lifetime Achievement Award. Vice President Al Gore nominated Cash for the award that honored his body of work for revealing "the entire range of existence, failure and recovery, entrapment and escape, weakness and strength, loss and redemption, life and death." In February 1998, *Unchained* won the Grammy for Best Country Album, and the following year the Recording Academy gave him the Grammy's Lifetime Achievement award.

It was in 1998 that he first had discussions about making a movie of his life story called *Walk the Line*. He approached James Keach, movie-producer-husband of Jane Seymour, who had first met him when he and June had guest starred on *Doctor Quinn, Medicine Woman* and had grown to be a close friend. "John said that he'd like me to be involved because he didn't trust the intentions of most people in Hollywood," says Keach. "He wanted a film that wasn't just sex and drugs and rock-'n'-roll but his journey as a man and his love with June and the fact that God was at the core of his story."

An original script by Gil Denis, written in close consultation with Cash, was eventually sold to Sony with director James Mangold and his producer-wife Cathy Konrad attached to the project but was put into turnaround and then picked up by

Fox 2000. Production started in 2004 with Joaquin Phoenix playing Cash and Reese Witherspoon as June.

In April 1999, the industry gathered at Hammerstein Ballroom in New York for the All-Star Tribute to Johnny Cash. Many of Cash's closest friends and greatest admirers in the business sang their choice of his songs. Filmed highlights included performances by U2 ("Don't Take Your Guns to Town"), Bruce Springsteen ("Give My Love to Rose"), and Bob Dylan ("Train of Love"). Cash watched the show offstage on TV monitors, but after Tim Robbins read the liner notes to *Johnny Cash at Folsom Prison,* the honoree graced the audience with both "Folsom Prison Blues" and "I Walk the Line." In 2001, President George W. Bush presented him the National Medal of Arts.

Being off the road did have its benefits—Johnny now had the time to focus on creating music. He had found a large part of his identity in being a performing artist and now he had to rediscover it as a recording artist. His relationship with Rick Rubin reinvigorated him. He derived great pleasure from researching songs to record in the future, and he enjoyed sending CDs to Rubin for his opinion. He recorded in his cabin, where, through the window, he could watch the goats, deer, and peacocks wandering among the trees. His son, John Carter, would join him and make suggestions. He, along with Cash's son-in-law Jimmy Tittle, would both work on all the *American Recording* sessions—John Carter as associate producer and Tittle as production assistant. Periodically, Rubin would fly in from L.A. to monitor the progress.

Thoughts of sin and redemption preoccupied him less during the building of this album, possibly because he'd left the arena of his greatest temptations. Spending so much time sick and at home, Cash was not so easily tempted by the lusts of the flesh. "They [the demons] don't come knocking on a regular basis," he admitted. "They just kind of hover in the distance." Instead, he became preoccupied with the transience of life and the consciousness of mortality. The subject even crept into the songs he dredged from his memory—songs he used to sing to his girlfriends back in Dyess—like "That Lucky Old Sun."

> Oh, Lord above, don't you hear me cryin'
> Tears are rollin' down my eyes.
> Send in a cloud with a silver linin,'

> Take me to paradise.
> Show me that river, take me across,
> Wash all my troubles away
> Like that lucky old sun, give me nothing to do,
> But roll around heaven all day.[1]

For the same album, Rubin chose more contemporary songs, like Neil Diamond's "Solitary Man," Tom Petty's defiant "I Won't Back Down," and Nick Cave's sombre "The Mercy Seat," which told the story of an execution from the point of view of the condemned man. In Cash's hands "The Mercy Seat" became not only a song of compassion for those facing the electric chair but the testimony of anyone under a death sentence.

> And the mercy seat is waiting
> And I think my head is burning
> And in a way I'm yearning
> To be done with all this measuring of truth
> An eye for an eye
> A tooth for a tooth
> And anyway I told the truth
> And I'm not afraid to die.[2]

The process of collecting material infused Cash's creative juices. He wrote three new songs, cowrote another and coadapted a fourth. "It's the first time I've ever had them bombard my brain like that," he told *Rolling Stone*. "I hadn't written for more than a year since I got sick, but when I started recording, the ideas started coming."[3] Again the songs depicted endings, departures, transitions. The last verse of "Wayfaring Stranger," a song from an 1858 hymnal, summed up his situation:

> I know dark clouds will hang 'round me
> I know my way is rough and steep
> Yet beauteous fields lie just before me
> Where God's redeemed their vigils keep.

I'm going there to see my mother
She said she'd meet me when I come
I'm only going over Jordan
I'm only going over home.[4]

His voice had grown noticeably weaker. He could no longer reach the high notes, and at times he was reduced to a vocal style that was closer to the spoken word. He was conscious of his loss of vocal power and range, but Rubin urged him on, telling him not to bother with continuous retakes. The fragility added to his art. When he sang about "this world of woe," his weary, broken voice supplied conviction. When he sang of "that bright world to which I go," that voice gathered a soulful yearning. As Bono perceptively observed, the initial revolution at Sun Records in the 1950s gave young people a voice to celebrate youthfulness, and now Cash, with great dignity, was leading another revolution against the ravages of age, as the first of his generation to sing about the dying of the light.

"Every time I recorded Johnny Cash I knew that it would be around forever," says David Ferguson, who increasingly found himself at Cash's cabin engineering these sessions. "You take extra time with stuff like that. As far as recording him went, you could take the cheapest microphone in the world and put it in front of that guy's voice and you'd know exactly who it was as soon as he opened his mouth. He had so much character in his voice. It got harder during *Solitary Man* because his voice would change so much. It got harder, but it was still so much fun."

For Cash, the loss of vocal power brought frustration. He felt that he was performing beneath his ability. Rubin recalls, "Some days he would sing well, but you could hear the age in his voice. I would tell him that it didn't sound as though he was tired, it sounded like he was emoting the song. Eventually he'd come around. There were times when he'd even joke about it, saying that no songs out there were safe, because he was going to get hold of them and ruin them."

Whenever Cash completed a batch of material he'd send copies to Rubin in California for review and then, health permitting, fly out to finish the tracks. In Los Angeles, guest vocalists joined him in the studio: Sheryl Crow on "Field of Diamonds" and Will Oldham on "I See a Darkness"; in Hendersonville Merle Haggard joined him on "I'm Leavin' Now" and Tom Petty on "I Won't Back Down" and "Solitary Man."

Two unexpected trips to the hospital interrupted recording in October 1999. The first trip was short—stitches for a gashed leg. Though the second stay for pneumonia was longer, good news came in the form of a revised diagnosis. After reviewing his condition, doctors decided that instead of the terminal Shy-Drager's syndrome, he suffered from the less lethal (but more vague) condition, autonomic neuropathy. At the news, Cash shrugged, "I knew I didn't have such a nasty-sounding disease anyway."

Despite the physical setbacks, Cash always remained positive. He never complained he'd been handed a bad deal nor did he question God's plan. He maintained an unwavering gratitude for every blessing—those received and those to come. On August 16, 2000, he wrote in the sleeve notes for *Solitary Man*: "I wouldn't trade my future for anyone's I know." His unexpected reference to his future may seem strange, especially knowing that his future held little more than the promise of declining health and diminishing faculties. But not to Cash: "The Master of Life's been good to me," he wrote. "He gives me good health now and helps me to continue doing what I love. He has given me strength to face past illnesses, and victory in the face of defeat. He has given me life and joy where others saw oblivion. He has given new purposes to live for. New services to render and old wounds to heal. Life and love go on. Let the music play."[5] The album came out on October 17, 2000, and again met with critical acclaim.

Almost immediately Cash set about collecting and writing for his next album. The most ambitious song was "The Man Comes Around." Unlike anything he'd written before, he mixed prophetic judgment with visionary insight and delivered it half in speech and half in song. It came, he said, from a dream he'd had of meeting the queen of England who told him, "Johnny Cash! You're like a thorn tree in a whirlwind." He remembered the phrase, he said, and later traced it to a passage in the Old Testament book of Job.

The phrase, however, did trigger an extensive search of prophetic and apocalyptic literature. The song, crammed with ringing phrases lifted from various parts of the Bible and pieced together as a collage, depicts events surrounding the Final Judgment when "the man" (Jesus Christ) "comes around." The image of "the potter's ground" refers to the burial ground for foreigners bought with the thirty pieces of silver Judas was paid for his betrayal (Matthew 27:3–8). The phrase "Alpha and Omega" is God's description of himself as the beginning and the end

(Revelation 1:8). The admonition "whoever is unjust let him be unjust still" is also attributed to the Lord God (Revelation 22:11).

Cash admitted that he spent more time on this song than any other he ever wrote. It shows. "The Man Comes Around" exudes an intensity of something written by someone who knows time is short. The warning is stark—the man is returning to decide "who to free and who to blame," and lest anyone should think that the concept of a loving God means that heaven is inevitable for all, he adds the reminder, "Everybody won't be treated all the same." He underscores the importance of being ready for the return of Christ when he uses the line "the virgins are all trimming their wicks" (Matthew 23:7).

This track could never have been as effective had he recorded it as a young man. Cash's cracked and sometimes breathless voice sounds both urgent and compassionate. It's not the voice of youthful zealousness or sheltered naiveté. It's the voice of the pilgrim at the end of his journey.

The song's construction presented a musical challenge. "We cut it a few times," says David Ferguson. "We first cut it with Marty Stuart and Johnny as a tick-tock sort of thing. Then he worked on it again with Randy Scruggs. It was then edited to make it meter out. The way Johnny laid it out, only he knew where the changes were going to be in the instrumental parts. It was something you had to learn. Rick would take a bar out here and a couple of bars out there to make the whole thing uniform."

Cash's deteriorating eyesight meant that the words of each song had to be printed in eighteen-point boldface type for him to be able to read. Nick Cave was visibly shocked when he met him for the first time in Rubin's studio, where he recorded a duet on the Hank Williams song "I'm So Lonesome I Could Cry" and the traditional song "Cindy." "There were steps into the studio and he had to be led down them very slowly by two people," he says. "One of his illnesses meant that when he went from light to dark he couldn't see for a while. He looked real sick, and he just sat down and was blind. He asked me if I was there and I told him I was. His eyes adjusted but it wasn't immediate. But when he started working he came alive. This man who I had seen virtually having to be carried down the stairs was utterly transformed when he started singing. In his own words, 'This is what I love to do. This is what I want to do. I want to do as much of it as possible.' It was his cause for living."

The other experimental track on the album was Trent Reznor's song "Hurt." Few would have spotted a Johnny Cash classic lurking inside the Nine Inch Nails rendition, but Cash did.

While still a junkie, Reznor had written the song about the despondency of someone addicted to heroin who not only hurts himself but those who love and try to help him. Although Cash never shot heroin, he could certainly relate to the sentiment. It was a song about disengagement from friends, feelings, surroundings, and even conscience. Yet in Cash's mouth the words took on another dimension. The numbness of the opening lines became the numbness of living on medication. The needle came from the familiar IV unit. The "sweetest friend" referred, of course, to June. The "everyone I know" who "goes away in the end" included Ray and Carrie, Maybelle, Ezra, Anita and Helen Carter, Roy Orbison, Waylon Jennings, Luther Perkins, and Jack Cash. His "empire of dirt" manifested itself in his possessions, awards, and earthly reputation.

"Hurt" could also be about vicarious atonement. From this perspective, the "sweetest friend" is Christ, the "empire of dirt" becomes Cash's collection of sins, and the pain at the heart of the song reflects the pain of the Crucifixion. The song, then, becomes an admission of his unfaithfulness to Christ. At the same time, it provides an assurance that this unfaithfulness is included among the sins for which Christ died.

> I will let you down
> I will make you hurt.[6]

Though a recurring theme in Cash's life, pain never made him bitter. "He lived in constant physical pain for the last ten years of his life," says John Carter. "He struggled with it for a long time, and it got to the point where you never heard him complain. There was a great sadness inside him but at the same time a great strength. He would never draw attention to himself. He owned those pains. He took them all on as his own, and he didn't blame anybody for it."

The song that Cash thought best summarized his faith was "Personal Jesus," written by Martin Gore and recorded by Depeche Mode. He once wished that he had composed it. It's easy to see why. The language is direct ("Reach out and touch faith / Your own personal Jesus / Someone to hear your prayers . . .")[7] and the message seems unambiguous: Jesus is ready to forgive anyone who calls on him and to establish a personal relationship with them. However, it was written as satire, mocking the tendency of people to turn lovers into savior figures. Gore wrote it after reading Priscilla Presley's book *Elvis and Me.* "It's a song about being a Jesus for somebody else," he said. "It's about how Elvis was her man and her mentor, and how often that happens in love relationships."

Departures and farewells permeated the new Cash album. The men in "Give My Love to Rose," "I Hung My Head," and "The Streets of Laredo" try to make amends before they die. "Danny Boy" is a plea to a soldier leaving for war. The Beatles' song "In My Life" is a lament for a disappearing world. "We'll Meet Again," a song made popular in World War II by Vera Lynn in Britain and the Inkspots in America, captured the mood of people thrown together by circumstance who never knew whether they'd ever reunite. Cash defined the theme as "the human spirit fighting for survival."

The album's packaging, coupled with Mark Romanek's video for "Hurt," intensifies the somber mood of the tracks. The front cover, dominated by a black background, features a bespectacled Cash in profile. His head is slightly tilted and his eyes appear to be closed. All but the front of his face is in shadow, giving the impression that he is slowly slipping from view. Photographs inside the CD booklet cast Cash almost as an apparition—his hair white and his fingers gnarled. In a closeup of his left hand, his black onyx ring displays a crucifix.

"On that record he was really showing his age," says Martyn Atkins, who did the cover photography. "There was a lot of frailty to the music, and the pictures tell the same story."

The video for "Hurt" must rank as one of the most tear-inducing ever made. Cash was filmed at home performing the song with June standing nearby watching him and then footage of his younger more vigorous self was edited in, giving the undeniable impression that he was singing about his own demise. The contrast between the powerfully built, dark-haired singer of the 1960s and this frail, balding man sitting on a sofa was painful to watch. Images from the House of Cash Museum, now obviously in a state of disrepair, were also used to underline the impression of a life drawing to a close.

Romanek had not planned to shoot the video this way. He originally wanted to film something inspired by images from a Samuel Beckett play, on a set in Los Angeles, but Cash got sick and couldn't travel. With four days left before the Cashes disappeared to Cinnamon Hill, Romanek had no choice but to shoot the video at home. When he arrived in Hendersonville on October 18, 2002, he picked out three or four areas in the house to film and then saw the museum, which had not only been closed for a long time but had been damaged in a flood.

Says Romanek, "I think I shot the museum the way it was and didn't try to gloss over the state of John's health and his advanced years because I was bolstered by the bold truthfulness and unusual candor that defined most of John's songs and public life. The use of archival footage wasn't part of the plan. We discovered this trove of material in a storage house while we were there and asked if we could take some back to L.A. Frankly, I didn't think it would be of much use, but when my editor Robert Duffy and I put a little piece in the first cut, the hairs on our necks stood up. We knew then that this footage would make up a huge part of the video. It then took us three weeks to comb through all the footage we'd brought back."

The result was an intensely moving study of someone facing the indignities of illness and aging but doing so without shame. It fit perfectly into Cash's *oeuvre* as a man known for his honesty and directness. He had for many years sung about the fleeting nature of life and the ravages of death, and now he courageously shared his own walk through the valley of the shadow of death. He'd started his career in a business that exalted youth, and now he exemplified the dignity in growing old.

Romanek sent a copy of the finished video to Cash in Jamaica. "Rick Rubin told me that the family watched it together as a group," he says. "Tears were shed. I think John was initially unsure about it, but the family convinced him that it was a strong, unusual, well-intentioned piece." Rosanne didn't see it for a while because her sisters thought it might upset her. She finally saw it when Cash played it for her in his office. "I was devastated," she says. "I was crying like a baby. He was sitting next to me patting me on the shoulder. I told him that it was the most powerful video I had ever seen. I said it wasn't even a video. It was a documentary."

The Man Comes Around hit stores on November 4, 2002. On November 26, Cash appeared in an hour-long interview with Larry King on CNN, which had been recorded six weeks earlier on October 11. Larry asked whether Cash was angry about his physical setbacks. He said he wasn't. Things had been good and things would get better. Did he have regrets? He said he didn't. Was he bitter? No, he wasn't. "Why should I be bitter? I'm thrilled to death with life! Life, the way God has given it to me, was just a platter—a golden platter of life laid out there for me.

It's been beautiful." Was he angry at God? "Oh no," said Cash. "I'm the last one that would be angry at God."

Cash and June retired to Cinnamon Hill while *The Man Comes Around* started to make waves. The video received instant accolades. *Rolling Stone* called it "one of the most intense and affecting videos in memory." The album went on to sell over a million copies and became his first platinum studio album.

He started feeling bad again in Jamaica, so the Cashes returned early to Hendersonville. Cash was admitted to the hospital in January suffering from pneumonia. "It was a really hard time for him," says his niece, Kelly Hancock. "He came out in January and was then back again in February (after gashing his knee) and then back again in March (after falling out of bed and losing consciousness). I believe he was released either on the last day of March or the first day of April, but this was the first time that he was unable to walk. He had to have a wheelchair and a walker and he found this really difficult. Two days later his sister Louise died of cancer and he was so fragile that he couldn't go to the funeral. The doctor forbade him from leaving the house."

The house Cash had moved back to was the house his mother had lived in before she had died. Being on one level it was more convenient for him now that his legs were weak, and the need to build an elevator in the house on Old Hickory Lake meant there was building work going on at home. June, as ever, was busying herself with making sure that he was as comfortable as possible, sticking resolutely to her belief that his needs were her number-one priority.

Karen Adams and Kelly Hancock would go over regularly with mail delivered to the House of Cash and talk over business decisions that needed to be made. "I noticed that June was taking all this special time with him and how important it was to her," says Kelly. "I remember thinking later that it was so sweet, and it was amazing to me that they had been married for so many years and yet they were still like that with each other. That's how they were. She wanted to be his caregiver. I don't think that he really wanted that for her, but a lot of times she would take over that role and see that things were done by her. Looking back, we realize that she was sick herself."

It was during the third week of April, after her brief stay in the hospital, that those who visited the house regularly noticed that June seemed different. Her energy seemed depleted, and her breathing seemed more labored, but she was so involved in looking after her husband that she didn't have time to mull over her ailments. On April 18, Good Friday, she told Kelly that she didn't have long to live. She told another friend that "something's going on in here," pointing to her chest.

On April 28 June was taken into the hospital. Whereas Cash was not initially aware of the seriousness of her condition, she appears to have instinctively realized that something major was wrong. "I think that she knew," says John Carter. "Before she left for the hospital, she had me come in with her to the room and go through stuff. She wanted to talk to me about things, about what should happen if she died. I think she knew she was going."

When she underwent the tests, June was apprehensive about her chances of survival. "I just don't have the energy," she told Michele Rollins, who went with Cash to visit her. They discussed the options until it became clear to everyone that there were really only two options—certain death almost immediately or the chance of an extended life. Cash was distraught about the possibility of losing June, telling her how much he loved her and how his life would be over if she were to leave him. They chose the possibility of life.

When Merle Kilgore visited, Cash seemed remarkably composed. "He was sitting in his wheelchair at the hospital and he reached out both hands to greet me," says Kilgore. "I remarked to him that he seemed so strong. He said, 'No. I'm really weak inside.' He said, 'I can talk about June without breaking up because I'm dehydrated. I can't make any tears.'"

The next two weeks proved the most harrowing of Cash's life. Hopes of a remarkable recovery were soon dashed by June's lapse into coma. The devastating moment when they agreed to unplug the life-support machine was closely followed by the excruciating period of waiting for her body to finally close down. "Part of him was gone," says John Carter of the effect of her death. "The two were one. When she left, part of him just wasn't there anymore."

"He was the most alone person I had ever seen in my life," remembers Kelly. "It was so strange to walk into his house and not to see June and to know that we were never going to see her. I don't think he'd ever been alone. He'd always had very strong women around him. June was someone who had been stable for him, and I looked at him and realized that for the first time he was alone and he was lost."

Cash never went back to their marital bed. Instead, he slept on a twin bed in his office with the pillows propped up to avoid acid reflux. Surrounding him were the things he loved: his guitar, his Bible, more than five hundred books of theology, history, poetry, music, fiction, and Western lore, a TV almost always tuned to CNN, and a framed photograph of June that he spoke to constantly. He napped there in the afternoon and slept there at night, waking around 5:00 a.m. for his first coffee of the day.

"John struck me as a quiet, pensive man," daughter-in-law Laura Cash says. "After June passed in May, he seemed to withdraw even more from having much conversation. Many times John Carter and I would sit with him for long periods with no words spoken. I believe it was a comfort to him to have someone there who didn't feel it necessary to talk."

After a time of grieving he knew the only way to cope with his loss was to get back to his music. "He said to me, 'I've got to get into the studio, son,' and so that's what we did," says John Carter. The first project he worked on was a collection of Carter Family songs, and then he continued with what he wanted to be the follow-up to *The Man Comes Around*, an album already being referred to as *American V*. John Carter continued in the role of associate producer.

One of the musicians working on these sessions was his old friend Jack Clement, now into his sixth decade of working with Cash. "I was pretty proud of the way John Carter rose to the occasion," he says. "Cash got to the point where he couldn't even read, much less decipher lyrics. But John Carter would sing them in the sessions so that he could learn to play them."

Cash had been taping new songs ever since completion of the last album. At the same time, preparations were underway for a five-CD box set that would contain the best of the *American Recordings* already released, as well as the best of the work not used. David Ferguson flew back and forth between Nashville and Los Angeles to sift through hundreds of hours of tape with Rick Rubin for the box sets and work with Cash in his home studio.

"He was weak by now," says Ferguson. "His voice would come and go. He never knew from one day to the next whether he was going to be able to sing. He was real weak. He was in a wheelchair and sick, but whenever he could and whenever he felt like it he wanted to record because he really wanted to finish up that record."

On June 21 he played seven songs at the Carter Family Fold in Virginia to celebrate what would have been June's seventy-fourth birthday. The concert, organized by Janette Carter, June's eighty-year-old cousin, attracted almost sixteen hundred people—twice the venue's normal capacity. With his wispy gray hair and sunken features he was a husk of the man he'd once been and seemed wrapped in a cloak of loneliness. "I don't know hardly what to say tonight about being up here without her," he said. "The pain is so severe there is no way of describing it."

"He'd bury himself in his music," says Ferguson. "He was lonely. He had fun when he was recording because he was surrounded by his friends. I've been working with him a long time and I know that's one reason that he liked to work—to have buddies around him. He had people like Pat McLaughlin, Jack Clement, Mark Howard, Randy Scruggs, Marty Stuart."

His daughter Cindy came to stay with him in June. Although he was 80 percent blind, he had her bring more photographs of June to his office. He even had Mark Burckhardt, an artist from Austin, Texas, paint June's face on the elevator doors. "He missed her so bad," says Cindy. "He sobbed for her daily. He would pick up the phone to talk to her as if she was on the other end."

Cindy would take him to sit outside in the sun, but after thirty minutes he was ready to come back in and lie down. Almost all of his enjoyments had now been taken away from him. One time she took him in his wheelchair to see June's grave. "He stared at it awhile and tried to focus so that he could see the tombstone," she says. "As soon as he had focused, he said, 'I'm coming baby. I'm coming.' That upset me. I had to tell him that I didn't want to hear those kinds of things."

Her sister Tara came to visit for three days in July, and she spent hours sitting with him in his office or outside the house. Knowing that it was almost certainly going to be their last time together, she made tapes of their conversations and of a game he enjoyed playing where she would throw a random topic at him and he had to dig up an appropriate song from his encyclopedic mind. "I'd say, 'Dad, sing a song about a rock,' and he'd break into one," she says. "Then I'd say, 'Sing one about grass,' and he'd break into one. I did that for maybe thirty subjects. He loved it. I think it helped to keep his mind active, and he loved the challenge."

As Cash's eyes and legs grew weaker, his faith appeared to grow stronger. He had a light box that projected pages of his Bible onto a screen so that he could read it with his 20-percent vision. He talked regularly on the phone with Billy Graham, someone whom he'd always relied on as a rock to lean on in times of trouble. "I think that God had given him such faith, almost to the point of it being unreal," says Kelly. "I think that's the only way he made it. I think he had the utmost faith in God and he looked to God for his strength and direction. After the funeral he could have gone to bed and told everyone that he wasn't going to get up again. He could have gone into isolation. But he chose not to. He could have got angry, but I never saw him angry. What I saw from him was that he was lost and he was still trying to find his way without her, but I didn't see the same man that I saw that day in the hospital who was utterly broken. I didn't see that again."

Cash had always said that he didn't fear death, but he now seemed to yearn for it—not in a morbid way, or even because it promised a relief from the pain. He believed that for a Christian, death was the gateway to eternal life. His sister Joanne remembers the times they spent together in his office, especially after June's death, when they would sit and discuss the Bible. "He would look at me, a couple of times with tears in his eyes, and he would say, 'I can hardly wait to see heaven, to see the Lord and to see our family.' I know him and I know how real it was to him."

As late as August 14, 2003, he was in the studio working on two songs: a humorous one called "Asthma Coming Down Like the 309" and a song called "1 Corinthians 15:55" about death, based on the verse "Where, O death, is your victory? Where, O death, is your sting?" And the following week, on August 21, he recorded his last song. It was at the Cash Cabin Studio, with John Carter Cash producing. The song was called "Engine 143," a story song about an engineer running to get to the station on time. He crashes the train, and dies. The song ends with the words, "And the very last words poor Georgie said were, 'Nearer my God to thee.'" This final song in his legendary catalog was for an album called *Unbroken Circle: The Musical Heritage of the Carter Family*. Three days later, his emergency trip to the hospital with peritonitis prohibited him from attending the MTV Awards in New York. Up for six category awards, the video of "Hurt" ultimately only won the award for cinematography. He was released on Tuesday, September 9, and was already making plans to fly to Los Angeles to do more work in Rick Rubin's studio.

On Thursday, September 11, he was taken ill again, this time with respiratory problems brought on by an asthma attack and complicated by his reflux condition. His lungs, which had very little healthy tissue left, began to fail. He was coughing up blood and was in a state of delirium when the ambulance came. "When I got to the hospital he was conscious," says Rosanne. "He wasn't eyes-open-and-sitting-up conscious, but he squeezed my hand. He had come back from death so many times that, as bad as it looked, we were still hoping that he would recover."

It wasn't to be. At 2:00 a.m. the next morning, John R. Cash died. The only people with him were John Carter, Rosanne, and Kathy. Courtney Wilson, his former pastor at First Baptist Church in Hendersonville, who had visited him during his previous stay, observed that though Cash hadn't lost the will to live, he was calm in the face of death. "There was no one else in the room," he says. "We just spent a little time together because I knew he wasn't feeling good, and after we had prayed, we shook hands and it was like two old friends saying good-bye. I might even have had a tear in my eye. I think he was at peace. Well, I know he was. He was really ready to go. Ready to go home to be with God."

The private funeral took place at First Baptist Church on Monday, September 15. It featured some of the same artists who'd performed at June's funeral. Emmylou Harris and Sheryl Crow sang "The Old Rugged Cross" and Bob Dylan's "Every Grain of Sand." Franklin Graham, representing his father Billy, spoke and said that Cash was "a good man who also struggled with many challenges in his life." Kris Kristofferson offered what was perhaps the most memorable description when he referred to Cash as "Abraham Lincoln with a wild side." Larry Gatlin, Marty Stuart, and Randy Scruggs were among the pallbearers of Cash's black coffin with silver handles.

Cash was laid to rest next to June. Close by were the graves of Mother Maybelle, Ezra, and Anita. On his grave marker, beneath his name and the dates of his birth and death, was Psalm 19:14: "Let the words of my mouth and the meditation of my heart be acceptable in thy sight, O Lord, my strength, and my redeemer." Then followed the familiar flourish of his signature.

Obituaries teemed with praise for the man universally regarded as a great artist, a great humanitarian, and a great American. The *New York Times* said, "His gravely bass-baritone was the vocal bedrock of American country music for more than four decades." To the *Village Voice* he was, "the most important country artist of the modern era." Robert Hilburn of the *Los Angeles Times* called him "a standard of integrity and craft that not only helped reshape country music but also served as a standard for any artist of merit in all pop music. People from Bono to Dylan to Springsteen admired this man and his work."

In Britain, the *Guardian* described him as "a country musician who was too big for country music, and his work as artist, humanitarian, and patron of songs and song writing will endure indefinitely." The *Independent* saw him as "one of the last great icons of American country music." *Time Out* said, "If America as a nation could speak . . . it would sound something like Johnny Cash. His voice was America's voice, just as America's voice was his."

The next weeks and months brought a steady stream of tributes: television and radio documentaries, special newspaper sections, prepared statements by everyone from President George W. Bush to Bob Dylan. Cash's image graced the cover of *TIME* magazine, and in November a televised tribute aired from the Ryman Auditorium, featuring most of his close friends and members of his family. Actor Tim Robbins hosted the show, which included taped appearances from Bono, Billy Graham, Whoopi Goldberg, Dan Rather, and Ray Charles. Particularly moving was a montage of photographs of Cash playing with his children and grandchildren over which was played the last recording he made with Rosanne, a song called "September When It Comes."

> So when the shadows link them
> And burn away the clouds
> They will fly me like an angel
> To a place where I can rest.
> When this begins, I'll let you know
> September when it comes.[8]

—

SIX WEEKS AFTER CASH'S DEATH, his stepdaughter Rosey was discovered dead in a parked tour bus alongside a bluegrass fiddle player, Jimmy Campbell. She was forty-five years old. Though emergency medical workers found drug paraphernalia on the bus, authorities attributed her death to carbon monoxide poisoning. Hers was the fourth death in the family in seven months. The family began to refer to this dark period as a "season of grief."

In November 2003, as planned, the first copies of the lavish box set that Cash had approved before his death made their way into the market. *Unearthed* consisted of seventy-seven songs spread over five CDs. Presented with the set was a beautiful book written by Sylvie Simmons that told the back story of the recordings and included a song-by-song explanation by Cash. All of the songs had been recorded during his decade-long relationship with Rick Rubin. Besides the fifteen tracks on the *Best of Cash on American* CD, none had ever been officially released. The songs ranged from simple acoustic renditions of hymns his mother had taught him as a child to covers of songs by Bob Marley, Neil Young, and Steve Earle. Guests on the album included Joe Strummer (formerly of the Clash), Nick Cave, Tom Petty, and Carl Perkins.

Though some critics thought Rubin had squeezed every last drop of creativity out of Cash and that the recordings lacked consistency, *Unearthed,* for the most part, received an enthusiastic welcome. Reviewing the collection for the music magazine *Mojo,* Mat Snow raved, "For those of us who hold that music is the noblest expression of what it is to be human, here is the final installment of a body of work that, almost uniquely, transcends the legend." Steve Volk of *Philadelphia Weekly* wrote: "Cash was a real flesh and blood man who took on the staggering proportions of myth. The image *Unearthed* leaves us with is something far humbler, yet no less grand: A sharecropper who dug down into the earth, discovered himself, and discovered us."

In his final decade, Cash had not only produced some of his best work, but he had done some of his best living. Closer than ever to June, he had healed many of his broken relationships and had, by all accounts, become more loving, caring, and forgiving. He had faced death neither with resignation nor with anger but with cheerful fortitude. "I don't understand death," he told Larry Gatlin, "but I'm not afraid of it."

In the end Johnny Cash achieved his aim of living a life that exemplified the power of redemption. He fought the good fight. He ran the race. He kept the faith. "You could look at the last days of his life and say that he died a sad, miserable soul," says John Carter. "However, that's not the full picture. Yes, he was sad. Yes, he was alone. But he had purpose, he had belief, and he had a peace in spite of himself that God granted him. I think that is what the grace was in his life and that is where the redemption lay. Even though there was great pain, he didn't live in misery. He was able to keep pressing on."

14

Touched by Grace

E VERYONE WHO KNEW JOHNNY CASH will attest to the fact that he was not an unhappy man. Despite his penchant for black clothing and songs about murder, Cash was an optimistic, loving, kind, and humorous person. Anyone less in love with life would have soon been beaten down by the setbacks he suffered. He delighted in friendships, in knowledge, in family, in music, in nature, and in God. "I can sing songs of death. I've seen a lot of it," he once said. "But I'm obsessed with life."

Yet pain characterized Cash's life—emotionally, physically, and spiritually. It made him the man he was and gave him great compassion for others. The trauma of witnessing the death of his beloved brother Jack was the catalyst for his art. Introspective analysis produced poetry and songs. The humiliation meted out by his father left him insecure and shy, but, as with so many other performers with tyrannical fathers, it gave him the desire for acclaim and the determination to prove his worth.

Cheating on Vivian and shirking his family duties added guilt to his pain. His drugs of choice not only alleviated the pain but also assuaged the guilt. While high, he could behave abominably without remorse. Some drugs, he discovered, could save a man from his sins, not by nullifying them, but by camouflaging them. No wonder he felt they'd been sent to him by God.

The short-term effect of the drugs left behind a tiredness laced with unresolved insecurity and unacknowledged sin. The longer Cash remained under the influence of drugs, the deeper he became mired in regret and insecurity. For years he dealt with this dilemma by taking more drugs and so maintained the downward spiral.

Indescribable physical pain, affecting virtually every part of his body, only added to his affliction. He broke his nose, his upper and lower jaw, a kneecap, a foot, five ribs, a thumb, an ankle, and more than twenty other bones. His heart, duodenum, spleen, stomach, eyes, mouth, toes, and intestines all underwent surgery, and he suffered at different times from tonsillitis, laryngitis, glaucoma, diabetes, compressed vertebrae, asthma, pneumonia, cystic sinusitis, and peritonitis. In the 1960s, he flirted on numerous occasions with death, usually with the help of amphetamines or alcohol.

By the time Cash reached what would have been his retirement age, he suffered from a multitude of separate problems. No wonder he had such an attraction for painkillers, particularly the synthetic opiate derivative Percodan. Taking them after surgery to facilitate the healing process almost always led to the conclusion that the pills would heal just about anything—if he took enough.

Perhaps Cash's greatest achievement was that he ultimately rose above all the pain. He came to see his trials, physical and mental, not as enemies to be defeated but as tests from God to make him a stronger person. His physical suffering alone would have left many people bitter, but for him it never became a source of doubt or resentment. It was as if instead of asking, "Why me?" he learned to ask, "Why *not* me?"

He took great comfort from the Old Testament book of Job and wrote a thesis on it to help his understanding. Job was a rich farmer who worshiped God, but the devil argued that Job's trust was in direct proportion to the lack of challenges in his life. Were Job to face sickness, loss, poverty, and destruction, he would moderate his faith. In order to prove the devil wrong, God allowed Job a period of severe testing, during which even his closest friends turned on him, convincing him that he brought the evil upon himself through his own wrongdoing.

Of course Cash took solace from this story. Job stuck to his beliefs even when all the evidence appeared to contradict them. Like Job, Johnny trusted in a loving God even when completely engulfed by pain. "I never questioned God," Cash said in 2002. "I never doubted God. I can't understand people saying they get angry with God. I walked with God all the way through this. That's why I didn't fear. I never feared anything. Not at all. I can honestly say that."

His emotional wounds could have made Cash an introvert, but instead of isolating himself he spent his entire life reaching out to others. He treasured his quiet times and the solitude of fishing, walking, or losing himself in books, but he spent the bulk of his time in the company of friends, family, and fans. Lacking love from his father made him determined to be someone who gave it in abundance.

Cash's suffering made him acutely aware of the suffering of others. At his funeral service and later at the tribute concert, artist after artist told how he had bought them food, paid for accommodations, donated guitars, or even clothed them when they fell on hard times. He used his music to raise money for prisoners, AIDS patients, orphans, drug addicts, alcoholics, autistic children, the illiterate, and countless other disadvantaged people. He said, "As I got to studying the Bible more, I found it part of my religion, not only an obligation but a privilege, to perform for people in bondage, especially those behind bars."

He spoke most often of his spiritual pain. A battle waged within him, he said, between his divinely inspired desire to do right and his natural inclination to do wrong, between serving God and serving himself. He understood only too well what the apostle Paul meant when he wrote, "We know that the law is spiritual; but I am unspiritual, sold as a slave to sin. I do not understand what I do. For what I want to do I do not do, but what I hate I do" (Romans 7:14–15).

His weakness bothered him. Why couldn't he defeat his temptations once and for all and live a consistent and placid life? Surely not every Christian was tempted as frequently as he was and with such uneven results. "I fight the beast in me every day," he once said. "I've won a few rounds with God's help."

Not everyone could identify with Cash's spiritual battle. Those immersed in the rock-'n'-roll lifestyle saw temptation as an opportunity rather than an obstacle and thought that excess led to the "palace of wisdom," as the poet William Blake put it, rather than to the gates of hell. But Cash held tightly to the orthodox Christian position. He believed that although he was redeemed, maybe even *because* he was redeemed, he was subject to spiritual attack. He believed in a devil who posed as an angel of light.

The Rev. Jack Shaw, a pastor whom Cash took on the road with him in the 1990s to keep an eye on his spiritual condition, says that Cash expected to be subject to greater tests of faith because of the uniqueness of his gift and his frankness when discussing spiritual issues in public. "They say that you get shot at the most when you are closest to the target," he says. "They never let up on Johnny. He was always fighting temptation, but I believe that he had a powerful anointing on his life. He also had a compassionate heart, especially for those who were hurting."

Yet Cash's Christian outlook never became self-righteous. He had too much in common with the drug addict, the alcoholic, the vandal, the thief, and the adulterer to ever want to disassociate himself from them. In his eyes the only difference between him and them was that he was forgiven. "I used to have regrets," he once said, "but then I forgave myself. When God forgave me, I figured I'd better do it too."

When Larry Gatlin found himself in a drug rehabilitation center in California in 1984 Cash was one of his first visitors. He didn't come to reprimand or chastise him; he came to show that he cared. "He never did preach to people," says Gatlin. "He shared his faith and his shortcomings with the whole world. John and June's lives were a book. They were open for everyone to see. They weren't perfect, but they were forgiven, and that was the message they shared."

In 1974, perhaps mindful of some of his own early zealousness, he wrote a song admonishing those who prided themselves on their own righteousness and ignored the rest of the world.

> Come heed me my brothers, come heed one and all
> Don't brag about standing or you'll surely fall
> You're shining your light and shine it you should
> But you're so heavenly minded you're no earthly good.
>
> ("No Earthly Good")[1]

Pain was a necessary part of his growth. Without it he would not have been the Johnny Cash we know. He took comfort from the apostle Paul's story of the unspecified "thorn in the flesh." Paul pleaded three times for this suffering to end but said that God told him, "My grace is sufficient for you, for my power is made perfect in weakness" (2 Corinthians 12:9). In other words, the weakness produced by the pain was necessary in order for God to reveal his power and forgiveness. "That is why, for Christ's sake, I delight in weaknesses, in insults, in hardships, in persecutions, in difficulties. For when I am weak, then I am strong" (1 Corinthians 12:10).

Cash seemed to understand this. The times of his greatest suffering were paradoxically the times of his greatest spiritual strength. When on top of the world he tended to trust in his own invincibility. He said himself that during the 1960s he thought he was indestructible, that he could do anything he wanted to his body without any adverse consequences. It was only as his frailties emerged that he developed humility, caution, and concern.

In his final years, as Cash was gradually stripped of everything—his sight, his mobility, his strength, his looks and, finally, his wife—he became more confident than ever in the object of his faith. "I think that after June died he was different," says Kelly Hancock. "He became even more compassionate towards people. He was kinder. He was more thoughtful. He worried about people. He took everyone in a bit closer and he treasured everyone."

He particularly loved being with his grandchildren, who brought out his playfulness and made him laugh again. Laura Cash recalls, "Most days we would bring our daughter, Anna Maybelle, with us. She would come in the front door and head like a bullet for 'Grandpa's room.' He took much delight in her company, as he did with all of his grandkids. He'd say, 'Hi, sweet baby' over and over. She would crawl up in his lap, and he would immediately produce some sugar-free chocolate for her. Even in those sad and lonely times, she could really draw the laughter out of him.

"There were some champagne grapes at the house one day, and John was so patient as Annabelle fed him one after the other for what seemed like an hour. He would brighten up at the mere sight of her and our son, Joseph. He had an electric recliner that, of course, our kids loved to operate. As soon as he sat down, they would be over pushing buttons and have him laid out flat before I knew it. Up and down and up again. I tried to get them to stop, but John wouldn't have it. He was a very loving, patient grandpa."

He restored his relationship with Marshall Grant despite the bitterness of their separation. "In the end," says Marshall, "we became closer than we'd ever been."

According to Kelly, Cash's life became characterized by a spirit of gratefulness. "He felt that he had had a blessed life and that he wouldn't trade one minute of it," she says. "He felt that his struggles he'd been through made him a stronger man, had given him a footstool to climb up to God that he might never have had. I never heard him complain. There were days when I could see that he didn't feel good and didn't look good, and yet he'd get up and go do a session and I would think, 'How is he doing this?' So many times we wondered, 'How can he go over there to the cabin and stay for four or five hours when he's barely able to walk across the room?' We didn't know. We know now that it was a divine strength that he was given. But it continued to amaze us."

His son, John Carter, embraced the same Christian faith and became a close spiritual companion. They spent many hours praying together and discussing the Bible. According to John Carter, he felt that his spiritual strength resulted from all the adversity he had faced. "It's like the strongest sword is made by the hottest fire," he says. "He was like Peter to Christ. Peter was a greatly tortured soul who was in misery and pain but who had something in him that brought him close to Christ. That's how it was with my dad. I think God knew that he would struggle, that he would fall down, but he saw something in him that would be a foundation for a lot of people just as Christ saw something in Peter."

Cash was an unusual figure in American popular music—a Christian with traditional evangelical beliefs who was revered by icons of the subculture as well as figureheads of mainstream culture. Few Christians would find themselves the subject of accolades by such diverse personalities as Snoop Dogg and George W. Bush, Nick Cave and Billy Graham, Trent Reznor and Dolly Parton.

Cash's acceptance didn't come from keeping his light hidden under a bushel. He was as explicit about his beliefs in personal conversation as he was in his songs, but he never appeared sanctimonious and he resisted relying on cliché. When he spoke about God he gained respect because he spoke from his heart— he wasn't merely reciting a creed. And the God of Johnny Cash, the God that shone through Johnny Cash, seemed interesting and relevant.

Rick Rubin tells a story of inviting Cash to a meal at his home, along with some musicians and friends from the film industry. Before eating, Cash asked everyone to hold hands while he prayed and then read from the Bible. "I know that some of these people had never experienced that before," said Rubin. "Some of them were even atheists. But his belief in what he believed was so strong that what you believed didn't matter so much. . . . It was really beautiful."

Everyone who worked with Cash knew of his beliefs because he spoke of God in such a natural way, without proselytizing. He preferred to wait for others to open up to him. "I don't compromise my religion," he said in 1979. "If I'm with someone who doesn't want to talk about it, I don't talk about it. I don't impose myself on anybody in any way, including religion."

His friends agree. "He was a deeply religious man," says David Ferguson, "but he didn't drive it down anybody's throat." Surprisingly Kris Kristofferson says that the two of them never discussed religion. "I think John respected people enough to let them do their own deciding about what they do spiritually," he says. "He got me along to a couple of Billy Graham events and that was enough. I think he was sensitive to the fact that I didn't want to talk about it."

To those who wanted to talk about spiritual matters, he was more than willing to share his thoughts. He and Rick Rubin engaged in deep debates about meditation, mysticism, Jesus, and Eastern thought. "I think that the depth of our connection was always about spirit, and we used music as a vocabulary for that," he says. "It was always about other worldly things, beyond worldly things." In April 2003, they took Communion together for the first time and continued the ritual over the phone every time they spoke over the next five months. Producer Larry Butler was so affected by Cash's faith when he worked with him in Israel on the *Gospel Road* film that he was baptized in the Jordan River and remains a committed Christian more than thirty years later.

Dyann Rivkin, who produced and wrote the TV Special "Ridin' the Rails" for him in 1974 was another person affected by his faith. "I saw something very special in him as we were doing the show," she says. "I asked him what it was, and he said simply, 'Jesus Christ.'" He bought her a Bible and spent hours answering her questions. She became a Christian as a direct result of his interest and patience, and fourteen years later Rivkin produced him as he recorded the entire New Testament for a cassette collection.

Almost a quarter of the songs he wrote were in some way about his faith or the Bible. Many others, although not specifically about faith, were influenced by his Christian world-view. "I Walk the Line," with its declaration of marital fidelity contained an unconscious Christian impulse as did a lot of his songs about justice and poverty. When he wrote about work he did so from a biblical framework. Work could be a source of dignity and pride, but in a fallen world work could also be degrading and exploitative. He accentuated the nobility of labor but never failed to point out how backbreaking it could sometimes be. In doing so, he celebrated the lives of ordinary hardworking people—from shoeshine boys to police officers, stone cutters to truck drivers—and made them feel that they were important.

He wrote about death, but not as a morbid subject. When people died in his songs it was usually the result of an injustice or a love affair gone wrong. His best known murder line, "I shot a man in Reno just to watch him die," appears in a song about imprisonment, freedom, and longing. Murder isn't the focus of the song. Most often, his death songs were actually about salvation. He was looking beyond death to the life to come.

Another quarter of the songs Cash wrote dealt with love—half of them about the joy of it and half about the loss of it. As a man who thrived in the presence of a strong woman, he preferred dark-haired women who were comfortable working in a man's world and who loved music as much as he did.

In June Carter he met his match. Although she always took great pains to say that she didn't "save" Johnny Cash, she certainly provided the stability, reassurance, encouragement, and care he so desperately needed. When they decided to marry, she said she was going to put God first in her life, her husband second, and herself last. She knew it sounded old fashioned, but she believed that inverting this order helped destroy her first two marriages.

June clearly delighted in Cash, and he in her. Not only did they live, work, and travel together, but they also read books, prayed, and listened to music together. Considering their history of relationships and the nature of the business, not many people would have believed their marriage could last thirty-five months, much less thirty-five years. "She's my companion and my friend," he once said. "We talk about things we don't talk to anybody else about. We understand each other. Sometimes it's scary; we can almost read each others' minds. She's my rock, my anchor. She's always there."

Without doubt June displayed tremendous fortitude over the years, calming Cash during his self-destructive periods, taking him back in when he wandered, staying by his side during his many illnesses. She considered caring for him as her life's great duty, and the music he made over the past three decades could not have been made without her. Indeed, we might well be talking of Johnny Cash, Brian Jones, Janis Joplin, and Jimi Hendrix in the same breath if not for June.

"I think they understood each other quintessentially," says Rosanne. "They were both very unusual people. It wasn't easy to understand either one of them. I think there was genuine passion, genuine chemistry. She amused him, and he loved being fussed over and taken care of. She was the talker and he was silent. She filled in the blanks for him. She made his life easy."

The rest of Cash's songs were equally divided between songs about family, justice, music, restlessness, trains, war, country living, the West, and America. He loved his country—its history, its beliefs, its landscape, and its people—and more than any other songwriter of his era, he was identified with the best of American values. He didn't voice disagreements with foreign policy in spite of his love but because of his love. He only got angry when he thought America was behaving in an un-American way.

"One of the last times I talked to him, we spoke about the war in Iraq," says Kris Kristofferson. "I said that we should just go to the table and say that this can't go on because it wasn't going to help us to bomb the country into oblivion. He said, 'I'm with you this time. We're bombing a tribal people.'"

A diligent student of U.S. history, he not only read books but projected himself into the lives of cowboys, early immigrants, Native Americans, pioneers, and Confederate soldiers. When he crawled through Nickajack Caves, dug up arrowheads on the Trail of Tears, or spent nights alone in the desert of California, he was trying to temporarily put himself in the place of his ancestors, to touch the things they touched, to feel the things they felt.

Cash explored his own family history. Earl Poole Ball can remember being with him in New England when they searched a house that he believed rested on the same spot where the first Cash settled in America. In Chesterfield, South Carolina, while en route to a concert in Georgia, he sought out Edgar Rivers, the oldest living member of his mother's side of the family, to learn about his grandfather, John. L. Rivers. "I showed him where the old farmhouse used to stand that his granddaddy was raised in," says Rivers. "I took him to the old spring where he would have got water. He said that if he'd had a jar he would have filled it with that water and taken it home."

In his own life Cash had had a front-row seat to many of the climactic events in recent American history. He'd felt the effects of the Depression, and when Mrs. Roosevelt visited Dyess, he shook her hand. He experienced the cold war firsthand in Germany during the early 1950s, participated in the birth of rock-'n'-roll in Memphis in 1954, was driving to a concert in Dallas the day John F. Kennedy was killed, turned down an offer to play at Woodstock in 1969 (on the advice of Bob Dylan), and traveled to Vietnam during the war. He attended the Watergate hearings; shook hands with Nixon, Carter, Reagan, Clinton, and Bush; and had a poem written for him by Muhammad Ali.

As with many legends in popular music, it's not easy to say exactly what made Cash great. He never became a great guitarist, his voice had a limited range, and his lyrics veered between poetry and doggerel. But the combination of that voice, those words, and that guitar far exceeded the greatness of any one element. He was a presence, a form of energy, a vehicle for truth. "I wouldn't call him a great musician," says Jack Clement. "I'd call him a great musical entity. He was a musical force and a great singer. People believed what he was saying. Most people don't understand that the voice is like an instrument and has to blend in with the other instruments. Somehow Cash understood that. Mostly because he didn't care. He would just sing. Somehow it worked."

His inspiration has been less one of musical form and more one of attitude. The people who have admired him—Steve Earle, Dwight Yoakam, the Dixie Chicks Emmylou Harris, Kid Rock, Joe Strummer, Elvis Costello, Bob Dylan, Kris Kristofferson, Bruce Springsteen, Keith Richard, Bono, Nick Cave—are not united by a sound but by an approach to their art. Cash encouraged people to be honest, to have integrity, to fearlessly explore within, to be compassionate, and to search for truth. "I'm sure I learned social consciousness from John," says Kristofferson. "I learned concern for your brother and independence—doing what you believe in spite of what other people tell you. I admired the way he spoke his own words. There was no question of me ever trying to imitate what he was doing because he was as unique as a snowflake."

Cash was an inspiration to Christians because of the candid way in which he discussed the problems that had affected his life. By admitting his mistakes he gave hope to the spiritually battered and abused. He also suggested a way of living the Christian life that was uncompromising yet compassionate, dedicated to timeless truths yet relevant to contemporary issues, in the world yet not of it, orthodox yet hip.

"Can you imagine being a believer in a population where other believers seem like freaks?" says Bono. "I'm talking of my own life as a believer. People were selling God like a commodity, and I couldn't relate to them. Then I met Johnny Cash and I felt like him. You read the Scriptures and you realize that he's actually like these guys in the Scriptures. He's not like these weirdos."

Ultimately what made Johnny Cash great was his unique way of viewing the world. "He didn't think like you and I do," is how his sister Joanne puts it. Rosanne elaborates, "You can't apply the template of a normal person to Dad and fit him into it. It doesn't work because he was such an unusual human being, and his mind worked so differently from anybody I have ever met in my life. He not only thought as a great artist but his thoughts *were* great art. That was the realm he lived in."

The realm Johnny Cash lived in was clouded by pain and colored by grace. He had the ability to transform the rough and commonplace into objects fit for heaven, just as he had been transformed. Rick Rubin remembers him taking Ewan McColl's song "The First Time Ever I Saw Your Face" and turning it from a love song into a devotional song. "He loved that," said Rubin. It came really naturally to him. It seemed like his devotion for life came from his devotion for God."

Interview with Johnny Cash

STEVE TURNER (BRIGHTON, ENGLAND, 1988)
PREVIOUSLY UNPUBLISHED

You've had the respect of most of rock-'n'-roll's key performers from Elvis through the Beatles and on to U2. Didn't you even suggest the title for "Blue Suede Shoes"?

It was my idea. I was in the air force in Germany, and I had a black friend named C. V. White from Virginia. He'd get dressed up for a three-day pass, and in his mind, when he put on his clothes to go out, his black shoes were blue suede shoes. He would say, "Man! Don't step on my blue suede shoes; I'm goin' out tonight." Carl Perkins and I were in Amory, Mississippi, with Elvis. Now Elvis, of course, was hotter than a pistol. He had his second record out. He'd had "That's All Right (Mama);" now he had "Baby, Let's Play House," and Carl hadn't had a hit. He'd had two country records. He asked me to write a song with him. I said, "You take this idea and write it yourself." This "blue suede shoes" line that my buddy used to say had been in my mind ever since I went to Sun. I told Carl about it and he said, "That's the one I'm looking for," and he wrote it that night. He started it backstage, but he went home and finished it.

When Elvis heard that song, he asked me to write him one; so I wrote "Get Rhythm," which was on the other side of "I Walk the Line." But before Elvis could

237

record it, he signed with RCA Victor, and Sam Phillips wouldn't let him have it. I put it down at Sun Studio, and Sam Phillips told him he couldn't have it.

Have you ever wished that you had written "Blue Suede Shoes"?

No. I gave the idea to Carl that night, and I'm still glad I did, because he was my best friend, and he deserved a hit. He'd worked hard for one.

Were blue suede shoes a fancy thing to wear at that time?

No. Not until the record came out. Maybe C.V. White had worn blue suede shoes before he came into the air force. I don't know. It was just something he used to say when he went out on a three-day pass.

What were your musical influences?

I always liked black gospel and rhythm and blues. I would listen to country music on the radio at night. I would tune into the Mexican border stations that played just country. I grew up just over one hundred miles from Cotton Plant, Arkansas, which was the hometown of Sister Rosetta Tharpe, and she was my favorite when I was a kid. I love songs like "This Train Is Bound for Glory." I think that song could be a rock-'n'-roll smash, if somebody recorded it right. Another song she did was "Didn't It Rain." She also did "Don't Take Everybody to Be Your Friend." She had some great songs that were spiritual but still had a universal message. Rock musicians have discovered these gospel and blues roots to an extent, but they haven't gone all the way. They've barely touched the source. When I want to play records to entertain myself, I play Robert Johnson, Josh White, Blind Lemon Jefferson, Pink Anderson, or the field recordings made by John and Alan Lomax. That is real gutbucket music. As far as I am concerned that is seminal rock-'n'-roll.

Do you see yourself as writing in that tradition?

I think so. From the Lomax album *Blues in the Mississippi Night* I got the idea to write "Going to Memphis," which is a song about chain-gang convicts talking about wanting to bust out and go to Memphis. Then there was "Another Man Done Gone" that I wrote new lyrics to. When I wrote "Big River" I wrote it [to be sung] real slow, not up-tempo as I did it on record. There was a guitar player named Roy

Nichols, who later worked with Merle Haggard, and he used to play that song with me, and he played some really black blues on it. It sounded like a real blues song. Sam Phillips wanted it upbeat, and he made it sound like a rockabilly song.

Did you feel comfortable with the original Sun sound?

As I said, I grew up on blues, gospel, and country, but at the time we recorded in 1955 every record that was coming out of Nashville had a fiddle and a steel guitar. One would take the first half of the instrumental, and the other would take the second half. I was just fed up with the sound that had been coming out on country records for the past six or seven years, and so I stuck with my own Tennessee Two sound, the boom-chicka-boom rhythm. I felt comfortable with it. It was not really rockabilly like Scotty Moore or "That's All Right (Mama)." But I was in that world for two or three years.

Did you feel a part of it?

Very much so. I toured almost exclusively with Sun people—Elvis, Jerry Lee Lewis, Sonny Burgess, Billy Lee Riley, Warren Smith. I even wrote "Rock-'n'-roll Ruby" for Warren Smith, which was a pretty good seller for him.

There was a feeling of artistic innocence about those days because there was no precedent.

Yes. We were having fun. We were really having fun. I don't think you could compare our tours to anything that had gone on the road before. Colonel Tom Parker had managed Eddy Arnold, who was a really big country singer in the late 1940s, but it didn't take him long to realize that he had to handle Elvis a little differently. I've seen that kind of reaction twice in my career—Elvis and the Beatles. I went to see the Beatles the first time I met Paul in 1964 [actually 1965] at Cow Palace in San Francisco. I saw the same thing that night that I saw in 1955 with Elvis. I haven't seen it since.

Was Paul McCartney a fan of your music?

I don't think so. I don't know. I was invited backstage, and their dressing room was in a trailer outside Cow Palace. I went in and met all four of them. I don't know if they were fans. I just went to meet the Beatles.

Why?

Well, *I* was a fan of *their* music!

Are you still a music fan?

I listen to a lot of music. If I hear a song I like, I sleep with it, I live with it, and I wake up with it. It doesn't matter whose it is.

Do you still want to meet the artist?

I sure do. I get a kick out of meeting an artist I admire. I had always wanted to meet Michael Jackson, just to say I had met him. And I did meet him. June and I had recorded a song called "Jackson," and I wouldn't have thought he would have made the connection in a million years, but there's a line in the song that says, "We got married in a fever / Hotter than a pepper sprout." I walked up and said, "Hi, Michael. I'm Johnny Cash," and he said [puts on falsetto voice] "Johnny Cash! Hotter than a pepper sprout!"

Would you risk embarrassment to go backstage and meet someone?

No. I'd never impose myself. I'd never go uninvited. I've been backstage at some rock concerts where my son would get tickets to see Twisted Sister, Metallica, Ozzy Osbourne, or Iron Maiden, and they would call up and tell him to come backstage and bring me. So I would go. I've met Iron Maiden in Toronto, during a soundcheck but, as I say, I never turn up uninvited.

How does Johnny Cash take to heavy metal?

It feels good. I like the way it feels in your liver. The vibrations! I did sixty networked television shows, and I had everyone on in the business. I had everyone you can imagine, from Burl Ives to Mahalia Jackson to Kenny Rogers and the First Edition.

If you were doing the shows today, would you invite Twisted Sister and Metallica?

If they wanted to do TV. I'm not sure that they would want to do TV. I like the people I've met. I like Dee Snider [of Twisted Sister] very much. He's a good man. I went to those heavy-metal concerts, because of all the concern about censorship and music. I wanted to see what it was all about. Of course, I'd heard it all before. Every day I would take my son to school, we'd listen to the car radio, and I probably heard more rock than I did country. I knew what was happening and, for the most part, I liked what I heard. Having seen all the craziness of working with Elvis Presley, and having seen the Beatles, I couldn't believe it was going to be that much different at a heavy-metal concert, and it wasn't. The main differences were that the sound was a little louder, and they had better lighting systems than we had back then. All I saw was a bunch of kids letting off steam in a good, safe atmosphere.

How do you think people perceive you?

As a conservative country singer who lives in the South somewhere. The misconception is that I'm regional, and they might even sometimes imply that I'm a redneck and, heaven forbid, a bigot. For instance, I did a TV show with Peter Falk *(Colombo),* and when we were rehearsing he told me what my line was, and he said, "You say so and so, or however you say that down there." I put my script down and said, "We say it almost exactly the way you do up there!" I looked him full in the eyes, and he smiled, and we were friends from then on. I could see right up front that he had that perception. But "I've been everywhere" and I've seen almost everything.

About what do you think you are best at singing? What causes are you best at representing?

I'm not blowing a bugle for any big causes right now, but in performance I love to do "Long Black Veil." I like just as much to do Springsteen's "Highway Patrol." That's one of the high points of my concert. I give Bruce the credit for writing that song. I wish I had written it. These are songs of the underdog, of the working man, of the down-and-out and, as is the case in a lot of country [music], of tragedy.

You cross over political boundaries in the issues that concern you.

You're right. I'm not really concerned about boundaries. I just follow my conscience and my heart. Kris Kristofferson has got a new song called "The Heart" that has the line "The heart is all that matters in the end." Follow your heart. That's what I do. Compassion is something I have a lot of, because I've been through a lot of pain in my life. Anybody who has suffered a lot of pain has a lot of compassion. Maybe I don't have enough. Maybe I do get jaded sometimes. I get tired after a concert, and I pass right by a panhandler to get to my room really fast and order room service. It's been a long time since I left the cotton fields.

Would you have been as powerful a performer if you had never strayed from your Christian upbringing?

I hadn't thought of that. Yes, if I had kept my head clear all of these years, I think I would have accomplished more, but I guess I'm right where I'm supposed to be in my life right now; so I'm happy with it. I don't have any regrets, and I don't carry any guilt trips around. I shook all that off with forgiveness and soul-searching. Forgiving myself mainly.

If you had stayed on the straight and narrow, would you have been Pat Boone rather than Johnny Cash?

No. I'm doing what I'm supposed to do. I always wanted a hit gospel song, but God gave me "A Boy Named Sue" instead, and I'm happy with it.

Since writing *The Man in Black* you returned to your drug habit. But, as I understand it, you're clean now?

Yes. I'm back out of that. I never lost my faith during that time, but I lost my contact with God because anyone chronically on drugs and alcohol becomes very selfish. You don't think about anyone else. You think about yourself and where your next stash is coming from or your next drink. I was at the point where I was thinking of nothing in the world but how long my supplies were going to last and where I was gonna get my next prescription. I wasted a lot of time and energy. I mean we're not just talking days, but months and years. So, I think I might have had a few more pinnacles in my life, if I hadn't gotten involved.

It must have been worse after you'd publicly admitted your problem and announced that God had rescued you. You must have felt a bit of a wretch.

Yes. I did it all again to show 'em I knew what I was talking about! No, chemical dependency is a progressive disease, and it hit me a lot harder the second time around because I was older. At the time I wrote *The Man in Black,* that's what I had to say. I made my point and was honest about it. I felt good about it. I'm straight now and have been for a long time. I'm drug free and alcohol free. But I may get stoned tomorrow. You never know with this disease. I don't intend to, and I'm hoping and praying I don't, but I might.

Does playing a concert give you a high?

It gives me a high like none other you can get. It's so good to get out there and perform without drugs. It is for me. But when I started taking them, it was so good to get out there and perform with drugs! I loved them! That's why you take them.

Almost all the Sun artists felt a tension between the rock-'n'-roll life and the values they had been taught growing up in church.

We were all roughly from the same area. We were all raised in the church and all greatly influenced by gospel music. That was Elvis's first love, and it was Jerry's, and Carl's, and mine. Carl Perkins has written hundreds of songs he has never recorded, and half of them are gospel. That's where our strength is. Regardless of how vocal you might be about your religion or you faith, it all comes down to the fact that it's a personal thing between you and God. It works. For me, it's where I get my strength.

It was as if they didn't totally reject it, and yet none of them stuck with it all the time.

Roy Orbison and I were talking about that very same thing. He quoted a line from a song of his, "Best Friend": "A diamond is a diamond / a stone, a stone / but a man's not all good, not all bad."

How do you live in Hendersonville?

I live in a house on a lake. I have about one hundred and seventy-five acres of land. The lake lot is only about five acres, but across the road is fifty acres that are fenced in, and that's where I keep wild animals and exotic birds. I also have a log cabin with a fireplace right in the middle of the woods, and that's where I go sometimes to write and to get away from everything. The other one hundred acres is pasture, wood, and fields. Sometimes we have cattle on it, sometimes not. Then there are twenty-five acres up by my office, which are just open field.

Where do you do most of your creative work?

Either in my log cabin, at a farm in a little town called Bon Aqua, Tennessee, or in my private library upstairs at my house. When I'm at home I write either very early in the morning or very late at night when things are really quiet. On the other hand, I've written as many songs on the road in the back of a bus, on an airplane, or backstage as I have in a quiet place. One energy generates another.

What makes you want to write one more song?

If the idea is there, it's a great feeling to put down a song. Sometimes I write without even touching a guitar. Sometimes I have a tune in my head, and then I see how the lyrics tie together. I love words; so I see how the story ties together. It's just the joy of writing. I love to write.

Do you find the form of the music too limiting?

No. I don't know if I've reached the limit or not. Every song I write is different; so I don't feel the need to burst out of anything. I enjoy writing a simple love ballad or a simple story. I just wrote a Scottish folk song called "A Croft in Clachan," and it's just a simple story set in the seventeenth century about this boy leaving the town of Clachan to fight the English and then coming back home to the girl he's going to marry. When I was writing it, Paul McCartney was talking about "Mull of Kintyre" and he said, "You should finish it. 'Mull of Kintyre' was the biggest song I ever wrote." That's something to think about! A Scottish song was the biggest song he wrote! So I finished it, and I'm going to record it with Glen Campbell.

Do you think that you've lost direction a few times in your career?

No. I haven't had any particular direction in my music. I just do it the way I feel it at the time.

Wouldn't you admit that there have been artistic troughs?

Oh, yeah. Sure. There have been times when I'd lose interest. There were times when I was tired of touring or tired of the whole thing, and so I'd just do a book or a movie, but I always came back to the music. I'm back to it stronger than ever. I'm just really into it now.

Now that you employ over forty people, does it make it harder to be a simple song writer like the blues musicians you admire?

When I start to write a song, I don't think of the colonial-style building where my offices are. I think of the song. When I was writing my Scottish folk song, I was seeing the boy who loved there. Whatever I'm writing I put myself into the song.

What books do you read?

I read all kinds of books. . . . I like American history. Right now June and I are reading *The Fatal Shore,* Robert Hughes's book about Australia. I've read everything James Michener has written. Colleen McCullough, Jack Higgins, Stephen King—I've read a lot of his. I like biblical novels like *The Robe, The Silver Chalice, Ben Hur.*

Did you write *The Man in White* during one of your spiritual "up" periods?

I wrote it over a period of nine years, when I was straight! That's why it took so long. I wasn't straight very much.

How did you come to correspond with Bob Dylan in the early 1960s?

We were writing together before we ever met. We'd write mainly about music, about what we were listening to, what we were writing, what we were recording. I wrote the first letter. It was 1963, and I was working Las Vegas. I got the album *Bob Dylan* and played it all the time. On the way home I took one of those vomit bags out of the back seat of the plane and wrote Bob a letter. He wrote me a little letter back and said that he was surprised to hear from me, because he was brought up in Hibbing on Hank Williams and Johnny Cash. He talked about "I Walk the Line" and a couple of my songs, and I wrote back. Then I got another letter from him, and so on. They weren't only about music but his observations of people and things he was doing. He'd talk about the Pacific Ocean or the plains of Kansas, "a two-thousand-mile wide beach" as he called it.

Did you influence him around the time that he recorded *John Wesley Harding?*

I don't think that I had anything to do with it at all.

Nashville Skyline?

They stayed at my house, Sara and the kids, the week he was recording, but it wasn't something I did. It was his idea to do the album.

Would he ever ask advice on song writing?

No. Never. He might give advice, but he never asked for any. I don't think Bob Dylan would ask advice from anybody on song writing.

What did you think of his "born again" albums?

I didn't see him during that time. I don't think Bob was ever into organized church religion. Some of the songs were good gospel. I did "Man Gave Names to the Animals" in a Christmas TV special that I recorded in Scotland. I loved "Slow Train Coming," but through those years I was very much the observer. He lived in California in half seclusion. No one saw him that much. Bob is very much his own person. He is a loner and a very shy person. I can respect that because I like my time alone. I was sick in the hospital over a year ago, and I got a telegram from him. That's all I've heard from him in over seven years. I've had no influence at all on his religion.

You're a patriotic American, but you're likely to clash with other patriots over American foreign policy.

All of the men in my family over the past two hundred years have had to go into the military. I was in the air force during the Korean War. My father was a World War I veteran. His grandfather was a Civil War soldier. His grandfather's grandfather was a Revolutionary War soldier. But even though I spent four years in the air force, I'm not military minded at all. Our government scares the daylights out of me. They swooped down and raided little Grenada, Libya. We should defend ourselves, I guess, in the Gulf, but that scares me too. With Central America, Panama . . . what were we doing there? What have we got troops down there for? I'm not saying this because my son is now draft age. I've always felt this way.

When you're away from America and think of home, what image comes to your mind?

The farm in the country where I like to go. This little farm is one hundred and seven acres in the most rural county in Tennessee. It's an hour and fifteen minutes from my home, and at the back of the farm there is a spring. It's a little spring that runs year round, and it's always fifty-eight degrees, summer or winter. It comes from way deep in the ground. I think of that a lot when I think of home. I like to get up there and drink from that spring. I just lay on the ground beside it. That's paradise on earth to me, that little place with the dogwood and sycamore trees all around. You don't hear a car, a train, a plane, or anything. All you can hear is nature.

Your book suggests that June has been a tremendous source of spiritual strength for you.

She's a solid rock. She never changes. I'm very unpredictable in my moods, but she's an anchor. She's also been a victim of my craziness.

When you talk in the book of your brother's death, that is a very moving passage. Has that event remained an influence on your life?

My brother Jack? It really was and still is. He was two years older than I. He was a very devout Christian and a very good boy. A very tough boy. He was named after the boxer Jack Dempsey—Jack Dempsey Cash. He looked like Jack Dempsey. He was built like a heavyweight champion. At fourteen he was about six feet tall and was a solid rock. He was a very devout Christian, who read his Bible every day. He was a very wise person. He gave advice on a lot of things. We were very close. When he died, I felt a really great loss, but his memory has always been an inspiration to me.

Chronology

1929

June 23   Valerie June Carter born in Maces Spring, Virginia

1932

February 26   J. R. Cash born in Kingsland, Arkansas

1935

March 23   Cash family moved to Dyess, Arkansas

1937

January 16   Flooding in Dyess

1944

                     Christian conversion and baptism at First Baptist Church, Dyess, Arkansas

May 20   Death of brother Jack Dempsey Cash at age fourteen

1950

May 19   Cash graduated from Dyess High School

July 7	Enlisted in U.S. Air Force
September 21	Started Special Intercept Operator Course at Keesler AFB, Mississippi

1951

April 27	Graduated from Keesler AFB, Mississippi
	Transferred to Brooks AFB, Texas
July	Met Vivian Liberto in San Antonio, Texas
September	Arrived in Landsberg, Germany, where he served with Twelfth RSM

1952

July 9	June Carter married Carl Smith

1953

January 1	Death of Hank Williams
June	Brief mission in Foggia, Italy
October 16–25	Traveled to Paris, France, and London, England

1954

July 3	Received honorable discharge at Camp Kilmer, New Jersey
July 5	Elvis Presley recorded "That's All Right (Mama)" at Sun Studios, Memphis, Tennessee
July	Met bass player Marshall Grant and guitarist Luther Perkins
August 7	Married Vivian Liberto in San Antonio, Texas
September 9	Saw Elvis perform for the first time
	Auditioned for Sam Phillips at Sun Records

1955

	Studied part-time at Keegan's School of Broadcasting, Memphis, Tennessee
March 22	Recorded "Hey! Porter"
May	Recorded "Cry, Cry, Cry"
May 24	First child, Rosanne Cash, born in Memphis, Tennessee

June 21	First single released
August 5	Played Overton Park Shell, Memphis, Tennessee, with Elvis Presley
September 26	June Carter Smith gave birth to daughter, Rebecca Carlene
November 19	Wrote "I Walk the Line" backstage in Gladewater, Texas
December 12	Suggested "Blue Suede Shoes" story to Carl Perkins in Amory, Mississippi

1956

February 11	"Folsom Prison Blues" entered the country music charts
April 2	Recorded "I Walk the Line"
April 16	Second child, Kathy Cash, born in Memphis, Tennessee
June 15	Jack Clement began job as Sun's engineer
July 7	Debut on *Grand Ole Opry* (met June Carter)
August	Toured Texas with Faron Young, Roy Orbison, and Johnny Horton
December 4	Million Dollar Quartet session with Jerry Lee Lewis, Carl Perkins, and Elvis Presley
December 6	June Carter Smith granted a divorce from Carl Smith

1957

January 19	Appeared on *Jackie Gleason Show*
February 17	Started first California Tour
April 21	Started first Canadian Tour
July	Introduced to amphetamines
August 31	Met Don Law of Columbia Records in Los Angeles, California
September 10	Released first LP
October 11	First session with Jack Clement as producer ("Ballad of a Teenage Queen")
November 11	June Carter married Edwin "Rip" Nix

1958

May 15	Recorded Hank Williams's songs
July 14	Announced his departure from Sun

July 18	Final session at Sun
July 29	Third child, Cindy Cash, born in Memphis, Tennessee
August 1	Started Columbia contract
August	Moved family to California
November	First Columbia album released

1959

January 1	Played San Quentin prison, California (Merle Haggard was an inmate)
January 13	Recorded gospel songs for Columbia
February 3	Death of Buddy Holly
February 23	Subject of a feature in *TIME* magazine
March 23	Screen test in Hollywood
September 17	Performed on British TV
October 23	Appeared on Burl Ives's TV show
November	Departure of his manager, Bob Neal

1960

March 2	Elvis left the army
June	Filmed *Five Minutes to Live*
August 5	Drummer W. S. "Fluke" Holland joined the band, making it the Tennessee Three
November 5	Death of Johnny Horton
November 9	J. F. Kennedy elected president

1961

April 27	Started recording *Hymns from the Heart*
July	Saul Holiff took over from Stew Carnall as Cash's manager
August 24	Fourth child, Tara Cash, born in Encino, California
September	Cash family moved to Casitas Springs, California
November 14	Arrested for drunkenness in Nashville, Tennessee
December 7	In Dallas, Texas, June Carter appeared on Cash show for the first time

1962

February 11	June Carter joined the Cash show
May 9	Appeared on Mike Wallace show
May 10	Made his debut at Carnegie Hall, New York
June 15	Appeared at Hollywood Bowl, Hollywood, California
August	First British Tour dates
November	Played for troops in Korea

1963

January 1	Played San Quentin prison, California
February	Joined Avenue Community Church, Ventura, California
March 25	Recorded "Ring of Fire"
June 8	"Ring of Fire" entered pop charts
September 30	Appeared on TV show *Hootenanny*
October 28	Beginning of Beatlemania in Britain
November 22	Assassination of President John F. Kennedy; Cash concert in Dallas was cancelled

1964

February 7	Beatles arrived in America
March 5	Recorded "Ballad of Ira Hayes"
July 26	Played Newport Folk Festival and met Bob Dylan
August 22	Placed ad lambasting radio stations for not playing "Ballad of Ira Hayes"

1965

January 10	Appeared on *Shindig!*
June 27	Caused 508-acre forest fire in Los Padres National Park
July 25	Defended Bob Dylan in pages of folk magazine *Broadside* after Dylan went electric
August 31	Met the Beatles in their trailer at Cow Palace, San Francisco
October 4	Arrested in El Paso, Texas, with stimulants and tranquilizers
October 27	Folk singer Peter La Farge found dead
December 28	Appeared in court in El Paso, Texas

1966

	June Carter divorced Edwin "Rip" Nix
March	Kris Kristofferson arrived in Nashville, Tennessee
May 5	Second British Tour
May 11	Met Dylan backstage at Sofia Gardens, Cardiff, England
May 16	Bob Dylan's *Blonde on Blonde* album released
June 30	Divorce proceedings started by Vivian Liberto Cash
August 29	Beatles's final concert, San Francisco, California
October 10	Bought land in Hendersonville, Tennessee
December 13	Arrested for "picking flowers" in Starkeville, Mississippi

1967

January 11	Recorded "Jackson" with June Carter
March	Purchased home on Old Hickory Lake
June 27	Was sued for $125,000 because of forest fire
	Bob Johnston replaced Don Law as Cash's producer
November 2	Jailed overnight in Lafayette, Georgia,
November	Dr. Nat Winston brought in to wean Cash off drugs
November 5	Attended First Baptist Church, Hendersonville, Tennessee, with June

1968

January 3	Cash's and Vivian's divorce finalized
January 11	Vivian Liberto Cash married Dick Distin
January 13	Recorded concert at Folsom Prison, Represa, California
February 22	Proposed to June onstage in London, Ontario
March 1	Married June in Franklin, Kentucky
April 9	Martin Luther King assassinated
May 4–19	British Tour
May	Holiday in Israel
June 6	Robert Kennedy assassinated in Los Angeles, California
August 5	Death of Luther Perkins
October 23	Played Carnegie Hall, New York

October 25–	
November 3	British Tour
November 6	Richard Nixon elected president
December 3	Elvis Presley TV comeback
December 10	Visited Wounded Knee

1969

January	Far East Tour, including Vietnam
February 18	Recorded with Bob Dylan in Nashville for *Nashville Skyline*
February 24	San Quentin concert for album and TV documentary
June 7–	
September 27	First ABC television series
September 27	Sell-out at Hollywood Bowl, Hollywood, California
October 1	*Abbey Road* by the Beatles released
October 18	*Nashville Banner* reported Cash was outselling Beatles
December	Featured on the cover of *Life* magazine
December	Billy and Ruth Graham visited Cashes for the first time

1970

January 21–	
May 13	Second ABC television series
March 3	Fifth child, John Carter Cash, born in Madison, Tennessee
April 9	Break-up of the Beatles
April 17	Played White House as guest of President Nixon
May 24	Appeared as guest at Billy Graham Crusade, Knoxville, Tennessee
September 23–	
March 31, 1971	Third ABC television series
October 24	Release of *A Gunfight* starring Cash and Kirk Douglas

1971

February 16	Recorded the song "Man in Black"
February 17	Appeared on *This Is Your Life*
March	Australian Tour

May 9	Public declaration of his Christian faith at Evangel Temple
September 9	Biography *Winners Got Scars Too* by Christopher Wren was published
November 2	Flew to Israel to film *Gospel Road*
November	Baptized in Jordan by Rev. Jimmy Snow (second baptism)

1972

February 11	Performed on first *Grand Ole Gospel Time* show at Ryman Theater
June 17	Appeared at Explo '72 in Dallas, Texas, with Billy Graham
August 10	Lou Robin took over from Saul Holiff as manager
October 23	Nashville premiere of *Gospel Road*

1973

January 23	Vietnam peace treaty signed
September 1	Appeared with Billy Graham at SPRE-E '73 in London, England
October 15	Hosted Country Music Association Awards

1974

January	Guest appearance on *Columbo* with Peter Falk
August 8	Resignation of President Richard Nixon
December	Spent Christmas with Billy and Ruth Graham

1975

January 22	June's father, Ezra "Eck" Carter, died
August	Published first autobiography, *Man in Black*
September 9–25	European Tour
October 25–31	Japanese Tour

1976

| February | Broke ankle while in Montego Bay, Jamaica |
| March 20 | Johnny Cash Homecoming Day in Kingsland, Arkansas |

| July 4 | Was Parade Marshall in Bicentennial celebration, Washington, D.C. |
| July 6 | Recorded with Waylon Jennings |

1977

January	Earle Poole Ball joined on keyboards
May	Awarded associate degree of theology by Christian International School of Theology
May 15	With Billy Graham at crusade in South Bend, Indiana
August 16	Death of Elvis Presley Ordained as Christian minister
October 17	Filmed Christmas Special with Roy Orbison, Jerry Lee Lewis, Carl Perkins

1978

February 1–5	Five nights with Billy Graham in Las Vegas, Nevada
March	Unissued Cash material released by Bear Records, Germany
April 10–11	Played Prague with daughter Rosanne
September 28	Hospitalized with cystic sinusitis
October 23	Death of Mother Maybelle Carter
December	Took entire staff to Israel

1979

March 11–21	British Tour
March 31	Johnny Cash museum opened
May 4	Margaret Thatcher won British election
June 24–27	Appeared with Billy Graham in Nashville, Tennessee
August 13	Renewed marriage vows in Jamaica
September 4	Denied drugs and marriage problems
October 18	Received UN Humanitarian Award
December	Recorded in London, England, with Nick Lowe and Elvis Costello

1980

January	Vacationed in Britain, Italy, and Egypt
March	Bass player Marshall Grant fired
July 30–	
August 5	Los Angeles concerts cancelled due to Cash's illness
August 11	Appeared on the *Muppet Show*
October 13	Inducted into the Country Music Hall of Fame
December 8	John Lennon killed in New York City

1981

April 23	Stuttgart, Germany. Concert with Jerry Lee Lewis and Carl Perkins was recorded
June 15–23	Australian Tour
June 24	Marshall Grant sued Cash for $2.6 million
July 29	Prince Charles married Diana Spencer in London, England
September	Ribs broken by ostrich
December 21	Cash family held up by masked gang at their Jamaican home

1982

January 9	Part of Gallatin Road was renamed Johnny Cash Parkway, Hendersonville, Tennessee
April 17	Hosted *Saturday Night Live*
September 22	Started filming *Murder in Coweta County*

1983

May 20	Four days in the hospital to treat compressed vertebrae
October 17–22	Filmed Christmas special at Carter Fold in Virginia
November 10	Cut hand badly when in Nottingham, England
November 22–	
December 16	Hospitalized in Nashville, Tennessee, for bleeding duodenal ulcer
December 20	Taken to Betty Ford Center

1984

January 31	Checked out of Betty Ford Center
April 12	Recorded "Chicken in Black" single
May 23	Performed at Bob Hope's 81st Birthday Special
November 12–17	Filmed Christmas Special in Montreux, Switzerland
December	Recorded with Kris Kristofferson, Waylon Jennings, and Willie Nelson

1985

February 7	Appeared on the *David Letterman Show* with Waylon Jennings
April 22	Surgery on abdominal scar tissue
June 4–17	Australian Tour
July 13	Live Aid took place in London, England, and Philadelphia, Pennsylvania
September	Recorded in Memphis with Carl Perkins, Jerry Lee Lewis, Roy Orbison, and others
September	Filmed *The Last Days of Frank and Jesse James*
October	*Rainbow,* last album for Columbia, released
December 23	Death of Ray Cash at age eighty-eight

1986

January	Filmed TV movie *Stagecoach*
	Challenger space shuttle exploded
June	Published novel *Man in White*
July 17	Columbia did not renew Cash's contract, after twenty-eight years
August 21	Signed with Polygram
September	Started recording for Polygram label, Mercury

1987

April	Sang duets with Kris Kristofferson at Bottom Line, New York
May 16	Developed irregular heartbeat during concert at Council Bluffs, Iowa
August 22	Played in Gdansk, Poland

1988

February 12	Endorsed Senator Al Gore's bid to run as a presidential candidate
February	Rosanne Cash had a hit with "Tennessee Flat Top Box"
March 22	Johnny Cash exhibit opened at Country Music Hall of Fame
April 20–28	German Tour
April 30–May 12	British Tour
December 12	Routine medical check-up detected artery blockage
December 19	Hospitalized for bypass surgery

1989

January 3	Left hospital
May	Johnny Cash tribute album, *Till Things Are Brighter*, released in Britain
May 3	Life-threatening chest problem in Paris
August 24–26	Canceled three shows because of bronchitis and respiratory infection
November 19	Entered a drug treatment center for relapse prevention
December 6	Left drug treatment center

1990

January	Had tooth removed, which later caused cyst problem
February 7	Stopped TV taping due to jaw pain
March 1	Highwaymen press conference at Country Radio Seminar in Nashville, Tennessee
March 3–17	Highwaymen Tour
September 17–October 9	Highwaymen Tour

1991

February 20	Won Living Legend Award at Grammies
March 11	Death of Carrie Cash at the age of eighty-six
May 1	Creation of Cash Country in Branson, Missouri, was announced

May 5–23	Highwaymen tour Australia and New Zealand

1992

January 15	Inducted into the Rock and Roll Hall of Fame
April 1–26	Highwaymen tour Scandinavia and Europe
May	Failure of Cash Country announced
October 16	Appeared at Bob Dylan's 30th Anniversary Celebration at Madison Square Garden, New York

1993

February 8	Recorded "The Wanderer" in Dublin for U2 album *Zooropa*
February 27	Met Rick Rubin backstage at Rhythm Café, Santa Ana
May 17–20	Did first recordings for Def American in Rick Rubin's Hollywood living room
July 8	Death of Ray Cash at the age of seventy-one
December	Played the Viper Room, Hollywood, California

1994

February 13–	
March 3	Toured Australia and New Zealand with Kris Kristofferson
April 18–21	Filmed video for "Delia's Gone" with Kate Moss
April 26	Released *American Recordings*
June 26	Played Glastonbury Festival, England
October 17	Filmed *Dr. Quinn, Medicine Woman* with Jane Seymour
October 31–	
November 8	Recorded third Highwaymen album in Santa Monica, California

1995

February	*American Recordings* wins Grammy for Best Contemporary Folk Album
May 4	Canceled European Tour after jaw surgery complications
May 31–June 28	Highwaymen Tour
September 7–29	European Tour

| November 3–
December 3 | Highwaymen tour New Zealand, Australia, and Far East |

1996

November	Released *Unchained,* second album with Rick Rubin
November 11	Filmed *Dr. Quinn, Medicine Woman*
December 9	Appeared on *Larry King Live*

1997

September 16	Told band of his retirement plans, Washington, D.C.
October 15	*Cash: The Autobiography* published
October 25	Final concert in Flint, Michigan
October 22	Book tour cancelled due to ill health
October 29	Entered hospital for tests

1998

January 19	Death of Carl Perkins
February	*Unchained* won Grammy for Best Country Album
June 24	Joined Kris Kristofferson onstage in Nashville, Tennessee
August 6	Hospitalized for four days

1999

January	Given Lifetime Achievement Award at Grammies
April 6	All-Star Tribute to Johnny Cash, New York
April 20	June Carter released her album *Press On*
July 1–2	June Carter played the Bottom Line, New York
July 29	Anita Carter died at age sixty-six
October 20	Hospitalized with pneumonia

2000

January	Started recording third album with Rick Rubin
April 23	Awarded Living Legend medal by Library of Congress
May 23	Triple CD compilation *Love, God, Murder* released by Legacy
October 17	Released *Solitary Man*

2001

February	Hospitalized with pneumonia
February 21	Won his tenth Grammy for Best Male Country Vocal Performance
August 24	June fitted with a pacemaker

2002

February 13	Death of Waylon Jennings
February 26	Columbia launched 70th birthday promotion
September	Appeared at Americana Music Association event in Nashville, Tennessee
October 11	Filmed *Larry King Live*
October 17	June's leaking heart valve detected
October 18–19	Video for "Hurt" shot in Hendersonville, Tennessee
November 4	Released *The Man Comes Around*
November 4	Traveled to Jamaica with June
November 26	*Larry King Live* episode aired

2003

January–March	Hospitalized three times
April 1	Released from hospital
April 4	Death of sister, Louise
April 11–16	June hospitalized
April 28	June hospitalized
May 7	June had heart surgery
May 15	Death of June Carter Cash
May 18	June Carter Cash funeral
June 21	Appeared in concert at Carter Fold
August 21	Recorded final song, "Engine 143," at Cash Cabin Studio
August 25–	
September 9	Hospitalized for pancreatitis
August 28	Wins MTV video award for Best Cinematography for "Hurt"
September 11	Returned to the hospital in the evening
September 12	Died of respiratory problems

September 15	Funeral at First Baptist Church, Hendersonville, Tennessee
November 10	Tribute concert at Ryman Auditorium, Nashville, Tennessee
November	*Unearthed* 5-CD box set released

Discography

Singles

These are the primary Johnny Cash singles with the highest US pop chart position indicated to the right. The list does not include re-releases, records on which he was a guest vocalist, or Sun singles released after he had signed with Columbia.

June 1955	Hey! Porter / Cry! Cry! Cry!	
January 1956	Folsom Prison Blues / So Doggone Lonesome	
August 1956	I Walk the Line / Get Rhythm	17
November 1956	There You Go / Train of Love	
June 1957	Don't Make Me Go / Next in Line	99
September 1957	Home of the Blues / Give My Love to Rose	88
January 1958	Ballad of a Teenage Queen / Big River	14
May 1958	Guess Things Happen that Way / Come in, Stranger	11
August 1958	The Ways of a Woman in Love / You're the Nearest Thing to Heaven	24
November 1958	All Over Again / Why Do I Care	38
January 1959	Don't Take Your Guns to Town / I Still Miss Someone	32
April 1959	Frankie's Man, Johnny / You Dreamer You	57
September 1959	Five Feet High and Rising / I Got Stripes	43
December 1959	The Little Drummer Boy / I Remember You	63

April 1960	Seasons of My Heart / Smiling Bill McCall	
July 1960	Second Honeymoon / Honky-Tonk Girl	
October 1960	Going to Memphis / Loading Coal	
January 1961	Locomotive Man/ Girl in Saskatoon	
May 1961	The Rebel—Johnny Yuma / Forty Shades of Green	
September 1961	Tennessee Flat-Top Box / Tall Men	84
January 1962	The Big Battle / When I've Learned	
May 1962	In the Jailhouse Now / Little at a Time	
August 1962	Bonanza / Pick a Bale O' Cotton	94
November 1962	Were You There? / Peace in the Valley (with the Carter Family)	
March 1963	Busted / Send a Picture of Mother	
May 1963	Ring of Fire / I'd Still Be There	17
October 1963	The Matador / Still in Town	44
February 1964	Understand Your Man / Dark as a Dungeon	35
December 1964	The Ballad of Ira Hayes / Bad News	
February 1965	Orange Blossom Special / All of God's Children Ain't Free	80
October 1964	It Ain't Me, Babe / Time and Time Again	58
June 1965	Streets of Laredo / Mister Garfield	
September 1965	The Sons of Katie Elder / Certain Kinda Hurtin'	
November 1965	Pickin' Time / Happy to Be with You	
February 1966	The One on the Right / Cotton Pickin' Hands	46
July 1966	Everybody Loves a Nut / Austin Prison	96
October 1966	Boa Constrictor / Bottom of a Mountain	
January 1967	You Beat All I Ever Saw / Put the Sugar to Bed	
July 1967	Jackson / Pack up Your Sorrows (with June Carter)	
September 1967	You'll Be All Right / Long-Legged Guitar- Pickin' Man	
November 1967	Red Velvet / The Wind Changes	
January 1968	Rosanna's Going Wild / Roll Call	91
May 1968	Folsom Prison Blues (live) / The Folk Singer	32
December 1968	Daddy Sang Bass / He Turned the Water into Wine	42
July 1969	A Boy Named Sue / San Quentin	2
November 1969	Blistered / See Ruby Fall	50

February 1970	If I Were A Carpenter / 'Cause I Love You (with June Carter)	36
April 1970	What Is Truth? / Sing a Travelling Song	19
August 1970	Sunday Morning Coming Down / I'm Gonna Try to Be that Way	46
December 1970	Flesh and Blood / This Side of the Law	54
March 1971	Man in Black / Little Bit of Yesterday	58
June 1971	Singing in Vietnam Talking Blues / You've Got A New Light Shining	
September 1971	I'll Be Loving You / No Need to Worry	
November 1971	I Promise You / Papa Was a Good Man	
March 1972	A Thing Called Love / Daddy	
May 1972	Kate / The Miracle Man	75
August 1972	If I Had a Hammer / I Gotta Boy (with June Carter)	
October 1972	Country Trash / Oney	
December 1972	The World Needs A Melody/ A Bird With Broken Wings Can't Fly	
February 1973	Any Old Wind that Blows / Kentucky Straight	
June 1973	Help Me Make It Through the Night /A Loving Gift (with June Carter)	
August 1973	Children / Last Supper	
October 1973	Ballad of Barbara / Praise the Lord and Pass the Soup (with the Carter Family)	
October 1973	Allegheny / We're For Love (with June Carter)	
November 1973	Diamonds in the Rough / Pick the Wildwood Flowers (with Mother Maybelle Carter)	
December 1973	Christmas as I Knew It / That Christmas Feeling (with Tommy Cash)	
February 1974	Jacob Green / Orleans Parish Prison	
April 1974	Ragged Old Flag / Don't Go Near the Water	
August 1974	Crystal Chandeliers and Burgundy / The Junky and the Juicehead (Minus Me)	
October 1974	Father and Daughter / Don't Take Your Guns to Town (with Rosey Nix)	

January 1975	The Lady Came from Baltimore / Lonesome to the Bone
May 1975	My Old Kentucky Home / Hard Times Comin'
November 1975	Look at Them Beans / All Around Cowboy
January 1976	Texas 1947 / I Hardly Ever Sing Beer Drinking Songs
March 1976	Strawberry Cake / I Got Stripes
April 1976	One Piece at a Time / Go on Blues 29
July 1976	Sold Out of Flagpoles / Mountain Lady
September 1976	Riding on the Cotton Belt / It's All Over
November 1976	Far Side Banks of Jordan / Old Time Feeling
	(with June Carter Cash)
April 1977	The Last Gunfighter Ballad / City Jail
September 1977	Lady / Hit the Road and Go
December 1977	Calilou / After the Ball
April 1978	I Would Like to See You Again / Lately
June 1978	There Ain't No Good Chain Gang /
	I Wish I Was Crazy Again (with Waylon Jennings)
September 1978	Gone Girl / I'm All Right Now
January 1979	It'll Be Her / It Comes and Goes
March 1979	I Will Rock and Roll with You / A Song for the Life
October 1979	Ghost Riders in the Sky / I'm Gonna Sit on the Porch
	and Play My Old Guitar
December 1979	I'll Say It's True / Cocaine Blues
March 1980	Bull Rider / Lonesome to the Bone
October 1980	Song of the Patriot/ She's a Go-er
December 1980	Cold Lonesome Morning / The Cowboy Who Started to Fight
February 1981	The Last Time / Rockabilly Blues
April 1981	Without Love / It Ain't Nothin' New, Babe
October 1981	The Baron / I Will Dance with You
January 1982	Mobile Boy / The Hard Way
March 1982	The Reverend Mr. Black / Chattanooga City Limit Sign
November 1982	I've Been to Georgia on a Fast Train / Sing a Song
January 1983	Ain't Gonna Hobo No More / John's Fair Weather Friends
April 1983	I'll Cross over the Jordan Some Day / We Must Believe in
	Magic

October 1983	Brand New Dance / I'm Ragged but I'm Right (with June Carter)
January 1984	Johnny 99 / New Cut Road
April 1984	That's the Truth / Joshua Gone to Barbados
October 1984	Chicken in Black / Battle of Nashville
October 1985	Desperadoes Waiting for a Train / The Twentieth Century Is Almost Over
December 1985	I'm Leaving Now / Easy Street
June 1986	American by Birth/ Even Cowgirls Get the Blues (with Waylon Jennings)
September 1986	The Ballad of Forty Dollars / Field of Diamonds (with Waylon Jennings)
August 1987	The Night Hank Williams Came to Town / I'd Rather Have You
January 1988	The Ballad of Barbara / Sixteen Tons
October 1988	Ballad of A Teenage Queen / Get Rhythm
January 1989	That Ole Wheel / The Last of the Drifters
February 1990	Cat's in the Cradle / I Love You, I Love You
April 1991	The Mystery of Life / I'm an Easy Rider
November 2002	Hurt / Personal Jesus

Albums

These are Johnny Cash's main albums with the highest US pop chart position indicated to the right and the producer(s) in parentheses. It does not include re-releases, re-recordings, compilations, live recordings released out of sequence, bootlegs, some gospel or albums released by Sun after he had signed with Columbia.

October 1957	*Johnny Cash With His Hot-and-Blue Guitar* (Sam Phillips)	
January 1959	*The Fabulous Johnny Cash* (Don Law)	19
January 1960	*Songs of Our Soil* (Don Law)	
June 1960	*Hymns By Johnny Cash* (Don Law)	
October 1960	*Now There Was a Song* (Don Law)	
December 1960	*Ride This Train* (Don Law)	
1962	*Hymns from the Heart* (Don Law, Frank Jones)	
1963	*The Sound of Johnny Cash* (Don Law, Frank Jones)	

March 1963	*Blood, Sweat and Tears* (Don Law, Frank Jones)	80
December 1963	*The Christmas Spirit* (Don Law, Frank Jones)	
March 1964	*Keep on the Sunny Side* (Don Law, Frank Jones)	
January 1965	*Bitter Tears* (Don Law, Frank Jones)	47
March 1965	*Orange Blossom Special* (Don Law, Frank Jones)	49
September 1965	*Ballads of the True West* (Don Law, Frank Jones)	
July 1966	*Everybody Loves a Nut* (Don Law, Frank Jones)	88
November 1966	*Happiness Is You* (Don Law, Frank Jones)	
March 1967	*From Sea to Shining Sea* (Don Law Productions)	
October 1967	*Carryin' on with Johnny Cash and June Carter* (Don Law Productions)	
June 1968	*Johnny Cash at Folsom Prison* (Bob Johnston)	13
February 1969	*The Holy Land* (Bob Johnston)	54
June 1969	*Johnny Cash at San Quentin* (Bob Johnston)	1
February 1970	*Hello, I'm Johnny Cash* (Bob Johnston)	6
November 1970	*The Johnny Cash Show* (Bob Johnston)	44
March 1971	*Little Fauss and Big Halsy* [soundtrack] (Bob Johnston)	
	I Walk the Line [soundtrack] (Bob Johnston)	
June 1971	*The Man in Black* (Johnny Cash)	56
May 1972	*A Thing Called Love* (Larry Butler)	
November 1972	*America* (Larry Butler)	
November 1972	*Johnny Cash Family Christmas* (Larry Butler)	
February 1973	*Any Old Wind that Blows* (Larry Butler)	
June 1973	*The Gospel Road* [soundtrack] (Larry Butler)	
October 1973	*Johnny Cash and His Woman* (Don Law)	
January 1974	*Children's Album* (Don Law Productions)	
March 1974	*Ragged Old Flag* (Johnny Cash, Charlie Bragg)	
October 1974	*The Junkie and the Juicehead* (Johnny Cash, Charlie Bragg)	
January 1975	*Precious Memories* (Johnny Cash)	
May 1975	*John R. Cash* (Gary Klein)	
November 1975	*Look at Them Beans* (Don Davis)	
March 1976	*Strawberry Cake* (Charlie Bragg)	
June 1976	*One Piece at a Time* (Charlie Bragg, Don Davis)	
February 1977	*The Last Gunfighter Ballad* (Charlie Bragg, Don Davis)	

August 1977	*The Rambler* (Charlie Bragg, Don Routh)
April 1978	*I Would Like to See You Again* (Larry Butler)
April 1979	*Gone Girl* (Larry Butler)
September 1979	*Silver* (Brian Ahern)
March 1980	*A Believer Sings the Truth* (Johnny Cash)
October 1980	*Classic Christmas* (Bill Walker)
December 1980	*Rockabilly Blues* (Earl Poole Ball)
June 1981	*The Baron* (Billy Sherrill)
May 1982	*The Survivors* [with Jerry Lee Lewis, Carl Perkins] (Chips Moman)
November 1982	*The Adventures of Johnny Cash* (Jack Clement)
November 1983	*Johnny 99* (Brian Ahern)
September 1985	*The Highwayman* [with Kris Kristofferson, Waylon Jennings, Willie Nelson] (Chips Moman)
May 1986	*Believe In Him* (Marty Stuart)
June 1986	*Heroes* [with Waylon Jennings] (Chips Moman)
May 1987	*Johnny Cash Is Coming to Town* (Jack Clement)
October 1988	*Water From the Wells of Home* (Jack Clement)
February 1990	*Boom Chickaboom* (Jack Clement)
March 1990	*The Highwayman 2* [with Kris Kristofferson, Waylon Jennings, Willie Nelson] (Chips Moman)
March 1991	*The Mystery of Life* (Jack Clement)
August 1991	*Country Christmas* (Ralph Jungheim)
October 1994	*American Recordings* (Rick Rubin)
April 1995	*The Road Goes on Forever* [as the Highwaymen] (Don Was)
November 1996	*Unchained* (Rick Rubin)
June 1998	*VH1 Storytellers* [with Willie Nelson] (Rick Rubin)
October 2000	*Solitary Man* (Rick Rubin)
November 2002	*The Man Comes Around* (Rick Rubin)

Posthumously:

| November 2003 | *Unearthed* (Rick Rubin) |
| Fall 2004 | *American V* (Rick Rubin) |

Personal Interviews by the Author

Martyn Atkins, Leo Ard, Earl Poole Ball, John E. Bell, Marie Bergeron, Freddie Bienstock, Eddie Bond, Bono, Joyce Burfield , Sonny Burgess, Larry Butler, Allen Caldwell, Geoffrey Cannon, Patsy Carmichael, Bill Carnahan, Lorrie Carnall, Cindy Cash, Joanne Cash, Johnny Cash, John Carter Cash, Kathy Cash, Rosanne Cash, Roy Cash Jr,, Tara Cash, Tommy Cash, Nick Cave, Jack Clement, Rich Collins, Cohen Cox, Janet Curtis, Michael Darlow, Sue Deal, Braxton Dixon, Jo Durden-Smith, Robert Duvall, Andy Earl, Robert Elfstrom, Bobby Emmons, David Ferguson, Gene Ferguson, Tilman Franks, Lou Freeman, Noel Furr, June Gallop, Larry Gatlin, Jack Good, Jim Gosnell, Joy Gower, Marshall Grant, Myra Hall, Bill Hamon, Kelly Hancock, Charles Harnett, A. J. Henson, Everett Henson, Saul Holiff, Jack Hollingsworth, Billie Jean Horton, J. E. Huff, Don Hunstein, Stan Jacobson, Sonny James, Frank Jones, Ralph Jones, Nadine Johnson, Bob Johnston, James Keach, Ron Keith, Merle Kilgore, Kris Kristofferson, Glenda Lesher, Charlie Louvin, Nick Lowe, Dennis Lynn, Richardson Lynn, Jack Matheson, Richard McGibony, Bob Moodie, Scotty Moore, Willie Nelson, Louise Nichols, Edwin Nix, Glen E. Pennywitt, Ben Perea, Steve Popovich, Don Reid, Harold Reid, Orville Rigdon, Chuck Riley, Edgar Rivers, Dyann Rivkin, Karen Robin, Lou Robin, Michele Rollins, Mark Romanek, Rick Rubin, Billy Shaddix, Jack Sharp, Jean Shepard, John L. Smith, Paul E. Smith, Jimmy Snow, Gerry Stewart, Mark Stielper, Everett Strawn, Al Thurston, Johnny Western, Robert Whitacre, Penny White, Harry Wiland, Courtney Wilson, Christopher Wren, Frank Yonco, Reggie Young.

Endnotes

Reasonable efforts have been made to locate the primary copyright holders of all the material in this book. However, some authors and original sources are still unknown. If anyone can provide knowledge of the authorship, origin, and first publication source for these stories, please relay this information to Editorial Assistant c/o Editorial Department, W Publishing Group, P. O. Box 141000, Nashville, TN 37217.

Front Matter

1. "The Pilgrim" by Kris Kristofferson. © Resaca Music Publishing Co. EMI New York. Used by permission.

Chapter One • First to Cross

1. "Hurt" written by Trent Reznor. © 1994 Leaving Hope Music/TVT Music Inc. (ASCAP). Administered by Leaving Hope Music, Inc. All rights reserved. Reprinted by permission.
2. "Far Side Banks of Jordan" words by Terry Smith. Published by Silverline Music, Warner/Chappel Music.
3. "Loving God, Loving Each Other" words by William J. and Gloria Gaither. Music by William J. Gaither. Copyright © 1997 Gaither Music Company. All rights controlled by Gaither Copyright Management. Used by permission.

Chapter Two • The Promised Land

1. This tune was composed in 1835 by M. Durham, lyrics written by Samuel Stennett in 1787.

2. The words to *Just As I Am* were written by Charlotte Elliott in 1835, music written by William Bradbury in 1849.

Chapter 3 • Leaving Home

1. Johnny Cash, *Cash: The Autobiography* (San Francisco, CA: Harper SanFrancisco, 1997).
2. Johnny Cash, *Man in Black* (Grand Rapids, MI: Zondervan, 1975).
3. Christopher Wren, *Winners Got Scars Too* (New York: Ballantine Books, a division of Random House, 1973).
4. Johnny Cash, *Cash: The Autobiography.*

Chapter 4 • Walking the Line

1. "Seven Dreams" by Gordon Jenkins. © 1953. All rights reserved. Used by permission.

Chapter 5 • Amphetamine Blues

1. Ben A. Green, "Johnny Cash Achieves Life's Ambition. Wins Opry Hearts," *Nashville Banner,* July 16, 1956.
2. Ralph J. Gleason, "It Looks As Though Elvis Has A Rival—From Arkansas," *San Francisco Chronicle*, December 16, 1956.

Chapter 6 • Going Down, Down, Down

1. Larry Linderman, "Penthouse Interview: Johnny Cash," *Penthouse*, August 1975.

Chapter 7 • Busted

1. Nat Hentoff, "Interview: Bob Dylan," *Playboy,* March 1966.
2. Nick Tosches, "Chordless in Gaza: The Second Coming of John R. Cash," *Journal of Country Music* 17 #3, 1995.

Chapter 8 • The Voice of America

1. Jack McClintock, "From Drug Addict to Committed Christian," *Family Weekly.* January 15, 1978.
2. Larry Linderman, "Penthouse Interview: Johnny Cash," *Penthouse*, August 1975.

Chapter 9 • Personal Jesus

1. "Help Me" by Larry Gatlin. First Generation Music Co. EMI New York. Used by permission.
2. "The Last Supper" by Larry Gatlin. First Generation Music Co. EMI New York. Used by permission.
3. Johnny Cash, *Man in Black* (Grand Rapids, MI: Zondervan, 1975).
4. "Holy Spirit's Alive in Me, Cash Says." *Nashville Tennessean,* August 20, 1972.

Chapter 10 • The Beast in Me

1. Byworth, Tony. "Johnny Cash: An Exclusive Phone Call." *Country Music People.* October, 1976.

Chapter 11 • Riding the Highway

1. Bill Flanagan, "Johnny Cash. American," Published interview, May 1988.

Chapter 12 • American Recordings

1. Lisa Robinson, "Johnny Cashes In On His Dream," *New York Post,* May 27, 1994.
2. Jance Dunn, "Mr. Cool," Rolling Stone, June 30, 1994.

Chapter 13 • The Man Comes Around

1. "That Lucky Old Sun" words and music by Haven Gillespie & Beasley Smith, © 1949. EMI New York. Used by permission.
2. "Mercy Seat" by Nicholas Cave, © Windswept Holdings/LLC DBA Songs of Windswept Pacific. Used by permission.
3. "Johnny Sings for June," *Rolling Stone,* July 24, 2003.
4. "Wayfaring Stranger" Adaptation & Arrangement by John R. Cash and John Carter Cash. Published by Song of Cash, Inc. Bug Music.
5. Johnny Cash, *Solitary Man,* CD, Hal Leonard Publishing Corporation, 2000.
6. "Hurt" written by Trent Reznor, © 1994 Leaving Hope Music/TVT Music Inc. (ASCAP). Administered by Leaving Hope Music, Inc. All rights reserved. Reprinted by permission.
7. "Personal Jesus" by Martin Gore, © 1990 EMI New York. Used by permission.
8. "September When It Comes" written by Rosanne Cash and John Leventhall. Chelcait Music, Bug Music.

Chapter 14 • Touched by Grace

1. "No Earthly Good" written by John R. Cash. Published by Song of Cash, Inc. Bug Music.

Bibliography

Books

Bane, Michael. *The Outlaws: Revolution in Country Music.* New York: Doubleday, 1978.

Burk, Bill. *Elvis: A 30-Year Chronicle.* Tempe, AZ: Osborne Enterprises, 1985.

Campbell, Garth. *He Walked the Line 1932–2003.* London: John Blake Publishing, 2003.

Cash, Johnny. *Man in Black.* Grand Rapids, MI: Zondervan, 1975.

———. *Man in White.* San Francisco: Harper and Row, 1986.

———. *Cash: The Autobiography.* San Francisco: HarperSanFrancisco, 1997.

Cash, June Carter. *Among My Klediments.* Grand Rapids, MI: Zondervan, 1979.

———. *From the Heart.* New York: Prentice Hall, 1987.

Cash, Rosanne, ed. *Songs without Rhyme: Prose By Celebrated Songwriters.* New York: Hyperion, 2001.

Cave, Nick. *King Ink II.* London: Black Spring Press, 1997.

Cash, Cindy. *The Cash Family Scrapbook.* New York: Crown, 1997.

Conn, Charles Paul. *The New Johnny Cash.* Old Tappan, NJ: Fleming H. Revell Company, 1973.

Coomes, David. *Spre-e '73.* London: Coverdale, 1973.

Cusic, Don. *Hank Williams: The Complete Lyrics.* New York: St Martin's Press, 1993.

Davidoff, Nicholas. *In the Country of Country.* London: Faber and Faber, 1997.

Davis, Clive. *Clive: Inside the Record Business.* New York: William Morrow, 1975.

Dellar, Fred and Roy Thompson. *The Illustrated Encyclopedia of Country Music.* London: Salamander, 1977.

Eliot, Marc. *Death of a Rebel: Starring Phil Ochs.* New York: Doubleday Anchor, 1979.

Escott, Colin. *The Story of Country Music.* London. BBC Worldwide, 2003.

———. *The Man in Black 1954–1958.* Book with CD box set. Bear Family Records. BCD 15517 EH.

———. *The Man in Black 1959–1962.* Book with CD box set. Bear Family Records. BCD 15562 EH.

Escott, Colin and Martin Hawkins. *Catalyst: The Sun Records Story.* London: Aquarius Books, 1975.

Fine, Jason. *Cash by the Editors of Rolling Stone.* New York: Crown, 2004.

Jones, George. *I Lived to Tell It All.* New York: Dell, 1996.

Flippo, Chet. *Your Cheatin' Heart.* New York: Simon and Schuster, 1981.

Fong-Torres, Ben, ed. *The Rolling Stone Rock 'n' Roll Reader.* New York: Bantam, 1974.

Franks, Tillman. *I Was There When It Happened.* Many, LA: Sweet Dreams, 2000.

Guralnick, Peter. *Best Music Writing 2000.* Cambridge, MA: Da Capo, 2000.

———. *Last Train to Memphis: The Rise of Elvis Presley.* London: Little, Brown, 1994.

Haggard, Merle. *My House of Memories.* New York: HarperCollins, 1999.

Hinton, Brian. *Country Roads.* London: Sanctuary Publishing, 2000.

Hopkins, Jerry. *Festival.* New York: Macmillan, 1970.

Jennings, Waylon. *Waylon: An Autobiography.* New York: Warner Books, 1996.

Lewry, Peter. *I've Been Everywhere: A Johnny Cash Chronicle.* London: Helter Skelter Publishing, 2001.

Lomax, Alan. *The Land Where the Blues Began.* London: Methuen, 1993.

Lydon, Michael. *Rock Folk.* New York: Dell, 1971.

Mansfield, Brian. *Ring of Fire: A Tribute To Johnny Cash.* Nashville: Rutledge Hill Press, 2003.

McNickle, D'Arcy. *Indian Man: A Life of Oliver La Farge.* Bloomington, IN: Indiana University Press, 1971.

Miller, Bill. *Cash: An American Man.* New York: Pocket Books, 2004.

Miller, Jonathan. *Stripped: Depeche Mode.* London: Omnibus Press, 2003.

Miller, Stephen. *Johnny Cash: The Life of an American Icon.* London: Omnibus Press, 2003.

Perkins, Carl. *Go. Cat. Go.* New York: Hyperion, 1996.

Pond, Neil, ed. *Johnny Cash an American Original.* Country Weekly Special Collectors Edition, October 2003.

Selvin, Joel. Ricky Nelson: Idol for a Generation. Chicago, Il: Contemporary Books, 1990.

Simmons, Sylvie. *Cash Unearthed.* Book with Unearthed box set.

Smith, John L. *The Johnny Cash Discography.* Westport, CT: Greenwood Press, 1985.

———. *The Johnny Cash Discography. 1984–1993.* Westport, CT: Greenwood Press, 1994.

Snow, Jimmy. *I Cannot Go Back.* Plainfield, NJ: Logos International, 1977.

Streissguth, Michael, ed. *Ring of Fire: The Johnny Cash Reader.* Cambridge, MA: Da Capo Press, 2002.

Thomas, Cal. *Public Persons and Private Lives.* Waco, TX: Word Books, 1979.

Tosches, Nick. *Country: The Twisted Roots of Rock 'n' Roll.* Cambridge, MA: Da Capo, 1996.

Urbanski, Dave. *The Man Comes Around: The Spiritual Journey of Johnny Cash.* Lake Mary, FL: Relevant Books, 2003.

Waters, John. *Race of Angels: The Genesis of U2.* London: Fourth Estate, 1994.

Williams, Hank Jr., *Living Proof.* New York: Dell, 1983.

Williams, Roger M. *Sing a Sad Song: The Life of Hank Williams.* New York: Ballantine, 1973.

Wolfe, Charles. *In Close Harmony: The Story of the Louvin Brothers.* Jackson, MS: University Press of Mississippi, 1996.

Worth, Fred L. and Steve D. Tamerius. *Elvis: His Life from A to Z.* Chicago: Contemporary Books, 1988.

Zwonitzer, Mark and Charles Hirshberg. *Will You Miss Me When I'm Gone?* New York: Simon & Schuster, 2002.

News Stories & Features

Appleton, Charlie. "Missouri Town Gets Johnny Cash Park." *Nashville Banner.* April 30, 1991.

Battle, Bob. "Big John Loves His America." *Nashville Banner.* April 21, 1971.

———. "Star Johnny Cash's Life is Shared at Museum." *Nashville Banner.* March 24, 1981.

———. "Johnny Cash Parkway Dedication." *Nashville Banner.* January 12, 1982.

———. "Cash Family Enjoys Quiet Refuge." *Nashville Banner.* August 24, 1982.

Candler, Peter M. Jr. "Johnny of The Cross." *First Things.* December 2003.

Carter, Walter. "Johnny Cash Gets a Big Kick Out of Waldo the Ostrich." *Nashville Tennessean.* September 25, 1981.

"Cash, June. Walk Line In Kentucky." *Nashville Tennessean.* March 2, 1968.

"Cash Plans $25 Million Suit On Klan." *Nashville Tennessean.* February 4, 1966.

"Cash To Pay $82.000 Damage." *Nashville Tennessean.* July 4, 1969.

"Cash Due Murphy Patriotism Award." *Nashville Banner.* June 30, 1972.

"Cash Denies Baptism, Altar Call." *Nashville Tennessean.* August 16, 1972.

"Cash Leaves Center After 45-Day Stay." *Nashville Tennessean.* February 2, 1984.

"Cash To Be Honored For Work With Young." *Nashville Tennessean.* September 30, 1979.

"Cash Collapses During Show." *Nashville Tennessean.* May 17, 1987.

Churchwell, Robert. "Johnny Cash Gift Stirs Others To Help Ailing Man." *Nashville Banner.* September 19, 1970.

Cooper, Peter and Craig Havighurst. "Country Legend Johnny Cash Dead At 71." *Tennessean.* September 12, 2003.

Corliss, Richard. "The Man In Black." Time. September 22, 2003.

Daughtrey, Larry. "One Who Came In Off The Street." *Nashville Tennessean.* March 8, 1966.

"Dope Is Death, Cash Declares." *Nashville Banner.* March 5, 1970.

"Dyess Arkansas: A Brand New Town." *Atlanta Journal.* July 7, 2000.

"Dyess Band Wins Contest." *Dyess Eagle.* April 26, 1939.

"Ex-Manager Files Suit Against Cash." June 24, 1981.

Forrister, Brad and Doug Wyatt. "Taylor-made Audience Rocks Opry House." *Nashville Tennessean.* February 21, 1971.

Fortune, Ross. Obituary. *Time Out.* September 17–24, 2003.

Foyston, John. "Johnny's Cache." *The Oregonian.* November 29, 2003.

Gleason, Ralph J. "It Looks As Though Elvis Has A Rival—From Arkansas." *San Francisco Chronicle.* December 16, 1956.

———. "Cash At San Quentin: The Law From Out Of Town." *Rolling Stone.* May 31, 1969.

Graham, David. "Third Suspect Sought In Holdup of Cash." *Nashville Tennessean.* January 5, 1982.

Green, Ben A. "Johnny Cash Achieves Life's Ambition. Wins Opry Hearts." *Nashville Banner.* July 16, 1956.

Gumbel, Andrew. "In A Garden of Weeds, The Oak Tree." *Independent.* September 13, 2003.

Hance, Bill. "Cash Says Prison System Is A School For Crime." *Nashville Banner.* July 30, 1975.

Hand, Jill. "Johnny Cash, Home in Asbury Park." *Asbury Park Press.* January 12, 1986.

Harlow, Susan. "Cash Up Front always Satisfies." *Rutland Register.* June 20, 1986.

Havighurst, Craig "Cash Buried Himself in Work in Final Months." *Tennessean.* September 14, 2003.

Havighurst, Craig and Peter Cooper. "A Celebration of a Remarkable Life." *Tennessean.* November 11, 2003.

Hilburn, Robert. "Country Kings Hit The Road." *Los Angeles Times.* April 15, 1990.

Holden, Stephen. "Johnny Cash. Country Music Bedrock. Dies at 71." *New York Times.* September 13, 2003.

"Holy Spirit's Alive In Me," Cash Says. *Nashville Tennessean.* August 20, 1972.

Hurst, Jack. "Cash At Leavenworth." *Nashville Tennessean.* May 31, 1970.

———. "Cash Gets Honorary Doctorate." *Nashville Tennessean.* September 29, 1971.

"Johnny Cash Slightly Hurt In Auto Crash." *Nashville Tennessean.* March 26, 1965.

"Johnny Cash Charged In Pep Pill Smuggling." *Nashville Banner.* October 5, 1965.

"Johnny Cash Talks About His TV Show." *Nashville Tennessean.* November 29, 1970.

"Johnny Cash Hospitalized To Prevent Addiction." *Nashville Tennessean.* December 21, 1983.

"Johnny Sings For June." *Rolling Stone.* July 24, 2003.

Johnson, Robert. "Gleason Signs Cash For 10 Guest Spots." *Memphis Press-Scimitar.* January 7, 1957.

"Kansas Inmates Get Cash Check." *Nashville Tennessean.* May 8, 1970.

Kershaw, Andy. "Ride This Train." *The Word.* November 2003.

La Farge, Peter. "Johnny Cash." *Sing Out!* May 1965.

Lord, Lewis. "Cash Offers Inmates Words With Music." *Nashville Tennessean.* August 14, 1970.

Mansfield, Brian. "Johnny Cash Sees The Light." *USA Today.* April 15, 1999.

Martin, Gavin. Obituary. *The Independent.* September 13, 2003.

Millard, Bob. "Road Catching Up With Me Johnny Cash Says." *Nashville Banner.* May 20, 1983.

Miller, Bill. "The Man In Black." *Collecting Magazine.* July 1997.

McCall, Michael. "In Pain. Cash Quits TV Taping." *Nashville Banner.* February 8, 1990.

Minaya, Zeke. "Music Legend Johnny Cash Dies at 71." *Los Angeles Times.* September 12, 2003.

Mitchell, John. "Cash Lived. Worked in County." *Ventura County Star.* September 13, 2003.

Obermann, Bob. "Johnny Cash Hospitalized With Pneumonia." *Nashville Tennessean.* February 17, 1983.

———. "Man In Black Without A Label." *Nashville Tennessean.* July 16, 1986.

———. "Polygram Records Cashes In With Legendary Man in Black." *Nashville Tennessean.* August 23, 1986.

———. "Highwaymen Rendezvous for Second LP." *Nashville Tennessean.* March 10, 1989.

Obituary. *Daily Telegraph.* September 13, 2003.

Obituary. *The Times.* September 13, 2003.

O'Donnell, Red. "Cash To Buy Plantation Dinner Theater." *Nashville Banner.* December 11, 1969.

———. "Cash Delivers His Best in Song. Words." *Nashville Banner.* April 18, 1970.

———. "Johnny Cash Declares TV Moratorium." *Nashville Banner.* April 7, 1971.

———. "Cash Completes Filming Movie of Christ's Life." *Nashville Banner.* November 29, 1971.

———. "Cash Denies Drug, Marital Rumours." *Nashville Banner.* September 4, 1979.

Olsen, Ted. "Johnny Cash's Song Of Redemption." *Christianity Today.* November 2003.

Orr, Jay. "Cash Completes Course On Relapse Wednesday." *Nashville Banner.* December 5, 1989.

Orr, Jay and L. Carol Ritchie. "Johnny Cash in Alcohol. Drug Treatment Center." *Nashville Banner.* November 25, 1989.

Pareles, Jon. "Tracing The Line Cash Walked." *New York Times.* September 13, 2003.

———. "A Nashville Tribute to Johnny Cash." *New York Times.* November 12, 2003.

Reaney, James. "Ex-Londoner Remembers Cash." *London Free Press.* September 13, 2003.

Sawyer, Kathy. "Cash and Co. Say Hello-Goodbye." *Nashville Tennessean.* June 1, 1969.

Simmons, Sylvie. "Hello. I'm Johnny Cash." *Guardian.* September 19, 2003.

———. "He Walked The Line." *Mojo.* November 2003.

Snyder, Bill. "Open-Heart Surgery on Cash Successful." *Nashville Banner.* December 19, 1988.

Sullivan, James. "Johnny Cash: Voice of the Common Man." *San Francisco Chronicle.* September 13, 2003.

Sweeting, Adam. Obituary. *The Guardian.* September 13, 2003.

Tedford Jones, Jill. "The Delight of Words: The Elizabethan Sonneteers and American Country Lyricists." *Popular Music and Society.* Winter 2000.

"The Man In Black Is Back." *Tennessean.* April 17, 1999.

Whiteside, Jonny. "Free in L. A." *LA Weekly.* September 19–25, 2003.

Wren, Christopher, *Winners Got Scars Too* (London: W. H. Allen, 1973).

"Write Is Wrong." *Time.* February 23, 1959.

Zimmermann, David. "A Stoic Man In Black." *USA Today.* October 30, 1997.

Published Interviews

Bane, Michael. "20 Questions With Johnny Cash." *Country Music Magazine.* January/February 1993.

Batin, Christopher. "Johnny Cash and Son Fish in Alaska." *Alaska Outdoors.* October 1986.

Berkowitz, Kenny "No Regrets." *Acoustic Guitar.* June 2001

Braun, Saul. "Good Ole Boy: Cash" *Playboy.* November 1970.

Byworth, Tony. "Johnny Cash: An Exclusive Phone Call." *Country Music People.* October 1976.

Carr Patrick, "What Now John Cash?" *Country Music.* December 1974.

———. "Cash Comes Back." *Country Music.* December 1976.

———. "Johnny Cash's Freedom." *Country Music.* April 1979.

———. "The Spirit Is Willing." *The Journal of Country Music.* 2002.

Cash, Rosanne. "Johnny Cash." Interview. December 1996.

Cooper, Peter. "Hello This Is Johnny Cash." *Tennessean.* October 2, 2000.

DeCurtis, Anthony. "Johnny Cash Won't Back Down." *Rolling Stone.* October 26, 2000.

———. "An American Original Returns." *New York Times.* February 24, 2002.

DeYoung, Bill. "Johnny Cash: American Music Legend." *Goldmine.* July 19, 1996.

Dickie, Mary. "Hard Talk from the God-Fearin', Pro-Metal Man in Black." *Graffiti.* October 1987.

Dickins, Barry. "The Man In Black." *The Melbourne Age.* November 18, 1995.

Farren, Mick "Johnny Cash: The Gospel According to J. C." *NME.* October 4, 1975.

Fine, Jason. "A Day In The Life Of Johnny Cash." *Rolling Stone.* November 26, 2002.

Flanagan, Bill. "Johnny Cash. American." May 1988.

Fricke, David. "Rick Rubin on Cash's Legacy." *Rolling Stone.* September 23, 2003.

"From Out Of the Past." Interview on WIXR. Richmond, WI. October 21, 1996.

Frook, John. "Johnny Cash: The Rough-Cut King of Country Music." *Life.* November 21, 1969.

Gallagher, Dorothy. "Johnny Cash: I'm Growing. I'm Changing. I'm Becoming." *Redbook.* August 1971.

Gill, Chris. "Johnny Cash: Turning Stories Into Songs." *Guitar Player.* September 1994.

Hajari, Nisad "Next Big Resurrected Legend." 1994.

Hilburn, Robert. "Rolling Stone Interview with Johnny Cash." *Rolling Stone.* March 1, 1973.

Hoskyns, Barney. "Johnny Cash: A Law Unto Himself." Mojo December 1996.

"The Johnny Cash Press Conference." *Country Music People.* December 1971.

King, Larry. "Interview With Johnny Cash." CNN. November 26, 2002.

"The Last American Hero." Unknown interviewer. Unknown month 1994.

Lanham, Tom. "Renaissance Man In Black. Unknown publication. 1996.

Linderman, Larry. "Penthouse Interview: Johnny Cash." *Penthouse*. August 1975.

McCabe, Kathy and Nui Te Koha. "Cash Bonus." *Daily Telegraph Mirror*. February 19, 1994.

McCabe, Peter and Jack Killion. "An Interview with Johnny Cash." *Country Music Magazine*. May 1973.

McClintock, Jack. "From Drug Addict To Committed Christian." *Family Weekly*. January 15, 1978.

Moss, Phil. "Music's Always Been Food For My Soul." *USA Today*. November 6, 1985.

Obermann, Robert K. "Johnny Cash Still Speaks for the Hearts of Americans." *Tennessean*. April 26, 1987.

Rader, Dotson. "I Can Sing of Death but I'm Obsessed with Life." *Parade Magazine Orange County Register*. June 11, 1995

Robinson, Lisa. "Johnny Cashes In On His Dream." *New York Post*. May 27, 1994.

Shaw, Bill. "Easing Back With Johnny Cash." *People*. July 11, 1994.

Tosches, Nick. "Chordless In Gaza: The Second Coming of John R. Cash." *Journal of Country Music* 17 #3. 1995.

Vovcsko, Jerry. "A Chat With Johnny Cash." *Evening Gazette and Worcester Telegram*. August 11–12, 1988.

Weisel, Al. "Johnny Cash." *US*. February 1997.

Yonay, Ehud. "Johnny Cash Tells It On A Mountain." *Nashville Tennessean*. November 21, 1971.

Index

Ace, Johnny, 53
Acuff, Roy, 39, 69, 137, 183
Adams, Karen, *xiii*
Ahern, Brian, 166–67, 171
Albums, 75–76
   listed by date, 269–71
Ali, Muhammad, 234
Allen, Joe, 168
American Recordings, 197–98, 200, 202, 261
Amphetamines, 72–73. *See also* Cash, Johnny, substance abuse
Anthony, 15
Ard, Leo, 34, 273
Armstrong, Garner Ted, 152
Arnold, Eddy, 56, 239
Asher, Dick, 182
Atkins, Jimmy, 78
Atkins, Martyn, 215, 273
Aucutt, Stephen, *xiv*
Automobile Sales, 45, 46, 50, 51
Autry, Gene, 77, 82, 103, 174

Baez, Joan, 92, 108
Ball, Earl Poole, 167, 168–69, 204, 233, 257, 273
"Ballad of Ira Hayes, The", 106–8, 253

Barnett, Tommy, 151, 152
Barnhill, Jesse, 25, 26, 39
Bates, George, 46
"Beast in Me, The", 196, 198, 202
Beatles, 58, 125, 135, 150, 237, 239–40, 241, 253, 254, 255
Bell, John E., 47, 273
"Belshazar", 51, 76
Bergeron, Marie, 273
Bernstein, Cecil, 132
Betty, 9
Bienstock, Freddie, 165–66, 273
"Big River", 74, 75, 108, 141, 238–39, 265
Bitter Tears, 106–10
Black, Bill, 46
Blackburn, Rick, 179, 181, 182–83
Blackwood Brothers, 48, 76
Blaine, Hal, 171
"Blue Suede Shoes", 65–66
   origin, 59–60, 237–38, 251
Blues in the Mississippi Night, 93, 94, 238
Bon Aqua, 177, 180, 244
Bond, Eddie, 273
Bond, Johnny, 85
Bono, 222, 223, 234–35, 273
   on Cash, 154, 190–91, 199–200, 211
Boone, Pat, 90

"Boy Named Sue, A", 134–5, 242
Bragg, Charlie, 159
Brando, Marlin, 53
Broonzy, Big Bill, 93
Bull, Sandy, 108
Burfield, Joyce, 273
Burgess, Sonny, 239, 273
Burnett, Beverley, *xiii*
Burton, James, 171
Bush, George W., 209, 223, 230, 234
Butler, Larry, 147, 231, 273

Caldwell, Allen, 50, 273
Caldwell, Doug, 170
Campbell, Jimmie, 223
Campbell, Mike, 196
Campus Crusade for Christ, 150–51
Cannon, Geoffrey, 131, 132, 273
Carmichael, Patsy, 273
Carnahan, Bill, 39, 40, 41, 43, 44, 54, 59, 273
Carnall, Lorrie Collins 91, 273.
    See also Collins, Lorrie
Carnall, Stew, 71–72, 79, 83, 86, 91, 252, 273
Carr, Patrick, 204
Carson, Johnny, 81
Carter, A.P., 68, 105
Carter, Anita (sister of June), 9, 68, 99, 105, 207, 214, 222, 262
Carter, Dale, 10
Carter, Eck (father of June), 32, 105, 117, 144, 256
Carter Family, *ix*, 10, 68, 92, 97, 103, 105, 109, 124, 137, 142, 154, 166, 219, 221, 266, 267
Carter, Helen, 68, 105, 207, 214
Carter, Janette, 10, 219
Carter, Joe, 10
Carter, John (Johnny's son).
    See Cash, John Carter.
Carter, June. *See* Cash, June Carter
Carter, Maybelle (mother of June), 9, 68, 97, 105, 116, 117, 118, 214, 222, 229, 257, 267

Carter, Sara, 68, 166
Carter Sisters and Mother Maybelle, 68, 97
Cash, Carrie Rivers (Johnny's mother), 3, 15, 16, 18, 19, 20, 45, 95, 103, 214, 260
    encouraging Johnny, 28
    tributes, 187–88
Cash Country, 188–89, 260, 261
Cash, Joanne, 20, 25, 145, 179, 221, 235, 273
Cash, John Carter (Johnny's son), *xiv*, 6, 7, 9, 10, 142, 153, 155, 163, 170, 171, 173, 174, 180, 183, 209, 214, 218, 219, 221, 222, 224, 230, 255, 273

Cash, Johnny, biography
    ancestry, 15–16
    background, 13–14, 26–29.
        See also Dyess, Arkansas
    birth, 16
    birth name, 16–17, 29, 53, 54
    brother's death, 22–25, 247
    childhood music, 19–20, 25-26
    Dyess years, 17–29
    father's influence, 14–15, 143–44
    his air force years, 29, 31–44
    life on tour 84–92
    marriage to Vivian, 46, 47–48
    marriage to Vivian ends, 109, 116–17, 118, 126
    marries June, 126
    midlife, 131, 153–54, 159–60
    Nickajack Cave, 119–20, 174, 187, 233
    Old Hickory Lake, 13, 117–18
    ordained as minister, 160–61
    sickness in last days, 207–221
    traumatic hostage-taking, 170–71
    tributes, 222–23
    where buried, 222.
    See also Cash, Johnny, character; Cash, Johnny, his art; Cash, June Carter

Cash, Johnny, character
  ambivalence, 13–14, 16–17, 127, 179–80, 198–200
  as pilgrim, *xvii*
  effect of pain, 214, 220, 225
  embellished recollection, 35–37
  gratitude, 212, 216–17, 229–30, 242
  lack of self-knowledge, *xiv–xv*
  on racism, 37–38
  pensiveness, 43.
  See also Cash, Johnny, faith life

Cash, Johnny, faith life, 7, 14, 126, 128, 224
  as Christian artist, 20, 198–200, 228–29
  backsliding, 22, 35–36
  Billy Graham's influence, 141–42
  church, 21–22, 62, 95, 144–45, 163–64
  commitment, 38, 21–22, 140–41, 143–61
  country music culture, 76–77
  ecumenism, 150–52
  gospel music, 82, 158–59
  near death, 3, 221, 226–27
  witness, 230–32, 234–35.
  See also Cash, Johnny, health issues; Cash, Johnny, substance abuse

Cash, Johnny, health issues, 170, 226
  jaw problems, 185–87, 203
  lapsed into coma, 203–5
  late life, 1–4
  nervous system issues, 212
  operations, 172, 184–85
  pain, 214, 220, 225
  substance abuse, 208.
  See also Cash, Johnny, his art; Cash, Johnny, substance abuse

Cash, Johnny, his art, 244
  acting, 81, 84, 172
  drawing, 41–42
  early creativity, 25, 26
  lifelong themes, 20
  movies, 143
  novel, 172–73

  reading tastes, 245
  short stories, 41
  TV, 241.
  See also Cash, Johnny, his music

Cash, Johnny, his music
  air force, 38–44
  alternative rock, 190, 200–201
  as rebel, 128–29
  broad tastes, 92, 244
  guitar, 39, 57
  hard rock, 193
  heart folk songs, 195–96
  heavy metal, 240–41
  key influences, 92–94, 238
  key themes, 17, 52, 203
  rock-'n'-roll, 67
  Rubin's role, 195–200
  songs he chose, 202–3
  songwriting, 40, 43
  sound, 239
  techniques, 74–75
  uniting generations, 157
  violent themes, 60–61
  voice, 211, 219
  with Luther and Marshall, 48–49, 51–52.
  See also Cash, Johnny, his music career; Country music; Gospel music; Rock-'n'-roll

Cash, Johnny, his music career
  as voice of America, 123–42
  career decision for music, 43
  comebacks, 125, 135, 188, 189, 191
  creates Tennessee Two, 45–46
  early years, 49–50, 54, 55–63, 66
  escapes "Southern" label, 70–72, 81
  inducted into Grand Ole Opry, 67–69
  international audience, 91–92
  lost by Columbia, 181–82
  Mercury label, 182–83
  midlife decline, 158
  prison concerts, 124–26
  radio, 47, 53–54, 61–62
  rivalry with Elvis, 165–66

Sam Phillips, 50, 66, 75, 77–78
seen as "hip", 189–90, 94, 200–201
stress of touring, 66–67, 82–91
tributes, 208–9
TV, 135–42
Viper Room test, 196–97.
See also Cash, Johnny, his music career,
  awards

Cash, Johnny, his music career, awards
  Audie Murphy Patriotism award, 156
  CMA Album of the Year, 130
  Country Music Hall of Fame, 168
  Flameworthy, 4
  Grammies, 208, 262
  honorary doctorate, 155–56
  Kennedy Center Lifetime Achievement,
    208
  Living Legend awards, 188, 260, 262
  MTV award, 221, 263
  National Medal of Arts, 209
  Rock-'n'-Roll Hall of Fame, 188
  UN Humanitarian, 257.
  See also Cash, Johnny, relationship
    with June; Highwaymen; Johnny
    Cash and the Tennessee Two;
    Johnny Cash Show, The

Cash, Johnny, relationship with June, 5–9,
    68, 117, 247
  affair with June, 97–99, 103–5
  as "sweetest friend", 214
  bereavement, 9, 12, 218–20
  marries June, 126.
  See also Cash, Johnny, social justice;
    Cash, Johnny, substance abuse;
    Cash, June Carter

Cash, Johnny, social justice, 106–8,
    125–26, 138–39, 154, 155–56,
    190–91, 227, 228, 233–34, 241–42,
    246
  AIDS, 189–90
  Native Americans, 106–10, 130–31
  prisons, 133–34

radicals, 131–32.
See also Cash, Johnny, substance abuse

Cash, Johnny, substance abuse, 82–84,
    114, 115, 120–21, 242–43
  amphetamines' effect, 72–74
  and stress of touring, 69, 72
  behavior change, 95–97, 166–67, 172
  Betty Ford Center, 173–74
  busted, 90–91, 113, 120
  car crashes, 110–11, 112–13
  career setbacks, 94, 99, 111–12
  drug free, 131, 158, 175
  drug relapse, 164–65
  pain as factor, 170, 225–26
  suicide bid, 119
  TV years, 135, 138–39.
  See also Cash, June Carter, helping
    Johnny

Cash, June Carter, ix, v, xv, 14, 130
  death, 1–9, 217–18
  failing health, 4–5
  forecasts death, 5, 6
  funeral, xi, 8–12
  helping Johnny, 4, 97, 117, 119, 120,
    133, 143, 217–18
  marries Johnny, 126
  relationship with Johnny, 68, 232–33.
  See also Cash, Johnny, biography

Cash, Kathy, xiv, 6, 7, 81, 103–4, 117,
    203, 222, 251, 273
Cash, Laura, 10, 219, 229
Cash, Louise (Johnny's sister), 4, 14, 16,
    18, 27, 217, 263
Cash Museum, 207
Cash, Ray (Johnny's father), 14–20, 45, 95
  character, 14–15, 17–18, 61
  faith life, 24–25
  his death, 179
  on Johnny, 23, 179, 214, 259, 261
Cash, Reuben Moses, 15
Cash, Rosanne (Johnny's daughter), xiv, 7,
    9, 10–12, 41, 53, 81, 95, 109,

116–17, 169, 170, 173, 183, 187, 196, 207, 216, 221, 222, 232–33, 235, 250, 257, 260, 273

Cash, Roy (Johnny's brother), 16, 19, 20, 21, 45, 46, 48, 56, 63, 103

Cash, Roy Jr. (Johnny's nephew), 138, 273

Cash, Tara (Johnny's daughter), *xiv*, 7, 14, 17, 27, 94, 144, 180, 198, 220, 252, 273

Cash: The Autobiography, 35, 36–37, 51, 204, 262

Cash, Tommy (Johnny's brother), 20, 24, 66–67, 267, 273

Cash, Vivian Liberto, 33, 45, 46, 47, 52, 54, 59, 62, 66, 74, 87, 89, 98, 103, 103–5, 109, 120, 225, 250, 254
  as Johnny's sweetheart, 32, 43–44
  as Johnny's wife, 47–48
  as Klan target, 113–14
  breakdown of marriage, 56, 84–85, 95
  divorce from Johnny, 109, 116–17, 118, 126.
  See also Cash, Johnny, biography

Cash, William Henry, 15

Cass, Mama, 136

Cave, Nick, 136, 210, 213, 224, 230, 234, 273

Charles, Ray, 137, 223

Christian International School of Theology, 160, 164, 257

Cinnamon Hill, 15, 160, 170, 184, 215, 217

Clapton, Eric, 150

Clark, Roy, 177, 189, 202

Clayton, Adam, 190

Clement, Cowboy Jack, *x*, 75, 76, 77, 78, 79, 100, 114, 169, 170, 183, 219, 220, 234, 251, 271, 273

Cline, Patsy, 69, 71, 72, 82, 103, 105, 186

Cobaugh, John, 163–64

Collins, Judy, 92, 137

Collins, Larry, 85

Collins, Lorrie, 85, 86.
  See also Carnall, Lorrie Collins

Collins, Rich, 34, 35, 37, 38, 42, 44, 273

Colony Herald, xiv

Colter, Jessie, 8, 177

Columbia, *x*, 77, 78, 79, 81, 90, 95, 100–101, 105, 109, 114, 123, 124, 125, 129–30, 131, 132–33, 158–59, 166, 169, 178–79, 181–83, 251, 252, 259, 263

Coolidge, Rita, 150

Costello, Elvis, 170, 234

Cott, Jonathan, 131, 132

Country Music Hall of Fame, *xiii*

Country music
  and folk revival, 105–6
  conventions, 57
  going mainstream, 65–66
  postwar culture, 40
  religious culture, 76–77

Country music supergroup, 177–78

Cox, Cohen, 26, 273

Crow, Sheryl, 10, 211, 222

Crowell, Rodney, 172

"Cry, Cry, Cry", 52, 53, 54, 57, 58, 60, 250
  origin, 52

Cummins, Reid, 38

Curtis, Janet, 273

Dalton, David, 131, 132

Danzig, Glenn, 202

Darlow, Michael, 132–33, 134, 273

Davis, Clive, 125

Davis, Don, 159

Deal, Sue, 273

Deckleman, Bud, 54

Def American Records, 193, 194, 261.
  See also Rubin, Rick

Denis, Gil, 208

Depp, Johnny, 196, 197, 201

Distin, Dick, 126

Dixie Chicks, 234

Dixon, Braxton, 117–18, 273

Document, The, 115

"Don't Take Your Guns to Town", 40, 209, 265, 267

Donoho, W.J., 90

Douglas, Kirk, 143

Dr. Quinn, Medicine Woman, 10, 195, 261, 262

Duffy, Robert, 216

Durden-Smith, Jo, 132, 133, 135, 273

Duval, Robert, 273

Dyess, Arkansas, *xiii–xiv*, 249
  1937 flood, 19
  Johnny's return visit, 13–14
  life in Dyess, 17–29, 37–38, 66–67, 233

Dyess High School, *xiv,* 26–27, 249

Dyess, W.R., 17

Dylan, Bob, *ix, xi,* 71, 106
  Cash as friend, 106, 108–9, 129–30, 136, 189, 194, 203, 209, 222, 223, 234, 253, 254, 255, 261
    Cash as inspiration, 75
    faith life, 115, 246
    influence on Cash, 128, 245–46

Earl, Andy, 200, 273

Earle, Steve, 234

Edmunds, Dave, 170

Elfstrom, Robert, 13–14, 127–28, 129, 130–31, 141, 146–47, 273

Eliott, Ramblin' Jack, 92, 108, 110, 136

Emmons, Bobby, 178, 273

Eno, Brian, 191

Eschenbach, Walter and Monica, 6

Etue, Kate, *xiii*

Falk, Peter, 241

Farina, Richard, 92

Ferguson, David "Fergie", 183, 197–98, 202, 211, 213, 219, 220, 231, 273

Ferguson, Gene, 106–7, 112, 116, 117, 273

Fielder, LaVanda Mae, 28

First Baptist Church (Dyess), 21, 24, 249

First Baptist Church (Hendersonville), 9–10, 120, 145, 179, 222, 254, 264

"Five Feet High and Rising", 92

Flanaghan, Bill, 181

Flatt and Scruggs, 103

Flea, 196

Folk music tradition, 105–8

Folk rock, Cash's role, 75

Folk Songs of the Hills, 93

Folsom Prison, 124–25, 132, 137

"Folsom Prison Blues", 40, 51, 56, 60–61, 66, 68, 78, 108, 133–34, 41, 209, 251, 254, 265, 266
  Jenkins' earlier work, 61.
  See also Johnny Cash at Folsom Prison

Franks, Billy, 88

Franks, Tilman, 87, 88, 273

Freed, Don, 131

Freeman, Lou, *xiv,* 273

Freeman, Ted, *xiv,* 38, 39, 42, 43, 52–53, 53–54, 55, 56, 57–58, 60, 62, 68–69, 72, 75, 273

Fremmer, Ray, 170

Fullam, Albert, 120

Furr, Noel, 273

Gallop, Hal, 22

Gallop, June, 273

Galloway United Methodist Church, 49–50

Gantry, Chris, 128

Gatlin, Larry, 10, 147, 148–49, 151, 222, 224, 228, 273

Geiger, Mark, 194

Gibson, Don, 105, 202

"Give My Love to Rose", 74, 75, 209, 215, 265

Gleason, Ralph J., 71, 134

Glover, Tony, 108

Godspell, 150

Goldberg, Whoopi, 8, 223

Golden Gate Quartet, 92

Good, Jack, 112, 273

Gore, Al, 8, 208, 260

Gore, Martin, 214–15

Gosnell, Jim, 194, 197, 273

Gospel music, 82
  and religious belief, 76–77
  and rock-'n'-roll, 243

Gospel Road, 146–47, 148, 149, 151, 158, 231, 256

Gower, Joy, 19, 24–25, 273

Graham, Billy, 8, 138, 150, 151, 152, 166, 177

   and Johnny, 141–42, 154–55, 220–21, 223, 230, 255, 256, 257

Graham, Franklin, 222

Grand Ole Opry (broadcast), 62, 67

   and Johnny, 20, 28, 38, 251

Grand Ole Opry (music hall), 68, 105

   and Johnny, 67–69, 111, 128, 129, 185–86

Grant, Etta, 48

Grant, Marshall, 45–46, 47, 48, 59, 70, 78, 79, 103–4, 187, 250, 258, 273

   helping Johnny, 96–98, 135, 164–65, 167

   on Johnny, 97

   playing with Johnny, 49–56, 73–74, 167

   terminated by Johnny, 167–68, 229

Green, Ben A., 67

Green, David, 189

Gressett, Floyd, 95–96, 124

Gunfight, A, 143

Guralnick, Peter, 161

Haggard, Merle, 132, 136, 211, 239, 252

Hale, Jack Jr., 168

Hall, Myra, 273

Hall, Tom T., 172, 184

Hamblin, Stuart, 103

Hammond, John, 106

Hamon, Bill, 160–61, 163, 273

Hancock, Kelly (Johnny's niece), *xiii,* 4, 5, 6, 7, 9, 12, 217, 218, 220–21, 229–30, 273

Hancock, Reba (Johnny's sister), 4, 17, 18, 27, 147, 168, 170

Harnett, Charles, 273

Harrington, Bob, 152

Harris, Emmylou, 10, 166, 183, 222, 234

Hawkins, Hawkshaw, 69

Hayes, Ira Hamilton, 107

Hendersonville (TN), 215–16, 243.

   See also Bon Aqua; Cash Country; House of Cash; Old Hickory Lake

Hendersonville Memory Gardens, 4, 9

Henson, A.J., *xiii–xiv,* 21, 37, 273

Henson, Everett, *xiii–xiv,* 273

"Here Comes That Rainbow Again", 178

"Hey, Porter!", 40, 51, 52, 53, 71, 188, 250, 265

   origin, 40

Highwaymen, 177–78, 186, 188, 195, 260, 261, 262

Hilburn, Robert, 222

Hill, Eddie, 52

Holiff, Saul, 91–92, 95, 96, 97, 103, 112, 114, 115, 127, 132, 135, 180, 252, 256, 273

   marketing Johnny, 92, 94–95, 115, 135, 136, 137, 157–58

Holland, W.S. "Fluke", 90, 252

Hollingsworth, Jack, 24, 273

"Holografik Danser, The", 41

Holy Dance, Robert, 130

Holy Land, 146

Home Equipment Company, 46, 52, 60, 63

Hooker, John Jay, 114

Horn Cloud, William, 130

Horton, Billie Jean, 69–70, 86–87, 88–90, 98, 273

Horton, Johnny, 69–70, 86–87, 88–89, 251, 252

House of Cash, 189, 215

Huff, J.E., 21, 22, 273

Humbard, Rex, 152

Hungry for Heaven, xv

Hunstein, Don, 273

Hurst Motor Company, 50

"Hurt", 2–3, 4, 213–14, 215–16, 221, 263, 269

Husky, Ferlin, 56, 72

"I Get So Doggone Lonesome", 57, 69, 265

"I Saw a Man", 141

"I Walk the Line", 40, 66, 67, 68–69, 70, 78, 108, 125, 141, 209, 231, 245, 251, 265

   origin, 40, 59

Inside the Walls of Folsom Prison, 40

Irizarry, Christine, *xiii*
Iron Maiden, 240
Ives, Burl, 137, 240, 252

Jackie Gleason Show, 65, 72, 251
Jacobson, Stan, 135, 137–41, 157, 273
Jamal, Mumia Abu, *xi*
James, Sonny, 54, 71, 273
Jefferson, Blind Lemon, 92, 238
Jeffries, Bob, 120
Jenkins, Gordon, 61
Jennings, Waylon, 8, 117, 137, 161, 174,
    177, 178, 179, 181, 183, 184–85,
    186, 214, 257, 259, 263
Jerkins, Terry, 5, 8
Jesus Christ Superstar, 150
Johnny Cash and the Great Eighties Eight,
    168
Johnny Cash and the Tennessee Three, 53,
    90, 124, 151, 168, 252
Johnny Cash and the Tennessee Two, 53,
    56, 69, 71, 79, 81, 84, 85, 90, 92,
    168, 239
  becomes Tennessee Three, 90, 252
Johnny Cash at Folsom Prison, 61, 125,
    127, 130, 188, 209, 270. *See also*
    "Folsom Prison Blues"
Johnny Cash Enterprises, 81, 91
Johnny Cash Museum, 207
Johnny Cash Show, The, 82, 97, 105, 136,
    137–38, 141, 145, 157, 169, 187, 270
*Johnny Cash: The Man, His World, His
    Music*, 146
Johnson, Hoyt, 78
Johnson, Jude, 203
Johnson, Nadine, 27–28, 273
Johnson, Ralph, 50
Johnson, Robert, 77, 92, 238
Johnston, Bob, 123–26, 128, 129, 133,
    254, 270, 273
Jones, Brian, 132
Jones, Frank, 269, 270, 273
Jones, George, 71, 100, 128, 170
Jones, Ralph, 120
Jones, Tom, 201

Justis, Bill, 79
Keach, James, 10, 208, 273
Keith, Ron, 4, 6, 273
Kemp, Wayne, 159
Kennedy, Jerry, 99
Kenton, Stan, 38
Kernodle, A.W. "Red", 51
Kershaw, Andy, 201
Kilgore, Merle, 7, 70, 73, 92, 98–100,
    103, 126, 218, 273
King, Claude, 98
King, Larry, 216–17
Kingsland, 15–18, 19, 159, 249, 256
Kingston Trio, 92
Klein, Gary, 158
Klein, Marty, 174
Konrad, Cathy, 208–9
Kristofferson, Johnny, *xi*
Kristofferson, Kris, 7–8, 74, 128–29, 134,
    147–48, 149, 179, 191, 195, 200,
    234, 241, 254, 259, 261, 262
  faith issues, 147–48, 231
  on Johnny, *ix-xiii, xvii*, 111, 138–40,
    150–51, 177–78, 185–86, 222, 233,
    234
Ku Klux Klan, 113–14
Kuhlman, Kathryn, 152

La Farge, Peter, 106–7, 108, 110, 114, 253
Landsberg Barbarians, 39
Langford, Jon, 190
Law, Don, 77, 82, 100, 110, 113, 123, 251,
    254
Leadbelly, 55, 92, 106
Lee, Larry, 145, 147
Lennon, John, 128, 150, 258
Lesher, Glenda, 273
Lewin, Bob, 168
Lewis, Jerry Lee, 71, 75, 76–77, 140, 145,
    178, 190, 239, 251, 257, 258, 259,
    271
Lewis, Walter "Curly", 94–95
Liberto, Tom, 32, 44, 46, 66
Liberto, Vincent, 32
Liberto, Vivian. *See Cash*, Vivian Liberto

Lien, James, 201
Lightfoot, Gordon, 136
"Like a Soldier", 198–99
Little Richard, 140
Lloyd-Webber, Andrew, 150
Lomax, Alan, 93–94, 110, 238
Lomax, John, 238
Louisiana Hayride, 61, 62, 69, 70
Louvin Brothers, 28, 48, 56, 58, 77, 92
Louvin, Charlie, 48, 58, 273
Louvin, Ira, 48, 77
Love Song, 150
Lowe, Nick, 169–70, 196, 198, 257, 273
Luman, Bob, 85
Lydon, Michael, 66

Maddox, Rose, 82
Maffetone, Phil, 6
Mahr, Beverly, 61
"Mama Cash's House", 3–4
Man Called Cash, The, xiii
Man Comes Around, The (album), 216, 217, 219, 263
"Man Comes Around, The" (song), 212–13
Man in Black (book), 35, 147, 256
"Man in Black" (song), 139, 255, 267
Man in White (novel), 180–81, 184, 245, 259
Mandrell, Barbara, 82, 177
Mangold, James, 208
Mansfield, David, 171
Maphis, Joe, 85
Martin, Buzz, 131
Matheson, Jack, 40, 41, 42, 59, 273
Matlock, 24
Matthews, Randy, 150
Matthews, Vince, 128
Mayes, Charles E., 184–85
McCaig, Annie, *xiv*
McCartney, Paul, 184, 239, 244
McClintock, Jack, 137–38
McGibony, Richard, 120, 165, 273
McLaughlin, Pat, 220
Mellencamp, John, 7
Memphis music scene, 46–48, 65
Memphis Slim, 93

Mercury label, 182–83, 188, 194, 259. *See also* Polygram Records
Miller, Roger, 103, 137
Mitchell, Joni, 129, 134, 136, 189
Moberg, David, *xiii*
Moman, Chips, 177, 178
Moodie, Bob, 32–33, 41–42, 273
Moore, Scotty, 44, 46, 50, 239, 273
Moore, Sue, 27
Moss, Kate, 201
Mother Maybelle. See Carter, Maybelle
Muddy Waters, 92
Murray, Larry, 146
Music. *See* Country music; Gospel music; Popular music; Rock-'n'-roll

Nashville sound, 105, 128–29
Neal, Bob, 53, 56, 58, 71–72, 79, 81, 91, 252
Neal, James, 168
Nelson, Connie, 177
Nelson, Ricky, 85
Nelson, Willie, 177–78, 185, 195, 259, 271, 273
Newbury, Mickey, 128
Newport Folk Festival, *ix, x,* 105, 106, 108, 129, 253
Nichols, Louise, 27, 273
Nichols, Roy, 238–39
Nickajack Cave, 119–20, 174, 187, 233
Nix, Edwin, 98, 104, 251, 254, 273
Nix, Rosey (June's daughter), 7, 145, 223, 267
Nixon, Richard, 153–54
Nolan, Bob, 39
Norman, Larry, 150

Ochs, Phil, 92, 161
Odetta, 136
Old Hickory Lake, 3, 117–18, 165, 254
Oldham, Will, 211
Orbison, Roy, 55, 67, 71, 137, 178, 184–85, 188, 203, 214, 243, 251, 257, 259
Orlando, Tony, 177
Overton Park Shell, 55–56

Parker, Colonel Tom, 58, 71, 239
Parton, Dolly, 195, 230
Peggy, 9
Pennebaker, D.A., 115, 130
Pennywitt, Glen E., 34, 35, 273
Perea, Ben, 32, 33, 38–39, 40, 42–43, 46, 273
Perkins, Birdie, 48
Perkins, Carl, 55, 58–59, 65–66, 71, 76, 124, 128, 130, 151, 178, 207, 224, 237, 238, 243, 251, 257, 258, 259, 262, 271
Perkins, Luther, _x_, 45–46, 73–74, 168, 214, 250, 254
"Personal Jesus", 214–15
Petty, Tom, 196, 203, 210, 211, 224
Phillips, Dewey, 47
Phillips, Sam, 44, 50–53, 58, 66, 74, 75, 76, 77–79, 183, 238, 239, 250.
    See also Sun Records
Pierce, Webb, 54, 55, 57, 62, 70
Pink Anderson, 92, 238
Polygram Records, 178, 182, 259.
    See also Mercury label
Popovich, Steve, 182, 273
Popular music, 65. _See also_ Country music; Gospel music; Rock-'n'-roll
Presley, Elvis, 44, 50, 58, 65, 145, 165–66, 237–38, 239, 250, 251, 255, 257
    as Cash rival, 55–56, 62, 71, 165, 241
Price, Ray, 69, 71, 72
Ray, Nick, 53
RCA, 65
Red Hot Chili Peppers, 193, 194, 196, 197
Reeves, Jim, 47, 69, 71, 105
Reid, Don, 11, 118, 273
Reid, Harold, 105, 273
Reverend Ike, 152
Reznor, Trent, 2, 213–14, 230
Rice, Tim, 150
Rich, Charlie, 79
Richard, Keith, 234
Richardson, Dennis, 273

Richardson, Lynn, 273
Ricks, J. Bernard, 70
Rigdon, Orville, 38, 39, 40, 43, 46, 273
Riley, Billy Lee, 76, 239
Riley, Chuck, 36, 41, 273
Riley, Mark, 190
"Ring of Fire", 99–101, 103, 183, 253, 266
Rivers, Carrie, 15.
    See also Cash, Carrie Rivers
Rivers, Edgar, 233, 273
Rivers, John Lewis, 16, 233
Rivers, Rosanna Lee (Hurst), 16
Rivkin, Dyann, 156, 231, 273
Robbins, Tim, 209, 223
Roberts, Oral, 151, 152
Robin, Karen, _xiii_, 175, 273
Robin, Lou, _xiii_, 7, 9, 157, 158, 173, 174, 179, 181, 182, 184, 185, 189, 194, 195, 256, 273
Robinson, Lisa, 200
Robison, James, 151, 152
Rock-'n'-roll, _xv_, 46–48
Rock, Kid, 234
Rodgers, Jimmie, 25, 39, 51, 60, 95, 120, 202
Rogers, Kenny, 240
Rolling Stones, 132, 135, 150, 158
Rollins, John, 160
Rollins, Michele, 8, 160, 218, 273
Rollins, Ted, 8
Romanek, Mark, 2, 3, 215-16, 273
Ronstadt, Linda, 136
Rubin, Rick, 6, 12, 136, 193–95, 196, 197–98, 200, 202, 203, 209–11, 213, 216, 219, 221, 223, 224, 230, 235, 261, 262, 273
    choosing songs for Cash, 208
    on Cash, 194
    taking Communion with Cash, 231
Ryman Auditorium, 67, 130, 135, 136, 151, 223, 256, 264

San Quentin State Prison, 132–35, 137
Scheff, Jerry, 171

Schwarz, Stephen, 150
Scruggs, Randy, 213, 220, 222
Seaga, Edward, 171
Seven Dreams, 61
Seymour, Jane, 10, 195, 208, 261
Shaddix, Billy, 29, 273
Shaddix, Evelyn, 27
Sharp, Jack, 273
Shaver, Billy Joe, 172
Shaw, Jack, 227–28
Shelton, Robert, 108
Sheppard, Jean, 56, 69
Sherrill, Billy, 169, 181
Silverstein, Shel, 134
Simmons, Russell, 194
Simmons, Sylvie, 223
Simon & Garfunkel, 123
Singles, listed by date, 265–69
Sleepy-Eyed John, 50, 53
Smith, Arthur, 141
Smith, Carl, 67, 68, 250, 251
Smith, Carlene Carter (June's daughter), 7, 68, 169, 170
Smith, Chad, 196
Smith, Connie, 147, 148
Smith, John L, 130–31, 273
Smith, Paul E., 40, 273
Smith, Warren, 67, 71, 239
Snoop Dogg, 230
Snow, Clarence, 51
Snow, Hank, 25, 38, 39, 48, 51, 55, 99, 144, 203
Snow, Jimmy, 144–45, 147, 148, 151, 152, 153, 163, 174, 256, 273
Snow, Mat, 224
Snider, Dee, 240
Songfellows, 76
Springsteen, Bruce, 171–72, 203, 209, 222, 234, 241
St. Marie, Buffy, 136
Stars Incorporated, 71, 81
Statesmen Quartet, 48
Statler Brothers, 105, 111, 118, 124, 137, 142, 154,

Steele, Gene, 49
Stelter, Gayle, *xiv*
Sterling, Jeannie, 85
Stewart, Gerry, 50, 273
Stielper, Mark, *xiv,* 273
Storch, Lawrence, 116
Strawn, Everett, 23, 24, 273
Strummer, Joe, 234
Stuart, Marty, 168, 213, 220, 222
Sullivan, Bob, *xiii*
Sun Records, 44, 50–53, 54, 55, 56, 63, 65, 76, 79, 178, 183, 190, 211, 239, 250, 251, 252
"Sunday Morning, Coming Down", 128, 129, 139–40, 267

Taylor, Elizabeth, 173
Taylor, James, 129, 150, 189
Taylor, Steve, *xiv*
Tebelak, John Michael, 150
Tennessean, the, *xiii*
Terry, Gordon, 73, 82, 83, 103
"That's All Right (Mama)", 46–47
Thompson, Bruce, 116
Thompson, Hank, 72
Thurston, Al, 273
Tillis, Mel, 189
Tittle, Jimmy, 209
Tomlinson, Tommy, 87
Tosches, 23
Travis, Merle, 85, 93, 94, 103, 137, 177
Tubb, Ernest, 25, 39, 48, 51, 55
Tubb, Glenn Douglas, 90
Turner, Steve, *xiii–xv*

U2, 136, 189–91, 209, 237, 261
Unchained, 203–4
Unearthed, 223–24, 264

Volk, Steve, 224

Wagoner, Porter, 114, 128
Walk the Line (movie), 208–9
Weaver, Tom, 47

Webster, Kurt, 7
Weekley, Glenn, 9
"Welfare Cadillac", 154
Wells, Joy Leta, 27–28
Western, Johnny, 82–84, 85–86, 88, 91,
     94, 97, 103, 109, 111, 219, 273
Whitacre, Bob, 32, 38, 39, 273
White, C.V., 59, 237, 238
White, Josh, 238
White Lance, Jesse, 130
White, Penny, 273
"Why Me?", *xi*, 148, 149, 150, 151, 198
Wiland, Harry, 127, 273
Wilbur, Crane, 40
Wildwood Flower, 4
Wilkin, Marijohn, ix
Williams, Hank Jr., 39–40, 52, 62, 68, 69,
     77, 79, 86, 97, 106, 128, 183, 213,
     245, 250, 251

Williamson, Sonny Boy, 93
Wills, Bob, 77
Wilson, Courtney, 9–10, 121, 179, 222,
     273
Wine, Tony, 177
Winston, Nat, 118–19, 254
Wootton, Bob, 134
Wren, Christopher, 35, 36, 45, 120, 147,
     256, 273

Yoakam, Dwight, 234
Yonco, Frank, 273
Young, Faron, 62, 69, 71, 72, 73, 251
Young, Reggie, 86–87, 178, 186, 273

Zooropa, 189, 191, 261